THINKING SHAKESPEARE

A HOW-TO GUIDE FOR STUDENT ACTORS,
DIRECTORS, AND ANYONE ELSE WHO WANTS
TO FEEL MORE COMFORTABLE WITH THE BARD

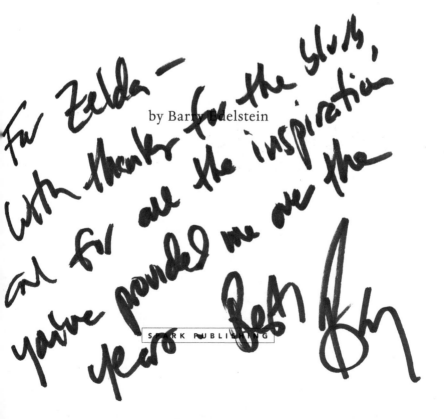

by Barry Edelstein

SPARK PUBLISHING

Cover photo—David McCallum in the title role of *Julius Caesar*, directed by Barry Edelstein, in the Public Theater's "Shakespeare in the Park," Central Park, New York City, 2000. Photo © Michal Daniel, 2000.

SPARKNOTES is a registered trademark of SparkNotes LLC

Spark Publishing
A Division of Barnes & Noble
120 Fifth Avenue
New York, NY 10011
www.sparknotes.com

ISBN-13: 978-1-4114-9872-3
ISBN-10: 1-4114-9872-0

Library of Congress Cataloging-in-Publication Data

Edelstein, Barry.
    Thinking Shakespeare: a how-to guide for student actors, directors, and anyone else who wants to feel more comfortable with the Bard / by Barry Edelstein.
        p. cm.
    Includes bibliographical references.
    ISBN-13: 978-1-4114-9872-3
    ISBN-10: 1-4114-9872-0
    1. Shakespeare, William, 1564-1616—Dramatic production—Handbooks, manuals, etc. 2. Acting—Handbooks, manuals, etc. 3. Theater—Production and direction—Handbooks, manuals, etc. I. Title.

PR3091.E34 2007
822.3'3—dc22

                                            2006100611

Please submit changes or report errors to www.sparknotes.com/errors.

Printed and bound in the United States.

1 3 5 7 9 10 8 6 4 2

For my beloved Hilit
"O! She's warm."

CONTENTS

PROLOGUE

Imagine the curtain falling at the end of a production of *Death of a Salesman* on Broadway, or at your nearest professional theater, or in a college drama department.

The actors bow to warm applause. As the audience members file out of the theater, they talk to one another about the show. "That was so powerful." "The guy who played Willy Loman broke my heart." "It reminded me of my grandfather." "I'm so glad I understood what they were saying."

Wait a minute! *What*?!

"I'm so glad I understood what they were saying" ??!!

That's a line you would never anticipate hearing from audiences at the movies, or in front of their TVs. Whether they like the show or not, audiences take it for granted that the words spoken on stage or screen will be clear and make sense. They expect to *understand*.

That's not always the case when it comes to Shakespeare in the theater.

Audiences approach the work of this one playwright with an entirely unique set of expectations. There are many reasons why. They might recall how impenetrable they found Shakespeare in Miss Baxter's 9th grade English class and brace themselves for the same difficulty in the theater. They may recall that the last time they saw a Shakespeare play, they couldn't quite keep up with the story and gird themselves to feel left out once again. To be sure, they may sense, based on conventional wisdom or from reading him now and then, that Shakespeare can be insightful, deep, moving, and sometimes even funny. Sitting in their assigned seats in the theater, however, audiences may have a very different and far less satisfying experience.

Shakespeare in the contemporary theater is many things. But he is not always comprehensible. And just as audiences can sometimes find him remote, baffling, long-winded, and downright hard, the actors and directors charged with bringing him to life can likewise feel intimidated.

These reactions are not surprising. Shakespeare wrote a long time ago, in a world very different from ours. The conventions of storytelling in the theater, the relationship between the verbal and the visual in society, even the English language itself, have changed enormously since Shakespeare's time. Making Shakespeare's words feel spontaneous, passionate, and real is one of the most difficult tasks today's theater artists face. And if *they* shrink from it, their audiences haven't even got a shot.

Thinking Shakespeare aims to help.

Thinking Shakespeare is based on a nearly twenty-year career directing America's leading classical actors in Shakespeare's plays and equally long experience teaching Shakespearean acting at this country's most prominent theater conservatories. It distills the complex work of making Shakespeare clear into an accessible and manageable process that can, with practice, be mastered by anyone.

This book is intended primarily for students working on productions of Shakespeare or enrolled in a class on Shakespearean acting or directing, but it is also a useful refresher for professional actors either facing Shakespeare for the first time or looking for a few pointers on specific problems. General readers with no background either in Shakespeare in particular or theater in general will find the book unintimidating and edifying, and scholars hoping to view Shakespeare from fresh angles will find much to interest them.

After this Prologue, *Thinking Shakespeare*, like every Shakespeare play, is divided into five acts.

Act I begins by exploring the book's central notion: that actors must regard Shakespeare's characters as living, breathing individuals who think for themselves and then choose language to express their thoughts. Chapter 1 describes an acting technique that makes speaking a character's thoughts a straightforward matter by asking the question, "Why am I using this word now?" The chapter shows how answering this question constitutes the basis of the Shakespearean rehearsal process. Chapter 2 builds on the first chapter's discussion of the relationship between thought and language on stage and links this relationship to the fundamental principles of acting. The chapter continues with an overview of the essential concepts and working methods employed by professional actors and directors.

Act II presents five primary approaches to analyzing Shakespearean language, along with practical techniques and exercises actors can use to conduct that analysis. Chapter 3 delves into scansion and meter—the arrangement of words in lines of verse organized according to the accents and stresses in certain patterns of syllables. Those patterns help determine the best way for an actor to say his lines. Chapter 4 explains that Shakespeare's characters always make arguments, thinking and speaking in a well-organized and linear fashion intended to make a case or express their point of view. The chapter describes the steps actors can take to identify and present the arguments in their speeches. Chapter 5 focuses on the crucial concept of antithesis.

Shakespeare's constant use of opposites in his characters' thought and utterance is a key feature of his writing, and this chapter outlines how emphasizing these oppositions helps bring the text vividly to life. Chapter 6 examines the way Shakespeare's language alternates between heightened, poetical speech of the sort we generally associate with him and simple, down-to-earth talk that doesn't necessarily sound "Shakespearean" at all. The chapter shows how observing the shifts between different kinds of language in a speech or scene leads to more specific and believable acting. Act II's last chapter recommends a powerful and necessary verse-speaking technique: phrasing with the verse line. The chapter demonstrates that saying, breathing, and thinking Shakespeare's text one verse line at a time is one of the best steps an actor can take in his quest to make the language immediately clear and tremendously exciting.

Chapter 8 is the book's Intermission, in which we break down a scene from *Henry V* in detail, rehearsing it in precisely the ways it would be rehearsed in preparation for a professional production. This sustained analysis serves as a review of all the techniques covered in the book's first two acts. (This will also be a good time to head to the lobby for a stretch and a bit of refreshment!)

Act III, in four chapters, presents how the basic material discussed in Acts I and II helps actors approach a wide range of other Shakespearean challenges with expertise and confidence. Chapter 9 encourages actors to look at the music of the text—its continual changes in rhythm, pace, and tempo—and offers exercises that set out how to use those changes to lend variety and interest to a performance. The unique power of verbs to animate language is the thrust of chapter 10. The chapter shows how giving prominence to a speech's verbs will help an actor speak the text with muscularity and stirring power. Chapter 11 examines irony, wit, and emotion in Shakespeare, revealing that sometimes the things a character says can be very far from the things he or she feels. By scrutinizing the relationship between the surface meaning of the words and the emotions swirling beneath them, actors add truth and believability to their portrayals. The final chapter of Act III concentrates on the interplay of stage business and the text and enumerates the various ways in which the structure of the language serves to direct the physical action called for in the play.

Act IV's subject is the application of the techniques in the book's first three acts to scenes involving multiple characters and to Shakespeare's non-verse writing. Exercises in chapter 13 focus on the importance of listening to the words other characters use and on the relationship between the structure of the language and the dynamics of the dramatic situation. Chapter 14 targets Shakespeare's prose, illustrating that the process an actor uses to bring verse to brilliant life is equally pertinent to this looser, freer form.

Thinking Shakespeare's final act points ahead to the next steps in the actor's work. Chapter 15 surveys the many approaches contemporary theater artists take to working on Shakespeare and shows how even the most provocative interpretive questions can be answered through the savvy and diligent practice of the techniques mastered while working through this book. The Epilogue lists helpful reference books and other resources actors should keep handy in the rehearsal room. It also recommends the most worthwhile Shakespeare on film and DVD. Acknowledgments and a list of illustrations can be found in the Curtain Call at the end of the book.

Thinking Shakespeare includes many passages from Shakespeare's plays. Each chapter is built around rehearsal time on one or more primary speeches chosen specifically to illustrate the central techniques under discussion. Other shorter passages develop points and provide perspective. Almost all of Shakespeare's plays will be excerpted or at least referenced.[1]

Read cover to cover, *Thinking Shakespeare* can serve as a textbook for a high school, college, or graduate school Shakespearean acting class. But it can also be used as a reference, dipped into as needed. Each chapter is subdivided into smaller sections that provide useful points of entry for readers who may want or need to solve specific problems rather than tackle overarching concepts. A shorter section called Things Further Thought On concludes most chapters. Here you will find succinct discussions of technical points raised by the material under study but not necessarily related to the chapter's main thrust.

Shakespeare's greatness is not just for the initiated, the professors, or the British. It's for actors and directors everywhere who love language and yearn to communicate with audiences, who in turn long to experience that most singular of theater experiences: understanding.

Thinking Shakespeare provides the tools to make Shakespeare's greatness something everyone can share.

---

1 Act, scene, and line numbers throughout the book are keyed to the Norton Shakespeare. Their format is (act.scene.line). For example, (2.3.47–49) means Act 2, Scene 3, Lines 47 through 49.

ACT I

John Turturro rehearses the title role of *Richard III* with director Barry Edelstein at Classic Stage Company, 2003. Photo © Dixie Sheridan, 2003.

ACT 1

CHAPTER
Nº
1

A THOUGHT AT A TIME

WHY AM I USING THIS WORD NOW?

Our work begins with two brief bits of Shakespeare:

> But look, the morn in russet mantle clad
> Walks o'er the dew of yon high eastward hill.
> Break we our watch up.
>
> —Horatio, in *Hamlet* (1.1.147–149)

> Come away; it is almost clear dawn.
>
> —Duke Vincentio, in *Measure for Measure*
> (4.2.226)

Both these lines, said by two very different characters in two very different sets of circumstances and in two very different plays, say the same thing: "The sun's coming up. Let's go."

The duke puts this simple idea simply, in language not terribly different from that which anyone awake at 4:30 tomorrow morning might use.

Horatio, on the other hand, speaks with more complexity. He employs metaphor (the sunrise is a person in a reddish cloak, walking on the wet grass in the east). He uses some poetic-sounding vocabulary (*morn* instead of *sun*; *o'er* instead of *over*). His phrasing is intricate ("yon high eastward" instead of "that tall eastern"). He structures his sentences in unusual ways ("Break we our watch up" instead of "Let's break up our watch").

Why do these two characters express the exact same idea in such different terms? Of all the countless ways they could say "the sun's coming up," why do they say it in the ways they do? Why do they say these specific things, in this specific manner, at this specific moment?

Why are they using these words now?

This is the central question of the Shakespearean rehearsal process, and it's the question at the heart of *Thinking Shakespeare*. We will ask it again and again. Our analysis of Shakespeare's text, no matter how deep or far afield it may go, will always return to this basic and powerful inquiry: "Why am I using this word now?"

It's a question that can be answered in a number of ways.

The Non-Actor's Answer

We could cut short our discussion by claiming simply that these characters talk the way they do because they're in Shakespeare plays, and that's how Shakespeare writes.

While certainly not incorrect, that answer is frustratingly vague. Horatio's complex words, "the morn in russet mantle clad / Walks o'er the dew of yon high eastward hill" may strike us as more typically Shakespearean than the duke's rather flat, "It is almost clear dawn." Yet Shakespeare wrote both lines, and only a few years apart, so the duke is every bit as "Shakespearean" as Horatio. As we'll see throughout this book, Shakespeare writes in so many different styles, voices, and ways that it's almost impossible to pin down what a "Shakespearean" sound truly is. Besides, the statement "The character is using these words now because he's in a Shakespeare play" doesn't give an actor the slightest clue about how to act these lines. We need a better answer to our central question.

We could take a more academic approach and observe that Horatio's image of the sun as a walking man is one that's seen with some frequency in the literature of Shakespeare's day, and that the Bard was not the first author to depict the sun as a guy in a red coat taking a stroll in the wet morning grass. We might even cite sonneteers of the Italian Renaissance, or epic poets of ancient Greece who love to imagine inanimate objects as people. We might then name this technique (it's called *anthropomorphosis*, "the process of giving human form") and talk about the various places in which Shakespeare uses it.

These observations are informative, but they won't quite do either, because they don't offer much to an *actor*. Someone playing Horatio might want to know the literary heritage of the images his character uses. That actor might be fascinated to read through a list of the various items of reddish-orange clothing that Shakespeare and other writers have draped over the shoulders of the anthropomorphized sun.

Or, more likely, he might not.

The Actor's Answer

Actors and directors and all the artists in the theater interpret Shakespeare's characters in a way that's very different from the way they are interpreted in the library.

To theater artists, these characters are not literary figures; they are *people*. They are not archetypes or symbols or the constructs of an author whose use of language can be seen in the light of a long and rich tradition that preceded him. Instead, they are three-dimensional human beings, with hearts and brains and lives and desires. They live in situations moment by moment. They have aims and wants and needs, and they take steps to fulfill them, whatever the obstacles. They have minds of their own. They think for themselves.

In the theater, unlike in the English class (as valuable and wonderful as that is), we start with the character's *thoughts* and work our way forward from there. Sure, those thoughts were written by an author in his study, but for an actor's purposes, the author is not there. All an actor is concerned with is the character and what's on the character's mind. The actor's notion is this: characters have ideas and choose language to express them.

Characters *think*, and then they *speak*.

Why am I using this word now? Because given who I am, and the situation I'm facing at this very moment, I have something I want to say, and of all the words in the English language, and of all the infinite ways of arranging them, I am choosing *these* words, in *this* order, to say it.

Thought on Stage

The word *thought* means something slightly different onstage than it does in ordinary life. In its day-to-day sense, *thought* is whatever idea, opinion, attitude, or deduction is ricocheting through our heads at any given time. Our thoughts are ephemeral—there one minute and gone the next. They are born and they die inside our brains. Other people can't see them, hear them, or know them, and when we consider them, our attention focuses inward.

On stage, however, *thought* moves outward. It starts in the brain of the character and then emerges. Thought onstage never dissipates into the ether or fades away into the recesses of the mind. Thought is material, forceful. It affects things. On stage, thought comes alive. And the vehicle that brings it to life is *language*.

Thought needs language to come into the world. A dramatic character *needs* the words he says, because without them his thoughts wouldn't exist in the world outside himself. His intention to communicate, his desire to effect some change in the reality around him—these are the engines that drive thought from deep inside a character's mind all the way to another's ear, and then out across the footlights and up to the back row of the balcony.

Shakespeare's characters understand well the connection between thought and language. "Speak to me as to thy thinkings," Othello requests of Iago, who refuses: "It were not for your quiet nor your good, / Nor for my manhood, honesty, or wisdom, / To let you know my thoughts." But the general wants to know what's on Iago's mind, so he gives an order: "By heaven, I'll know thy thoughts!" It's a philosophical tussle. Both men recognize that thoughts have force. Both believe that thoughts have effects. Both grasp that speech makes thought real, and both know that until they are spoken, thoughts are powerless.

Othello and Iago understand: *Thinking Shakespeare* is *speaking thought.*

Same Thought, Different Words

Let's examine how Horatio and the duke speak thought. Why do these two men mention that the sun is rising? What is the need for their words? And why does this simple thought find two such different utterances in their respective voices?

Consider the context of Horatio's three lines. It's nighttime on the battlements of Denmark's royal castle. It's a few weeks before Christmas. It's cold. Horatio has been invited here by two castle guards who have seen something disturbing: the ghost of King Hamlet, who died recently under mysterious circumstances. Tonight the king appeared again. A stern and terrifying vision, it seemed to want something from Horatio. Then a rooster crowed and the ghost took off. The same rays of the early morning sun that made the rooster cry are now visible to Horatio as they appear in the sky above the dew-drenched eastern hills.

Consider Horatio's situation in life. As we discover later in the play, he is a graduate student—of philosophy, most likely—at the University of Wittenberg in Germany. This suggests that he is comfortable with large thoughts, complex language, and figurative, elevated expression. So when he sees the sun—this thrilling, reassuring, gorgeous orb that signals the end of one of the most harrowing nights of his life—his deep sense of relief comes out in words suffused with a special energy that lifts them beyond the normal, that takes them outside the realm of everyday speech:

"The morn in russet mantle clad / Walks o'er the dew of yon high eastward hill." In this particular situation, because of who he is, Horatio uses charged words that give voice to the complicated, turbulent thoughts firing through his sophisticated brain. His words put his thoughts into the world, where they might affect his companions and bring change to the tense atmosphere of this cold, intensely frightening night.

That's why he's using these words now.

Duke Vincentio in *Measure for Measure*, on the other hand, keeps it simpler. For one thing, he's in a hurry. He's trying to carry out an audacious plan to entrap his wayward deputy. The plan involves beheading a convicted felon and swapping the detached cranium for someone else's. This strange switcheroo needs to be completed by 5 a.m., and it's already early morning so the duke has no time for Horatio-esque metaphor and poeticism. Nor is that kind of talk typical of the way he usually speaks. Throughout the play, he uses language more down-to-earth and straightforward than that of just about any other Shakespearean hero. Vincentio is a technocrat, a strong leader with a no-nonsense attitude. Hence, this terse line: "Come away. It is almost clear dawn." He has something urgent to say and he just spits it out.

That's why he's using these words now. [2]

---

[2] Why "clear" dawn? A modern audience might assume that this phrase describes a cloudless morning, sunny and crisp, which makes perfect sense. But in Shakespeare's time, according to the *Oxford English Dictionary*, "clear" was used to distinguish the time of morning when the sun is *entirely* up from the time when it's *coming* up. That is, while today we'd say that sunrise takes us from night into dawn into day, Englishmen in Shakespeare's period would say that sunrise brings us from night into dawn into *clear dawn* into day. The Duke uses "clear" to add urgency, to hustle his confederates along, to say that there is hardly any time to pull off the head-switch by 5 a.m. The thought is, "Let's get going—the sun is almost finished coming up!"

The Core of Shakespeare: Words and Emotion

To analyze Shakespeare one thought at a time, and to see how a character's language emerges from that character's thought, is to understand two crucial things about how Shakespeare's plays work on stage.

IT'S ABOUT THE WORDS   First and foremost, *the words are what count.* The spectacle in the plays is fun—battle scenes, lush costumes, lights, and sound and pageantry—but lots of playwrights are good at providing all that. The stories are interesting—hilarious and entertaining in Shakespeare's comedies, fast-moving and sweeping in his history plays, suspenseful and fearsome in his tragedies—but an hour in front of HBO can deliver all that, and we don't even have to leave home. We go to the theater to see a Shakespeare play not for stories or outfits or smoke and mirrors, *but because we want to hear his extraordinary writing.* We want the magical, transformative power of Shakespeare's words.

For example, consider this idea: "In the death of even the tiniest little bird, we can find evidence of God's presence." A philosopher might express such a thought, or a priest, or perhaps even a very spiritual ornithologist. Only Hamlet can tell you, "There's a special providence in the fall of a sparrow."

Another example. Many playwrights in the English Renaissance wrote about the victory of the ragtag English army of King Henry V over the vastly superior French forces at Agincourt. A number of these plays have survived, but only one is still performed in the modern theater: the one by William Shakespeare. Only in that play does the king say extraordinary things like, "Once more unto the breach, dear friends, once more, / Or close the wall up with our English dead!" and "We few, we happy few, we band of brothers."

When it comes to Shakespeare, the story is important, but *the words that tell the story are what it's really all about.* The Shakespearean actor's obligation is to deliver those extraordinary words with clarity, vitality, and élan to an audience that has given time, attention, and money to hear them.

IT'S ABOUT THE EMOTIONS   All this emphasis on thought suggests that acting Shakespeare is above all an intellectual process. It isn't.

Intellect is certainly involved. Characters like Hamlet and Falstaff and Iago are, like the genius who created them, astonishingly articulate, erudite, and witty. It takes a huge amount of brainpower to keep up with them. "What a piece of work is a man," says Hamlet. "How noble in reason! How infinite in faculty!" He might be talking about himself, or about the actors who play him, because it takes a noble reason and infinite faculties to think a thought like, "There's a special providence in the fall of a sparrow."

But thought in Shakespeare frequently comes from a *non-intellectual* place. Hamlet refers to his constant need to "unpack my heart with words." His notion is that talking makes him feel better, that words get rid of pain. It's an insight that every psychotherapist in the world would cheer. There's an emotional dimension to speech, because the thoughts behind speech engage the heart, the body, and the soul.

And because the thoughts behind Shakespeare's text frequently transcend intellect, the actor must open his own intellectual process to the possibility that his creative exploration may take him beyond reason. Sometimes the question, *Why am I using this word now?* can't be answered rationally. Sometimes the only answer is, "I'm using these words now because my heart is bursting," or "because my spirit is on fire," or "because my soul has plunged into the abyss," or "because my insides are churning around like a hurricane." King Lear, crouched over the lifeless body of his precious daughter Cordelia, despairs that she's gone and devotes one of his last mortal breaths to the thought that he'll not see her again: "Never, never, never, never, never." Ask the actor playing the role *why* Lear repeats this word five times, and the answer you'll get won't have much to do with Lear's reason or intellectual acuity. This thought comes from his guts, not his brains. Lear speaks as he does because of his infinite pain, because of his powerlessness before a random universe, because of his despair at the wretched and unjust fact that that those we love must one day die. *That's* why he's using those words now.

Thinking Leads to Feeling

Despair. Resignation. Grief. These are not intellectual notions any more than Horatio's relief or Duke Vincentio's alarm is. These are emotional states, pure feelings. Yet no matter how intense these emotions may be, their expression through language still involves thought. Actors experience their characters' feelings by looking deeply at their characters' language, finding the thought behind that language, *thinking it*, and then expressing it through speech.

That's the real substance of *Thinking Shakespeare*. When the actor thinks the character's thoughts and expresses them in the character's words, the actor *is* the character. His mind and heart merge with those of the person he's portraying. The character's thoughts become the actor's thoughts, and the character's feelings become the actor's feelings.

Think the thoughts behind the words "It is almost clear dawn," and you will feel the feelings behind them too. Understand what makes you envision the sun as a walking man in an orange cloak—the context of the thought, the need to say it—and you will feel what it's like to see the sun come up after the scariest night of your life.

Emotion flows from the exploration and expression of the thoughts in the text.

It sounds like a riddle, or the pronouncement of some guru. But in practice, as we will see as we work through the chapters ahead, the link between thought and emotion is concrete and easily made.

Nonetheless, this book is called *Thinking Shakespeare*, rather than *Feeling Shakespeare*, because *thinking* is the crux. Thinking is the beginning of a process that leads to speaking, and then to feeling. That's a truth that every one of Shakespeare's characters knows. Three of them, from *Much Ado about Nothing*, deserve the last word on it:

DON PEDRO   By my troth, I speak my thought.
CLAUDIO   And, in faith, my lord, I spoke mine.
BENEDICK   And, by my two faiths and troths, my lord, I
spoke mine.

(1.1.182–185)

Speaking your thoughts: the alpha and omega of Shakespeare.

WHAT ACTORS DO

ACT I | CHAPTER № 2

THE BASIC TECHNIQUES OF ACTING

To ask the central question of *Thinking Shakespeare*, *Why am I using these words now?* is to acknowledge that words *do* things.

Words make public whatever it is we need to communicate. They express our inmost selves. They transmit to others what is, up until the moment we speak, known only to ourselves. And when words arrive at the ears of our listeners, they have an impact. Actors know a lot about the impact of words. Their art depends on understanding how and why characters speak and on calculating the effect of words on other people.

The techniques in the remaining four acts of *Thinking Shakespeare* revolve around this special understanding of how words work.[3]

The Fundamentals: Objective, Obstacle, Action

Imagine you are cast in the role of Ricky in *Driveway Wars*, the newest work from the hot, young playwright Ed DeVere. Here's the script:

DRIVEWAY WARS

by

ED DEVERE

The curtain rises to reveal the suburban driveway of RICKY, who gets in his car, starts the engine, and shifts into reverse. A truck, driven by FRED, pulls up and parks, blocking Ricky's driveway. Ricky rolls down his window.

RICKY   Hey! Move your truck!

Fred smiles, waves, and drives off. Ricky pulls out of his driveway.

END OF PLAY

Okay, so Ed DeVere is no Shakespeare. Still, his play illustrates the basic principles of dramatic construction that every actor must understand.

---

3 Readers who have some acting experience may wish to jump ahead to chapter 3, although a quick refresher course is never a bad idea. I've begun rehearsals for every Shakespeare play I've directed with a day spent reviewing basic principles of how the text works, even when my casts have been full of trained classical actors with many years of Shakespearean experience. It's good to be reminded of the fundamentals from time to time, no matter how advanced your technique may be.

Just as we do with the characters in every Shakespeare play, we regard the characters in *Driveway Wars* as living, breathing people who think their own thoughts and choose language to express them. We know that a playwright wrote the words, but in a creative act of willful ignorance, we disregard the author and consider the words to be the spontaneous utterances of the characters in their respective situations. "Hey! Move your truck!" may well be one of Ed DeVere's finest lines, but for our purposes it is made up by Ricky in his own driveway, behind the wheel. Ricky chooses words to express his thoughts.

Why, then, is Ricky using these words now? Because he wants to drive off and he can't until the truck hindering him moves. Saying, "Hey! Move your truck!" is a way to get the truck to do so.

Ricky speaks to obtain a desired result, which, at this moment, he cannot otherwise obtain.

That's acting in a nutshell.

All acting essentially boils down to the things a character does to overcome the difficulties that prevent him from having what he wants. We describe the components of the acting process with these terms:

Objective: What the character wants.
Obstacle: Whatever blocks the character from what he wants.
Action: What the character does to surmount his obstacle and gain his objective.

Objective, obstacle, action. Every moment of every scene of every play has all three. Consider the following scenarios:

King Henry V of England wants to rule France. The current French king stands in his way, so Henry leads an invasion of France and seizes the crown.

Richard, Duke of Gloucester, wants to rule England. The current English king and his heirs stand in the way, so Richard murders them one by one and seizes the crown.

Both men have an objective (to rule a country), encounter an obstacle (the current occupant of the throne), and take action (waging war, committing murder).

Action Through Language

In *Driveway Wars*, Ricky's objective is to pull out of his driveway. The obstacle is Fred's truck blocking the way. Ricky's action is *to demand* that Fred move, which he does by saying the line, "Hey! Move your truck!" Had the playwright written the stage direction *Ricky honks his horn* instead of a line of text, the action would be identical. Just as the physical act of honking the horn demands that Fred move his truck, so too does the language Ricky speaks.

The key concept for our work (and the sole relevance of Ed DeVere to William Shakespeare) is that in the context of a dramatic scene, *speech is action*. Ricky is acting upon Fred by speaking to him. His words are chosen to effect change in his situation. His language is active.

An important part of the rehearsal process is the determination of the characters' actions through close analysis of their words. In rehearsal for *Driveway Wars,* you would interpret the dialogue and put forward your own ideas about what Ricky is trying to achieve by saying the things he does in the script. If the director were to ask you, "What's your action on Ricky's line?" you might answer, "To demand that Fred move," or, perhaps, "To order Fred out of the way." Over the course of many hours you would try all the actions you could think of, and others the director suggests, until you found an approach to Ricky's line that everyone would agree makes the scene believable and exciting.

STRONG ACTIONS, STRONGER LANGUAGE Now suppose that at the end of the first day of work, the playwright and director decide that *Driveway Wars* needs some development. The next morning, Ed DeVere arrives for rehearsal with new pages, which the stage manager distributes to you and the actor playing Fred. Here's the new material, which begins just after the opening stage direction:

RICKY	Would you mind moving your truck?
FRED	I won't be a minute.
RICKY	Hey! Move your truck!
FRED	Get lost.
RICKY	(*gets out of his car, cell phone in hand*) I'll call the police and *they'll* tell you to move.
FRED	(*runs toward RICKY*) And I'll see to it that you don't!

RICKY and FRED face each other, fists raised.
END OF PLAY

Unlike in DeVere's original draft, in this version of the scene Ricky's first line is not a demand but is instead more of a simple question. His action? *To request, to entreat,* or, perhaps, *to plead.* Also new in this draft, Ricky's first action does not result in Fred immediately driving off. His request goes unheeded; his obstacle remains. Because he is still in pursuit of his objective, Ricky must now speak a new set of words that express a new action. With the line, "Hey! Move your truck!" Ricky's action switches from a request to a demand (the same action this line expressed in DeVere's first draft). Once again, the action fails to eliminate the obstacle, so once again Ricky tries another action. He decides *to threaten* Fred, or, in another interpretation of his third line, *to intimidate* him. This too leaves the obstacle unmoved, so Ricky's only recourse is to turn away from words and toward physical action. He cocks back his fist and the curtain falls on a note of incipient violence and great suspense.

Notice how, as the scene continues, Ricky must resort to increasingly intense actions to obtain what he wants. In turn, these actions are manifested through increasingly emphatic language (and, eventually, brute force). This escalation in intensity takes place because although Ricky's objective—to back out of his driveway—remains strong throughout the scene, his obstacle grows more formidable the more he tries to eliminate it. And what is Ricky's obstacle? Fred.

Fred, too, has an objective in the scene: to park his truck, presumably because he has some business to conduct nearby. The action in Fred's first line ("I won't be a minute.") might be *to placate* Ricky, or perhaps *to brush him off*. In his second line ("Get lost.") Fred might be trying *to rebuff* Ricky or *to dismiss* him or, in a slightly different direction, *to belittle* him or *to mock* him. Fred's final line ("And I'll see to it that you don't!") serves *to defy* Ricky or, depending on how much violence you and your director wish to inject into your interpretation of the play, *to provoke* Ricky or *to attack* him or maybe even *to kill* him. Note that Fred's language grows more intense as the scene continues, just as Ricky's does, because his increasingly strong actions require increasingly strong speech for their expression.

Fred's actions are aimed at eliminating the obstacle of Ricky, and Ricky's actions are calculated to remove the obstacle of Fred. That is, their actions place the men in *conflict* with each other.

Conflict

Conflict is an essential component of acting. It's what makes drama exciting.

In DeVere's first draft of *Driveway Wars*, Fred moved his truck as soon as Ricky demanded it. Ricky's obstacle disappeared as quickly as it arrived, and he got what he wanted. Why would anyone go to the theater to watch a scene like that? It's not interesting. Nothing happens. No wonder DeVere and his director decided to rewrite it. No conflict, no scene.

Thanks to some excellent play writing—or, for our purposes, thanks to Ricky and Fred's powers of thought and speech—the second draft of *Driveway Wars* is full of conflict. It escalates rapidly from a polite exchange to a violent confrontation.

Just as a playwright must doggedly pursue conflict in the composition of his scenes, so too must actors and directors always be sure to interpret the text with conflict in mind. As they work on their lines, they must find in them objectives and actions that heighten the conflict in the situation. They must "raise the stakes," as the lingo of the professional theater puts it.

Ricky's third line is a good example: "I'll call the police and *they'll* tell you to move." We decided that Ricky's action here is *to threaten*, or *to intimidate*, both interpretive choices that increase the tension in the scene by escalating the conflict between the two characters. There are, of course, other directions the line might take. Ricky could choose *to avoid* Fred by running inside his house as he says the line. Ricky could choose *to snub* Fred, saying the line through his teeth as he dials 911 on his cell phone. Or Ricky might choose *to lord it over* Fred, sneering the line in a petulant and superior tone intended to make Fred feel powerless and small. All three choices are justifiable responses to the line that DeVere wrote—the line that Ricky thinks up in the moment. But none of these choices serves to raise the stakes of the scene. Instead, each one would actually de-escalate the conflict. Similarly, Fred's second line, "Get lost," which we decided was said *to rebuff* Ricky or *to dismiss* him, could just as legitimately function *to sidestep* a confrontation or *to disengage* from the situation or, simply, *to avoid* trouble. Choosing these actions, all of which put Fred in retreat, would soften the conflict between the two men and defuse the scene.

The same lines can be interpreted in many ways. The actions the actors choose to play with those lines influence the overall tone of the scene, heating it up if the actions are strong and confrontational, and cooling it down if they are gentle and oblique. In general, choices of avoidance serve to minimize conflict, whereas choices of engagement serve to increase it. Engagement makes for better drama.

This leads to one of the general rules of acting: *always play actions of engagement rather than retreat.* Whenever possible, make choices that amplify the conflict in the scene.

This rule is one reason why actors are trained to phrase their characters' actions using strong infinitive verbs. Such language reminds us that speech is active, that talking has impact, and that to act is to do. Consider the list of the actions we have found in *Driveway Wars: to request / to placate, to demand / to dismiss, to threaten / to defy.* Each pair of verbs is highly charged, and each verb within each pair is in conflict with the other. This list reminds us that the scene is energetic, tense, and exciting. It emphasizes the central importance of conflict to well-conceived dramatic action.[4]

Given Circumstances

The intensity of the scene's conflict is not the only consideration that informs the interpretation of a character's lines. As rehearsal continues and you hone in on the specific actions Ricky is taking in pursuit of his objective, a range of questions will arise. If Ricky's action is *to demand*, how forceful should that demand be? Should he scream at Fred? Should he grab him and shake him? Or if his action is *to intimidate* Fred, should Ricky do so from across the driveway, or inches from Fred's face?

The answers depend on the *given circumstances*—the environmental and interpersonal factors that put a character into a specific situation. Who is he? Where is he? What happened just before this scene? What are his relationships to the other characters in the story? The given circumstances determine the events, tone, and very nature of the scene.

A good playwright will write the given circumstances into the play. In cases in which he does not, good actors and directors will use their imaginations to supply given circumstances that make sense within the context of the story and that justify the actions each character takes and the words he uses.

We have stipulated that Ricky's objective is "to move his car," but we have not explored the reason why he needs to move

---

4 We will return to the dramatic value of verbs in Shakespeare in chapter 10.

it in the first place. Suppose *Driveway Wars* is a comedy, and Ricky needs to get out of his driveway because his wife, Lucy, has just gone into labor. Suppose the play is a drama, and Ricky is a mobster on his way to a hit, or a minister on his way to a funeral. Whatever the play's genre, suppose it's set in Buffalo, New York, in January, and, as the scene begins, Ricky has just spent thirty minutes digging his car out of the snow and twenty more trying to get it to start. Now suppose Fred isn't a stranger but Lucy's ex-husband, whom Ricky has always despised.

Any single line of dialogue in the scene—"Hey! Move your truck!"—will sound entirely different depending on whether Ricky is a temperamental mobster, a frazzled and half-frozen minister with an aching back, or a jealous rival. *The interpretation of the line is a function of the given circumstances in the scene.*

The actor's job is to come to a thorough understanding of the text and then say the line in a way that reflects all the aspects of the dramatic situation. Study the words to define the objective, identify the obstacle, and zero in on the most effective actions. Consider all these choices within the context of who the character is, where he is, what has just happened to him, and how he feels about the other people in the scene.

You're almost acting.

YOUR CHARACTER, YOUR LIFE: MAKING ACTING CHOICES PERSONAL

The most difficult task remaining is also the most fulfilling part of the actor's work: finding your own personal relationship to the actions, circumstances, and words in the play.

Especially when it comes to Shakespeare, the actor's personal stamp is part of what makes us return to the same plays again and again. I've seen *Hamlet* twenty times in my life. I know how it ends, so why should I bother going back for number twenty-one? The answer is that I want to see what yet another actor will bring to the role. The words will be the same, and the story won't change, but the individual interpretation of line after line and scene after scene will be brand new with each new Danish prince.

Stanislavski's System

Early in the twentieth century, the great Russian director Constantin Stanislavski recognized the importance of personal interpretation and devised a system through which actors might imagine themselves in their characters' circumstances. His work changed the course of modern acting.

Stanislavski gave his actors a technique for putting themselves in their characters' shoes. He urged them to ponder "the magic 'if.'"

In *Driveway Wars*, pondering the magic "if" would sound like this: *"If I were Ricky* trying to get a guy I hate to move his truck on a cold Buffalo morning while my wife Lucy clutches her belly inside the house, *how would I do it?"*

SUBSTITUTION   The key to pondering the magic "if" is *substitution.* The actor's task is to search his own life history for situations and relationships that parallel the ones in the play. Having identified them, he remembers the emotions he felt at the time and uses those as *substitutes* for what the character is experiencing.

An actor playing Ricky in our scene may have had an experience almost identical to Ricky's. Perhaps this actor's car was once blocked as he was on the way to do something important. If so, he can draw directly on that experience to bring authenticity to the scene. But even if the actor has never owned a car, let alone had one blocked by a truck, he can still achieve authenticity by drawing on another experience in which he felt something similar to what Ricky feels. Perhaps he remembers a time when he was in a hurry to get someplace and the subway station was crammed with commuters. The annoyance he felt as he struggled through the crowd parallels Ricky's frustration in his driveway, so the actor substitutes his own recollected experience to come nearer to an authentic version of Ricky's.

An actor can also think back on his own relationships to find substitutes for the other characters in a scene. He can find his private version of Fred: someone with whom his relationship is similar to that of Ricky's relationship with Fred in the scene. Perhaps the actor remembers some stubborn official he once clashed with, or, to really ratchet-up the conflict in the scene, perhaps he remembers his wife's ex-boyfriend, or his bitterest high school rival. Then, when looking into the eyes of the actor playing Fred, he can substitute that remembered person, turning Fred from an abstraction into a flesh-and-blood human being from his own life. Ricky's interactions with Fred will be much more real as a result.

SENSE MEMORY AND EMOTIONAL MEMORY   Substitution is enhanced by two special categories of memories, which actors call *sense memory* and *emotional memory*.

Sense memory involves drawing on your sensory experiences. An actor born and raised in El Paso may never have shoveled snow off his car, but he may have visited his grandmother in

Minneapolis once or gone skiing in Aspen. The feeling of the frigid air on his skin, the blinding white of the fields of snow, the unique scent of dry winter air—these are concrete sensory experiences he can use in his portrayal of Buffalonian Ricky. He doesn't have to pretend to be cold. Instead, he can remember a specific time in his own life when he *was* cold and allow that memory to inform his acting in the scene.

Emotional memory has to do with feelings. The actor playing Fred might believe that in the best interpretation of the scene, Fred should become immediately and violently confrontational with Ricky. But the actor may be a shy man in real life. Or he may find that when he is in character, his anger sounds false and inauthentic, blustery rather than frightening. He must then review his life history for a time when he lost his temper, when he did fly off the handle and explode terrifyingly at another person. He must find an emotional memory that corresponds to Fred's emotion in the scene.

The circumstances needn't match Fred's in any way; trucks and driveways are not required. Maybe the actor remembers screaming at someone who accidentally bumped into him on the street. Maybe he remembers losing his temper when his kid brother broke his prized model airplane. What matters isn't the circumstances that produced the emotion in his real life but the appropriateness to the scene of the remembered feeling itself. Emotional memory serves to ground and make personal the emotion required in the play.

Method Acting

Stanislavski's system spread through the American theater thanks largely to the work of Lee Strasberg, founder and guru of the legendary Actors Studio. Strasberg was famous—some would say infamous—for demanding that actors dig perilously deep into their psyches and emotional lives to find memories and substitutes for their characters' experiences. *Method acting*, as it came to be called, resulted in profound, powerful, and shockingly realistic performances. Method actors such as Marlon Brando produced work that was nothing short of revolutionary.

Strasberg's Method proved particularly well-suited to the psychologically rich dramas of Arthur Miller, Tennessee Williams, Clifford Odets, and Eugene O'Neill, which were being written at the time Strasberg was teaching. But the Method often foundered in the classical theater, whose highly elevated texts seemed to defy personalization. The psychologies, imaginations, personalities, and experiences of such characters from the classical canon as Oedipus, Alceste, Hamlet, and King Lear are simply too large to be approximated by some remembered episode from the life of a mere mortal. Furthermore, for actors not blessed with the genius of a Marlon Brando, the Method's reliance on intense personal emotion could lead to self-indulgent, sentimental performances.

One of Strasberg's contemporaries, the great teacher Sanford Meisner, was particularly attuned to the trap of self-indulgence. His techniques, developed at his Neighborhood Playhouse in New York City, emphasized that despite all the preparation an actress must complete in rehearsal and in private, she must never plan in advance what she's going to do in the heat of performance. Every actress, Meisner taught, must always remain open to what is happening right in front of her, on stage, right now. Accordingly, Meisner training places a huge emphasis on *listening*, and on the importance of not responding until one has fully absorbed what's just been said or done. It insists that actors develop extraordinary powers of observation, so that they are able to perceive even the minutest change in the environment and in the people around them and to let those perceptions affect their responses. The goal is to be "in the moment," as actors put it—alive in the present and experiencing the events of the play as if they are happening for the very first time.

Post-Method Acting

In the latter half of the twentieth century, actor training began to integrate the best of the Method and other Stanislavskian techniques with an approach derived from the European classical tradition. The Method's basic impulse is to bring the character to the actor, to view the character's existence through the lens of the personal experiences of the actor playing him. But the classical theater tends to require the opposite: that the actor come to the character. A classical actor subsumes his own persona to the character's, becoming a vessel for the larger truths embedded in and embodied through a timeless text. In this approach, the words lead the way. All the other homework an actor does is indispensable. She must analyze her character's objectives, obstacles, and actions. She must consider the given circumstances and imagine how she would react if she experienced them. But what really makes her work thrilling, and what best serves the play, is her facility with the words themselves.

As we continue through *Thinking Shakespeare*, we will find countless points at which a character simply *talks*. Like a patient on a psychiatrist's couch, a Shakespearean figure will go on for a while, unburdening himself for dozens of lines, and then stop. It can be difficult to identify the action behind a fifty-line speech and challenging to see how the given circumstances of the scene influence the way that speech unfolds. Trickier still is to see how one's own life experience might connect to such a torrent of complex and elevated language. Yet there always is an action, and the given circumstances always are relevant, and one's own personal background always does apply. It is the actor's joy to dig and explore and then to share his findings with the audience. And it is the actor's obligation to balance these findings against the fundamental importance of making the words clear and vivid and exciting.

REHEARSAL TIME

Let's look at a short passage from Shakespeare to see how to strike this balance. In this scene from *Hamlet*, Horatio has come to the prince to tell him something very important.

HORATIO	My lord, I think I saw him yesternight.	
HAMLET	Saw? Who?	
HORATIO	My lord, the King your father.	
HAMLET	The King my father!	
HORATIO	Season your admiration for awhile	5
	With an attent ear, till I may deliver,	
	Upon the witness of these gentlemen,	
	This marvel to you.	
HAMLET	For God's love, let me hear.	

(1.2.188–195)

Much can be said about even the shortest excerpts from Shakespeare, but let's confine our rehearsal to the basic exploration of the characters' circumstances, objectives, obstacles, and actions.

Given Circumstances

Here are the questions actors playing this scene might ask, followed by the answers they might find, based on their careful reading of the scenes that have taken place up to this point in the play:

Where are we? We're in Denmark. It's wintertime. We're in one of the large halls in Elsinore Castle, the seat of Denmark's royal family.

What has happened prior to this scene? Hamlet was in college at the University of Wittenberg when his father, Old Hamlet, King of Denmark, died. Hamlet came home for his father's funeral and discovered that "within a month" of the king's death, Hamlet's mother, Gertrude, married his uncle Claudius.

Horatio, a classmate of Hamlet's at Wittenberg, also returned to Denmark for the king's funeral. Last night, at the invitation of Marcellus and Bernardo, two palace guards who are also present in this scene, Horatio went to the castle ramparts, where he saw and tried to speak with the ghost of the dead king.

What has happened in the moments immediately prior to this exchange between Hamlet and Horatio? Claudius and Gertrude have just left the room after a celebratory public appearance that ended with some awkward moments between them and Hamlet. Left alone, Hamlet spoke at length of the pain he feels about his father's death and his anger at his mother and uncle for their unseemly, hasty marriage. He said he must keep quiet about his feelings, even though to do so breaks his heart.

What are the relationships? Hamlet and Horatio are college chums. Hamlet is a prince; Horatio is a commoner and, like so many university students, is broke. Despite this class difference, they are very close. They share confidences and speak frankly and openly with each other.

Objectives

What is Horatio's objective? Horatio wants Hamlet to know about last night's incredible events (after the ghost disappears at sunrise, he tells Marcellus and Bernardo, "Let us impart what we have seen tonight / Unto young Hamlet"). His objective in this scene, then, might be *to reveal* to Hamlet what he saw, or *to share* important information the prince should know, or *to alert* Hamlet to some remarkable news about his late father. An actor might even borrow Shakespeare's own verb and say that Horatio's objective here is *to impart* the facts to his friend.

These are good, clear answers to the question of Horatio's objective, expressed in strong verbs easily translatable into actions. But once Horatio tells Hamlet about the ghost, which he does in line 3 of this excerpt, this objective is achieved. He must then undertake a new objective, based on what he needs to achieve next or formed in response to Hamlet's reaction to this news or some other development in the story. In addition to fulfilling an immediate need, both of these moment-to-moment objectives support a larger objective that motivates Horatio throughout the entire play.

This larger objective is sometimes called the character's *super objective.*[5] The super objective envelops and includes everything

---

5 Some call the super objective the character's *spine.* Acting terminology is hardly standard, although the basic techniques it labels do not change.

the character does. It answers the question, "What does this character want in this play?" It is his all-encompassing need; it is the reason the character is in the story.

For example, Horatio's super objective might be *to help heal* the pain his friend feels over King Hamlet's passing and Gertrude's remarriage. *To support* Hamlet, *to be there for* Hamlet, *to love* Hamlet—these are also valid super objectives for Horatio.

What is Hamlet's objective? It changes as the scene progresses. At first, Hamlet's objective is *to be alone* with his thoughts, or *to ruminate*, or, more actively, *to find a solution* to his dilemma. (In one production I saw, Hamlet's objective at the beginning of this excerpt was *to chill out*, an objective he achieved with these actions: *to smoke* a cigarette and *to down* a shot of whiskey!) Once Horatio tells him about his father's ghost, Hamlet's objective changes: now it is *to digest* what Horatio has told him or *to interrogate* his friend or, perhaps, *to reject* Horatio's wild claim (or, conversely, *to rejoice* in his father's seeming return from the grave).

Hamlet's super objective is harder to pin down. Later in the play, after he speaks with the ghost, it becomes *to avenge* his father's death. At this point, it might be *to figure out* how to live in a world as corrupt as today's Denmark, or *to manage* overwhelming grief, or *to mourn* a great personal loss.

Obstacles and Actions

What is Horatio's obstacle? Horatio is afraid that Hamlet will think he's out of his mind. The outlandishness of his story—that the ghost of Hamlet's dead father is roaming about town—is an obstacle that might prevent Hamlet from believing it. This outlandishness is therefore also an obstacle to telling it. Hamlet's frail psyche and deep grief are potential obstacles as well: the news about his father might upset the prince, or worse, drive him mad. All these factors together are impediments to Horatio's objective of telling the prince what he saw.

Given his obstacle, what is Horatio's action? Look closely at Horatio's language. "My lord, I think I saw him yesternight." Horatio *did* see the ghost last night. Yet he doesn't say, "I know I saw him" or even "I saw him"; he says, "I think I saw him." The word *think* suggests that Horatio is stalling a bit. He's reluctant to come right out and say what he has to say. This makes great sense in light of the obstacles we've identified.

The best choice for Horatio's action in this line, therefore, isn't *to blurt out* the information or *to announce* it, but rather *to sidle up* to it, *to hedge* a little.

What is Hamlet's obstacle? Hamlet's first objective—to be alone—is of course flouted by the arrival of three people. They are his obstacle. His next objective, *to digest* the information about his father, or *to learn* more about it, is blocked by the same obstacle that blocks Horatio: the unlikelihood of the nonsensical information itself.

Given his obstacles, what are Hamlet's actions? His first action, intended to overcome the obstacle to his being alone, might be *to ignore* the three arriving men. It might be *to turn his back* on them. (Or, as I once saw in yet another production, it might be *to listen* to an iPod and *to block* them out.)

Hamlet's actions in response to the information Horatio gives him are more complex. Again, look carefully at the words he uses. His first utterance, "Saw?" is obviously intended *to question* Horatio. That's rather general, so we might say instead that Hamlet's line seems intended *to make sure* he heard right, *to confirm* what he thinks Horatio said. That "Saw?" might also suggest Hamlet's disbelief at what his friend has told him. Disbelief is a wonderful action to play—Shakespeare gives it to his characters again and again. Hamlet's action is *to disbelieve* what he's heard.

Horatio doesn't respond to the one-word question, "Saw?" Hamlet still has not gotten the further information he wants. So he asks another question: "Who?" The action here might be *to plead* for more information, or *to urge* Horatio to explain. But remember: we always want to make choices that intensify the situation, adding to the conflict in the scene. Hamlet's action on "Who?" then, is best interpreted as a reflection of his increasing need to know, and therefore increases in intensity from his previous action. *To challenge* Horatio, or *to insist* that he clarify matters, are two good, strong actions for this line.

Note that as our line-by-line analysis of each character's actions continues, it dovetails neatly with the central *Thinking Shakespeare* question: "Why am I using these words now?" All of our choices arise from a careful consideration of the text.

ACTIONS VERSUS STATES OF BEING   In line 3 of the excerpt, Horatio obliges the prince's demand for more information. He now knows from listening to Hamlet's skeptical questions and observing his disbelieving manner that the prince does indeed find the information outlandish. This obstacle continues to impede his need to tell more. On the line, "My lord, the King your father," the actor can continue to play Horatio's reluctance to speak, perhaps saying the line apologetically. But that's a choice of avoidance, not engagement, and it makes the scene weaker and less active than it could be. Instead, the actor can increase the conflict in the scene by throwing himself right up against the obstacle of Hamlet's doubt and interpreting Horatio's line aggressively. His action might be *to force* Hamlet to hear the truth, *to expose* all the facts, or *to administer* some tough love to his friend.

In response to Horatio's full and frank disclosure, Hamlet's next line, "The King my father!" could be played in a number of ways. He could continue to disbelieve, in which case his action might be *to scoff*, *to jeer*, or *to dismiss*. But Horatio's next line refers to the prince's "admiration," which in Elizabethan English means, roughly, "astonishment." This indicates that Hamlet believes what Horatio has said but is stunned by it. If you are playing Hamlet, therefore, you might be tempted to say that the prince's action in line 4 is *to be stunned*.

Be careful: *to be* something is not the same as *to do* something. Being stunned is simply an emotional state. An actor playing such a *state of being* shows the audience the result of someone else's action rather than an action of his own. States of being are passive, and what an actor must be is *active*. On "The King my father!" as on every line, Hamlet must play an action: *to disbelieve* might work again, or *to struggle* with the impossible, or *to puzzle* at the news, or *to wonder* at it. All of these choices are active and engaged with the scene and the other characters.

Later in the play Hamlet actually discusses the gulf between being and doing when he comes to the realization that he might "lose the name of action." He realizes this after asking in his most famous speech, "To be, or not to be, that is the question." For actors, the answer to Hamlet's eternal conundrum is clear: not to be. Simply being on stage won't do; actors must find the name of action, even if the Dane cannot. Acting is doing.

ACTION LEADS TO EMOTION Although the distinction between playing an action and playing a state of being is an important one, the two concepts are linked.

Hamlet's line, "The King my father!" illustrates this point. By playing the *action* of disbelieving or wondering, the actor playing Hamlet will automatically feel the *emotion* of being stunned (or being in "admiration," as Horatio says). It's one of the cardinal rules of acting: *action creates emotion.*

This is not an easy concept to embrace. Actors rightly want to make sure that they feel all the emotions their roles demand. But even in offstage life, we know that feelings almost never come out of the blue. They are always a function of events, of things that happen, of things we do.

Again, Hamlet provides an example. We found in our discussion of the scene's given circumstances that the speech he gives while alone prior to Horatio's arrival ends with him saying he has a broken heart ("But break, my heart," he says, in the final line of the speech that begins, "O that this too too solid flesh would melt" [1.2.129–158]). An actor playing Hamlet must of course feel that heartbreak, must portray that emotion in an authentic and believable way. But he can't do that by simply *being* heartbroken. This use of prefabricated emotion is certain to ring false. If the actor is trained in the Method, he could search his own past for a heartbreaking moment and remember it on stage. This too results in playing a state of being, inactive at best and self-indulgent at worst. A better approach is to arrive at the emotion through action. The thirty-line speech preceding Hamlet's heartbreak brims with active talk. Anatomizing the morally dubious shotgun wedding of Claudius and Gertrude, the speech serves *to rail* against an injustice, *to protest* a great wrong, *to decry* a grievous error. When, at the end of the speech, the force of all that verbal action collides with an immovable obstacle—the permanence of the marriage and Hamlet's inability to undo it—the pain, futility, and dejection of the situation automatically arise. The emotion washes over the prince, and the actor playing him, all by itself. Hamlet's broken heart appears on stage naturally, organically.

Doing comes before feeling. Always be doing. Always be in action. The feelings will follow.

Substitution

The actors playing Hamlet and Horatio, like those who played Ricky and Fred in *Driveway Wars*, will examine their own lives for parallels that might help them with the scene. Perhaps they have been to Denmark or inside a royal castle. They have almost certainly experienced winter, and they know what it's like to have a close friend. It may be that one or both of them have buried a father, and so the pain of talking about such matters may be easier to imagine.

These are the more straightforward aspects of the scene. But surely neither actor has encountered anyone's father's ghost, or any other ghost, or had to say so. How do you make *that* authentic and real?

Here we learn the value of the Method acting technique of substitution to the classical actor. The actor who needs to discuss an impossibility—what it's like to see a ghost—can scan his memory for a time when he had to describe something very difficult to believe. Perhaps he once went to the redwood forests of northern California and struggled to put into words how overwhelming those amazing trees are. Or perhaps he was in New York City on September 11, 2001, and recalls what it was like to describe the terrifying sight of two 110-story buildings collapsing into dust.

The actor playing Horatio will want to choose memories of prodigious things such as these, because they will better correspond to the prodigious turn of events the character is trying to describe. Remember that the issue for Horatio and the actor is not the specific reality of the ghost itself. After all, in Scene One of the play, the ghost actually appears to him. The actor will therefore have a concrete image in his mind when he talks about it. No, the issue is the awkwardness of talking about it at all. The power of substitution in this case is that it will help him bring authenticity and emotional truth to how difficult it can sometimes be just to talk, especially when the subject under discussion is so overpowering.

Substitution can make anything real, no matter how far-fetched. Being real is the actor's job. Playing actions and thinking thoughts and speaking words that convince the audience that a real situation is unfolding before their eyes—this is the actor's magic.

Doing. And imagining. And remembering. And feeling. This is the actor's art.

Shakespeare demands that it be practiced at its highest level.

ACT II

David McCallum as the title role, surrounded by the conspirators who stabbed him, in *Julius Caesar,* directed by Barry Edelstein at the New York Shakespeare Festival / Public Theater's "Shakespeare in the Park," 2000. Photo © Michal Daniel, 2000.

ACT II

CHAPTER
—№—
3

THAT WOULD
BE SCANNED

SCANSION AND THE ARCHITECTURE
OF THE VERSE LINE

Before we start thinking Shakespeare's text, it's crucial to explore some elemental principles of its composition.

One of these principles goes right to the DNA of the language, to the core precepts that govern how the words coalesce into groupings that express thought. That aboriginal precept is known as *scansion*.

Scansion is a complicated word for something very simple: rhythm. Just as notes on a staff tell a musician how to phrase a piece of music, scansion tells an actor working with poetic writing how to phrase a certain line.

Every line of verse in Shakespeare is written within a certain rhythmic framework. No matter how varied and complex that framework may grow, it arises from one tiny component: the syllable. The rhythm of the text is dictated by the stresses placed on syllables when they're spoken. Those syllabic stresses fall into patterns, and those patterns come together to make a kind of scaffolding—a rhythmic framework—that holds poetic language together.

Scansion is a tool that actors can use to understand and harness the rhythmic framework of the text as they work on it. *Scanning* poetry is naming and analyzing the way it works rhythmically.

Cities, States, Syllables, and Stresses

Here's how scansion works.

Think about *Detroit*. Not the city, but its name. When you say it, *-troit* has more stress than *De*. Cars are made in de-TROIT. Not DE-troit. The second syllable is stressed, not the first.

The nonsense syllables *dee-DUM* have the same pattern: first syllable unstressed, second syllable stressed.

Boston, on the other hand, is different. Its first syllable, *Bos*, is stressed, but the second isn't. Where's Fenway Park? BOS-ton. *DUM-dee*.

Tennessee has three syllables, the first two unstressed and the third stressed: *dee-dee-DUM*.

Iowa is the opposite: *DUM-dee-dee*.

Look at the pattern of syllables in this bit of language:

New York, New York	*dee-DUM dee-DUM*
It's a helluva town.	*dee-dee-DUM dee-dee-DUM*
The Bronx is up,	*dee-DUM dee-DUM*
But the Battery's down.	*dee-dee-DUM dee-dee-DUM*

We could create the exact same rhythm by saying this:

Detroit Detroit
Tennessee Tennessee
Detroit Detroit
Tennessee Tennessee

If you wanted to label the rhythm of these lines, you might say that the first line, two *dee-DUM*s, is a "Double Detroit," and the second line is a "Two Tennessee."

That's scansion.

All you need to know is what pattern the stressed and unstressed syllables make and how many repetitions of that pattern are found in each line of poetry.

The Language of Scansion, Part One: Feet

As diverting as it is to analyze Shakespeare with the names of American cities and states, scansion has a standard vocabulary that, though less colorful, is more useful.

Each unit of syllables is called a *foot. Feet* come in seven major varieties:

An *iamb* (pronounced *I am*; adjectival form *iambic*) has two syllables. The first is unstressed and the second is stressed: *dee-DUM*. Examples: *Detroit* (de-TROIT), *New York* (new YORK)

A *trochee* (*TROE-kee*; adjectival form *trochaic*) also has two syllables. The first is stressed and the second is unstressed: *DUM-dee*. Examples: *London* (LON-don), *Boston* (BOS-ton)

An *anapest* (*AN-a-pest*; adjectival form *anapestic*) has three syllables. The first two are unstressed and the third is stressed:

dee-dee-DUM. Examples: *Tennessee* (ten-nes-SEE), *New Orleans* (new or-LEANS)

A *dactyl* (DACK-till; adjectival form *dactylic*), which also has three syllables, is the opposite. The first syllable is stressed and the second two are unstressed: *DUM-dee-dee*. Examples: *Iowa* (I-o-wa), *Michigan* (MICH-i-gan)[6]

An *amphibrach* (AM-fi-brack; adjectival form *amphibraic* or *amphibractic*) has three syllables. The first syllable is unstressed, the second is stressed, and the third is unstressed: *dee-DUM-dee*. Examples: *Chicago* (chi-CA-go), *Alaska* (a-LAS-ka)

Two types of feet remain, and they are a little more unusual than the five above.

A *spondee* (SPON-dee; adjectival form *spondaic*) has two syllables. Both are stressed: *DUM-DUM*.

The *pyrrhic* (PEER-ick; adjectival form also *pyrrhic*), the spondee's opposite, also has two syllables. Both are unstressed: *dee-dee*.

Individual words that are spondaic or pyrrhic are hard to find, although both feet are common in poetry. Consider these famous verses:

----

6 Iambs and anapests are sometimes called *rising* rhythms because they start gently and build upward toward stresses. Trochees and dactyls, on the other hand, are sometimes called *falling* rhythms, because they start strong and then fall off, getting softer.

O say, can you see
By the dawn's early light
What so proudly we hailed
At the twilight's last gleaming . . .

The third line's rhythm is *dee-dee DUM-dee DUM-DUM*. That's a pyrrhic and a spondee separated by a trochee.

The Language of Scansion, Part Two: Meter

Once you identify the kind of feet in a given line, there's one more step involved in scanning it. You need to figure out the *meter*, or number of feet in the line. The meter is counted with these prefixes:

Mono = 1
Di = 2
Tri = 3
Tetra = 4
Penta = 5
Hexa = 6
Hepta = 7
Octa = 8

And so on.

Feet + Meter = Scansion

The scansion of a line is labeled by the adjectival form of the foot that composes it plus the word *meter* and the correct prefix.

For example, look at these lines from *A Midsummer Night's Dream*:

If we shadows have offended,
Think but this and all is mended . . . (Ep.1–2)

The rhythm of both lines goes *DUM-dee DUM-dee DUM-dee DUM-dee*. That's four trochees, a "tetra" meter of trochees, or *trochaic tetrameter* (tet-TRAM-iter).

Here's a line from *The Comedy of Errors*:

Ay, when fowls have no feathers and fish have no fin. (3.1.79)

The rhythm of the line is *dee-dee-DUM dee-dee-DUM dee-dee-DUM dee-dee-DUM*. That's four anapests, or anapestic tetrameter.

All these technical terms are a real mouthful. Don't worry about them too much. I've been directing Shakespeare professionally for the better part of two decades, which means that I've worked with actors on tens of thousands of lines of verse. I can count on one hand the number of times I've actually discussed the technical names for the meter. I may have pointed out a few times that a certain line began with a trochee, or that another phrase relied on spondees, but even those cases were exceptions. It's useful to know that scansion is a real thing, with terminology and methodology behind it. But all that really matters is that an actor is able to sense that there's a rhythm built in to the language he's speaking. That's the value of scansion. Go to a rehearsal of a professional Shakespeare production and you'll see people pounding through the beat of the lines, banging on tables like the late great Keith Moon and tapping their feet like Savion Glover. It's a cacophony of *dee-DUM*s and *DUM-dee*s. It's the percussion section in the Shakespeare Orchestra.

This fact—that the lines have a kind of music—counts for more than the technical names ever do, as useful as those names may be as tools for analysis and discussion.

Iambic Pentameter: The Most Important Meter

There is, however, one particular mouthful of Greek that's really good to know: *iambic pentameter*.

Five iambs. It goes like this:

dee-DUM dee-DUM dee-DUM dee-DUM dee-DUM

It's the most common meter in Shakespeare. It's his bread and butter.

Think of the Bard's most famous lines. They are all built on this rhythm:

The quality of mercy is not strained
= the QUAL-i-TY of MER-cy IS not STRAINED

To be or not to be, that is the question
= to BE or NOT to BE that IS the QUES-(tion)

Friends, Romans, Countrymen, lend me your ears
= friends ROM-ans COUNT-ry-MEN lend ME your EARS

Now is the winter of our discontent
= now IS the WIN-ter OF our DIS-con-TENT

Tomorrow and tomorrow and tomorrow
= to-MOR-row AND to-MOR-row AND to-MOR-(row)

It's all iambic pentameter. (For the record, it does have a plain English name: *blank verse*. The terms are interchangeable.)

Metric Stress Versus Natural Stress

Clearly, no actor in her right mind would say "the QUAL-i-TY of MER-cy IS not STRAINED," or "friends ROM-ans COUNT-ry-MEN lend ME your EARS." Most actors would follow their instincts with these lines and say them much more naturally. Try it. They will probably come out something like,

> the QUALity of MERcy is NOT STRAINED
> *dee-DUM dee-dee dee-DUM dee-DUM DUM-DUM*

That's iamb pyrrhic iamb iamb spondee.

> FRIENDS, ROMans, COUNTrymen, LEND ME your EARS
> DUM-DUM dee-DUM dee-dee DUM-DUM dee-DUM

That's spondee iamb pyrrhic spondee iamb.

You may even find other natural ways to say these lines. That's fine. While the scansion says the language is iambic pentameter, *the natural instincts of most speakers of English* will make the rhythm something else, something less rigorously structured and more free. In other words, there's a difference between the *metric stress* (the scansion) and the *natural stress*.

....

THINKING SHAKESPEARE RULE: Trust your instincts about which words need stress, but verify those instincts by comparing them with what the meter says.

....

I call this the Ronald Reagan Rule, after the president's famous admonition to Mikhail Gorbachev during nuclear treaty negotiations. He said, "Trust, but verify." (He actually liked to say it in Russian—*Dovyai no Provyai*—which apparently drove poor Gorby crazy.)

Remember that scansion is a rhythmic *framework*, not a rhythmic straitjacket. There is plenty of maneuvering room within it.

"There is a tide in the affairs of men," says Brutus in *Julius Caesar*, "which, taken at the flood, leads on to fortune." (4.2.270–272) The scansion says that for this to be iambic pentameter, the stresses must fall like this:

there IS a TIDE in THE af-FAIRS of MEN
which TAK-en AT the FLOOD leads ON to FORT-une

But say the line out loud, as if you're telling someone how important it is to seize opportunities in life:

there is a TIDE in the afFAIRS of MEN
which TAKen at the FLOOD LEADS ON to FORTune.

dee-dee dee-DUM dee-dee dee-DUM dee-DUM
dee-DUM dee-dee dee-DUM DUM-DUM dee-DUM dee

When these two lines are spoken naturally, they reveal not a regular and rigid march of ten iambs but instead a funky arrangement of mostly iambs, mixed in with some spondees and pyrrhics.

The Ronald Reagan Rule reminds us that scansion is there as a structure, a guide, a roadmap. If it doesn't help you communicate the thought behind the line, it's useless. There is no point in adhering to it slavishly. Let your instincts lead you.

Think of the interplay between metric and natural stress as good jazz. The drummer is the scansion. He keeps a beat going. The soloists are the actors speaking with natural stress. They play all kinds of improvisations around the drumbeat, flexing and changing their own rhythms in counterpoint to the pattern established by the drums. There's a word for this that jazz players know well: *syncopation*. Shakespeare knows it too. His rhythm is surprising, jazzy. Syncopated. He uses scansion the same way a nightclub combo uses the drums, hearing it as a baseline rhythm, then improvising all around it.

Writing the Scansion Out

As you're checking your instinctual line readings against the meter, it sometimes helps to write out the scansion.

Rather than rewriting the words with UPPERCASE and lowercase letters, try this accepted shorthand to indicate how they scan. First, separate the line into its individual feet with vertical lines:

Now is | the win | ter of | our dis | content.

Then mark the stressed syllables with accent marks (´) and the unstressed ones with carets (˘). Sometimes you'll see the unstressed lines marked with *x*'s or dashes. Whatever works; it's a matter of individual preference.

    ˘   ´   ˘   ´   ˘ ´   ˘   ´   ˘   ´
Now is | the win | ter of | our dis | content

That's the metric stress. Now say the line as your instincts tell you it should sound.

Now is | the win | ter of | our dis | content

Notice that if spoken naturally, the stress in the first foot falls not on *is* but on *Now*. The line starts with a trochee, not an iamb, which is a syncopation Shakespeare loves. Note also that *of* doesn't really get stress at all, creating a pyrrhic foot halfway trough the line. The framework is still iambic pentameter, but there are variations: that initial trochee and the pyrrhic in the middle.

The regular meter is the line's rhythmic framework. The sense of the thought being expressed by the line makes the natural expression twirl and pirouette around the meter in a lively and exciting dance.

REHEARSAL TIME

Here are two lines from *Hamlet*. They are spoken by the Ghost of Hamlet's father, the Old King, who has led Hamlet to an isolated part of the castle ramparts to tell him how he was murdered by Claudius, his brother. He bemoans the intimate relationship between Claudius, who is now the king, and Hamlet's mother—and the Old King's widow—Queen Gertrude, and he urges Hamlet to block it.

Let not the royal bed of Denmark be
A couch for luxury and damned incest. (1.5.82–83)

The sense of what he's telling Hamlet is "Don't let the bed where the Danish monarch sleeps turn into a sleazy place for a quickie."

Let's scan the lines, according to how the meter says they should sound.

   ˇ   ˊ   ˇ   ˊ   ˇ   ˊ   ˇ   ˊ   ˇ   ˊ

Let not | the roy | al bed | of Den | mark be

   ˇ   ˊ   ˇ   ˊ ˇ   ˇ   ˊ   ˇ   ˊ

A couch | for lux | ury | and damned | incest.

VARIATION ONE: THE NATURAL STRESS   But according to the natural stress of the first line, it's really more like this:

   ˊ   ˊ   ˇ   ˊ   ˇ   ˊ   ˇ   ˊ   ˇ   ˊ

Let not | the roy | al bed | of Den | mark be

The first foot is a spondee, not an iamb.

Look at the last word of the second line, "incest." Iambic pentameter says it's *inCEST*, which sounds odd. We know the word's pronunciation to be *INcest*. If we say it that way, the line scans like this:

   ˇ   ˊ   ˇ   ˊ ˇ   ˊ   ˇ   ˊ   ˊ   ˇ

A couch | for lux | ury | and damned | incest.

DAMNED INcest. Two stressed syllables jam up against one another, breaking the alternating iambic pattern. That sticks in the mouth as you say it. It hiccups; it's not smooth.

VARIATION TWO: AN "-ED" ENDING   What if "damned" has two syllables?

˘   ′   ˘   ′   ˘ ′   ˘   ′   ˘   ′   ˘

A couch | for lux | ury | and dam | ned in | cest.

DAM-ned INcest flows better, and it allows you to pronounce "incest" in the familiar way. But it requires you to pronounce the -ed ending on "damned" as its own syllable. The usually silent n in the word is pronounced, and the -ed is accented, or inflected. This is one of the old-fashioned sounds that we always associate with Shakespeare, those -eds that crop up everywhere. This line shows where they come from. They are in the text because the scansion puts them there.[7]

At this point, our central *Thinking Shakespeare* question enters into the analysis of scansion. *Why would Old King Hamlet say "DAM-ned" now?*

Remember, he was murdered by his brother, who is now married to his widow. Theirs is an incestuous relationship, and the king considers incest not merely a personal affront but horrid and evil in general. In a word, it's damned. In fact, it's even worse than damned. It's DAM-ned. The -ed ending gives the word more power. It expresses the idea of damnation with fury, with an almost biblical scope. The language articulates the thought in the most forceful possible way.

---

7 We still pronounce some words with this stressed -ed in modern English, as when we talk about caring for the *aged*, or a *learned* scholar.

VARIATION THREE: OVERCOMPLICATION But the scansion offers yet one more way to approach "damned incest." If "luxury" has not three syllables but only two, "lux'ry" then the line goes:

˘ ´ ˘ ´ ˘ ´ ˘ ´ ˘ ´

A couch | for lux | ry and | damned | in cest.

We still get the *-ed* ending on "damned," this time in a position of strong stress, plus we have to twist "incest" so that the stress again falls, unusually, on its second syllable. a COUCH for LUX-ry AND dam-NED in-CEST.

Although technically a possible way to scan this line, this is not a very natural way to say it. Stressing "and" is odd, as is saying "dam-NED," and that pesky "in-CEST" still comes out backward. Strange readings like this one show why it's important not to follow scansion blindly. If you do, overcomplicated, nonsensical line readings can be the unfortunate result.

VARIATION FOUR: THE CREATIVE ACTOR'S INSTINCTS Sometimes, though, even odd readings have value. Strict observance of the scansion when it does something that feels unusual can lead you to discover something you may have missed at first. Here's an example:

In one production I worked on, the actor playing the Ghost of Old Hamlet went through most rehearsals saying, "a COUCH for LUX-u-ry and DAM-ned IN-cest," the way we found the line naturally falls out in Variation One. One day, for reasons not entirely clear to me, he decided to sit down and re-scan all his lines. He found as we did that strict iambic pentameter makes the line end with "DAMNED in-CEST." Rather than dismissing that reading as odd-sounding, though, one night in performance he gave it a whirl, pouring into the words all of Old Hamlet's disgust and rage over Claudius and Gertrude's unwholesome relations. It sounded like this:

a COUCH for LUX-u-ry and DAMNED in-***CEST!!!!!***

It was a searing moment. The very idea of incest seemed to rack Old Hamlet's soul. The word stuck in his throat, then exploded out, as though he were vomiting up this evil practice he hated so deeply. The actor's odd twist on the shape of the language perfectly captured his character's agony. It was thrilling theater.

Was it the right way to read the line? Impossible to say. As we've seen, there's more than one "right" way according to the scansion—at least three in this case—so, therefore, there's no one "right" way at all. One way of saying the line worked well for this particular actor in this particular production. Another actor in another production might say it differently, perhaps even in some other way we've not yet imagined. Another actor might even say it one way for evening performances and another way at the matinees!

The point is that this actor trusted his instincts, and when he checked them against the scansion, he discovered something potentially useful to him. Combined with his actor's imagination and his actor's kit of expressive tools, this discovery resulted in an arresting moment on stage.

Trust your instincts, but compare them against the meter. *Dovyai no Provyai.*

....

THINGS FURTHER THOUGHT ON

....

Elision

Squeezing words to make them fit the scansion is called *elision*. In Old Hamlet's lines, for example, we compressed the three syllables of "luxury" into two in order to look at the many different ways one line could possibly scan.

To elide is to streamline the rhythm of a word by pushing syllables together. Usually, an apostrophe (') indicates where the missing syllable goes. *O'er* is an elision of *over*; "o'th'clock" is an elision of "of the clock." Shakespeare often uses these elisions, as well as less familiar ones such as *heav'n* for *heaven* and *sev'n* for *seven*. Here are two examples:

In *All's Well that Ends Well*, Helena confesses to the stern and elderly Countess that she is in love with her son, Bertram.

> . . . Then, I confess,
> Here on my knee, before high heaven and you,
> That before you, and next unto high heaven,
> I love your son. (1.3.175–178)

The first time "heaven" is said, it is elided so that it scans "heav'n." It becomes one syllable instead of two. The second time, it scans either elided as "heav'n" or unelided as "heaven." "Heav'n" is hard to say and can sound unnatural in the mouth of a modern actor. That's fine. Just say "heaven." As long as the stress is good and strong on the first syllable, the scansion will be fine. All that really matters is that the thought is clear.

Here's a more famous example:

O Romeo, Romeo, wherefore art thou Romeo? (2.1.74)

If Juliet were to pronounce all three syllables in Romeo's name each time she says it, it would scan like this:

˘ ´ ˘´ ˘ ´˘ ´ ˘ ´ ˘ ´ ˘´
O Romeo, Romeo, wherefore art thou Romeo?

That's seven iambs, and two different ways of saying the name: ROM-e-O and rom-E-o. It's a mess. If his name always has two syllables, however, with the first always stressed, the line becomes regular iambic pentameter again:

˘ ´ ˘ ´ ˘ ´ ˘ ´ ˘ ´ ˘
O Romeo, Romeo, wherefore art thou Romeo?

The two syllables "e-o" are elided into one, "-yo," and loverboy's name becomes ROME-yo, and the line sounds smooth and right.

Feminine Endings

Let's return one more time to the Ghost of Old Hamlet. When we scan the line "A couch for luxury and damned incest" with the inflected *-ed* ending on "damned" and with "incest" pronounced in its familiar way, we create an extra, eleventh syllable at the end of the ten-beat iambic line: *-cest.*

˘ ´ ˘ ´ ˘´ ˘ ´ ˘ ´ ˘
A couch | for lux | ury | and dam | ned in | cest.

That spare wheel has a name: *feminine ending*. In the iambic pattern, syllable number eleven will always be unstressed, or soft. And alas, because women were considered soft and dainty in the sexist worldview that prevailed when these techniques were first codified, unstressed endings are called feminine. A line that ends on beat number ten, which in the iambic pattern is a strong stress, is called *masculine*. (There is a gender-neutral term for a feminine ending, but it's rather less poetic: *hypermetrical*, meaning "having too much meter." With apologies, this book will use the more descriptive and more familiar term.)

What do feminine endings do?

Consider Hamlet's "To be or not to be" speech. (3.1.59–92) It is full of feminine endings, a fact that becomes apparent when we take them away:

> To be, or not to be: that is the ques
> Whether tis nobler in the mind to suff
> The slings and arrows of outrageous for
> Or to take arms against a sea of troub
> And by opposing, end them . . .

The final syllables of each line, "-tion," "-er," "-tune" and "-les" are eleventh beats, or feminine endings. Why are they there?

In this case, they serve to make the words they're part of sound more special. "Question," "suffer," "fortune," and "troubles" are very important ideas in this speech. We'll see later in this book that throughout Shakespeare's works the important words in a verse line tend to come at the end and that the energy of thought always moves forward toward them. The feminine endings in these four lines are the climax toward which each line drives. Try it:

To be, or not to be: that is the **question**.
Whether tis nobler in the mind to **suffer**
The slings and arrows of outrageous **fortune**,
Or to take arms against a sea of **troubles**
And by opposing, end them . . .

Those special words get special emphasis, thanks to their endings' femininity.

Modern Versus Shakespearean Pronunciation

Sometimes the scansion requires that a word be pronounced in a way unfamiliar to our modern ears, because in Shakespeare's period, that word *was* pronounced differently. *Revenue*, meaning income or property that earns income is one example. Shakespeare uses the word a few dozen times, always with the accent on the second syllable: re-VEN-ue. Here's an example from *A Midsummer Night's Dream*:

I have a widow aunt, a dowager
Of great revenue, and she hath no child. (1.1.157–158)

Some actors and directors might prefer to use the scansion-busting modern pronunciation, REV-en-ue. That's fine; the Shakespeare Police won't come and arrest you if you say it that way, and today's audiences might even be grateful that you're making Shakespeare a little bit easier to understand. But traditionalists would argue that re-VEN-ue, though more foreign-sounding to modern ears, is not only more authentic but also makes for a smoother flow and more harmonious sound. There's no right or wrong, but the debate can't even begin until the scansion is analyzed.

Impious, meaning not reverent (the opposite of "pious") is always stressed on the first syllable in Shakespeare, unlike how it's most often pronounced today. Claudio, in *Much Ado about Nothing*, insults his girlfriend, who he thinks has cheated on him, with the angry accusation, "Thou pure impiety, and impious purity!" (4.1.105) And in the first part of the three-play series named for him, King Henry VI says that he always thought "it was both impious and un-natural" (5.1.12) that good Christians would fight one another in a civil war. "IMP-yus" is how the word scans in both lines, as odd as that sounds to our modern and im-PI-ous ears. Again, some directors may choose to flout the meter and pronounce the word as we do today. *Thinking Shakespeare*'s view? It comes down not to right or wrong but simply to taste. Just check the meter first, then decide.

A related bit of tricky scansion has to do with many of Shakespeare's uses of words ending in the suffix *-tion*. Here's one example: In *Troilus and Cressida* there's a wonderful scene in which Cressida learns that she is about to be separated from her beloved Troilus. She explodes with emotion so extravagant and devastating that her uncle Pandarus tells her, "Be moderate. Be moderate." She thunders back,

Why tell you me of moderation? (4.5.2)

Scan this line, and you'll find it's got only nine syllables. The tenth syllable is missing.

why TELL you ME of MOD-er-A-tion _____

To be iambic pentameter, the scansion requires that *-tion* have two syllables ("shee-un"), and that "moderation" have five.

Why TELL you ME of MOD-er-A-shee-UN

That sounds odd. But remember the central *Thinking Shakespeare* question: *Why am I using these words now?* Cressida is a petulant, angry teenager in the middle of a rant. Her uncle tries to restrain her with a word that strikes her as offensive and irrelevant. So she throws it back in his face, mocking it—and him—by twisting it like a knife into his guts. MOD-er-A-shee-UN, scanned according to the meter, creates a dismissal, an insult, a sneer.

Can a good actor achieve that effect without a two-syllable suffix? Sure. But it's always good to let Shakespeare provide whatever help he can.

Should you pronounce familiar words in unfamiliar ways? Isn't Shakespeare hard enough to understand without crazy pronunciations of simple words? Those are harder questions to answer. Some modern directors refuse to use pronunciations they believe will confuse or alienate the audience, even when the scansion seems to demand those pronunciations. I respect that view, but I don't share it. To me, these little poetic details are what make Shakespeare's language so rich and wonderful.

One final example. In *The Merchant of Venice*, the Jewish moneylender Shylock explains why he despises his archenemy, Antonio:

I hate him for he is a Christian. (1.3.37)

Again, nine syllables; the tenth is blank.

i HATE him FOR he IS a CHRIST-ian _____.

"Christ-shun," the customary pronunciation, has two syllables. But the scansion here suggests something else:

˘ ´ ˘ ´ ˘ ´ ˘ ´ ˘ ´
I hate | him for | he is | a Christ | ian

"Christian" actually gets three syllables: "CHRIST-i-AN," "Christ-ee-an." Why? Christians have been Shylock's nemeses, enemies who have persecuted him all his life. The Jew reminds Antonio a few lines later that his anti-Semitism is particularly heinous: "You call me misbeliever, cut-throat, dog / And spit upon my Jewish gabardine." In Shylock's mouth, then, the word "Christian" is painful, loaded with emotion, and difficult to say. The third syllable helps make it sound that way. This small detail, indicated by the scansion, is a clue to the actor that he must give the word weight, point, and acid.

The word *Christian* appears twenty-four other times in *Merchant*, and each time it gets two syllables. This line of Shylock's marks the word's only three-syllable pronunciation. Similarly, the canon is full of words ending in *-tion* that don't get stretched to "shee-un." (Hamlet's famous "question" is just one obvious example.) Each line must be evaluated individually. And even when the scansion seems to call for something that sounds unusual, the actor has the final say about whether to disregard it in the name of some other theatrical value.

ACT II

CHAPTER
—№—
4

ACTING IS
ARGUING

THE ART OF USING LANGUAGE TO PERSUADE

Sharp and well-trained Shakespearean actors understand that there's no better way to approach a scene than to ask what all the arguing is about.

That's because William Shakespeare really knows how to write a good argument, or, to put it another way, because Shakespeare's characters really know how to argue.

Argue, argument, arguing. These words might suggest to modern ears that Shakespeare, and good Shakespearean acting, is all about fighting, bickering, and quarreling. The Bard does go in for that sort of thing now and again: Beatrice and Benedick mix it up something fierce in *Much Ado about Nothing*, as do Kate and Petruchio in *The Taming of the Shrew*. The history plays are full of tussles, and more than one of the tragedies ends in sword fights and screaming matches.

But William Shakespeare is not Edward Albee. Mr. and Mrs. Macbeth, despite their occasional fireworks, are not George and Martha in *Who's Afraid of Virginia Woolf.* Nor is William Shakespeare William Frawley; although Hotspur and Lady Percy take some well-aimed verbal shots at one another in *Henry IV, Part One*, they don't conduct themselves like Fred and Ethel Mertz, firing off put-downs and one-liners in a never-ending squabble about who's fat, who's lazy, who's ugly, and who's old.

Argument, in the sense that Shakespeare relies on it, is not about heated exchanges, angry disputes, or biting quarrels. Instead, it's about articulating a point of view, stating a position, laying out a line of reasoning, and building a convincing case.

This sense of the word still exists in modern English, as when an attorney *argues* before a judge, or when a White House spokesman summarizes the administration's *argument* for making a certain policy decision. To *argue* is to present a rationale, prove something through reason and logic, and convince someone else of your view.

To argue is to make your case.

This kind of arguing is something Shakespeare's characters do dazzlingly well. Every Shakespearean actor must learn to emulate this skill, first by understanding the argument his character is making and then by figuring out how to deliver that argument as plainly, powerfully, and passionately as possible.

Making Logical, Orderly Arguments

The central question of *Thinking Shakespeare*, "Why am I using this word now?" once again goes to work. The final word of the question, "now," means "at this particular moment in time." Shakespeare's characters choose words that express their thoughts moment by moment. They use words *now* to give form to the thoughts they're trying to express *now*. *Now*, and not a second ago or an instant into the future. Shakespearean thinking unfolds over time, in sequence, one idea after another—articulated by one word after another.

That is, Shakespeare's characters argue their thoughts *in order*. They think coherently and methodically. There's a system at work in their minds. One thought connects to the next. Ideas are strung together. They are arranged to be maximally clear, organized so that they will have a strong impact.

Why am I using this word now? Because to make the assertion I'm trying to make, this is the best next word for me to use. It's the word that will lead me to the next word I'll require as I build my case, and then to the next one after that.

Some acting teachers like to use the metaphor of a chain to describe this process, and it's a neat image for the way Shakespeare writes human thought. Each single idea is a link. Each link, strung together with others before and after it, forms a chain—namely, the argument the character wishes to express. For these teachers, the characters construct a *chain of thought*, and the actor's job is to find it, think it, and give it voice.

Others prefer the metaphor of a ladder, in which each individual idea in a Shakespeare speech is one rung in a larger idea, a *ladder of thought*. The mind of the character steps from one rung to the next, and then to the next, and the next, until the overall shape of the argument emerges.

Both of these images are helpful, because both suggest forward movement, whether it is up the ladder or along the chain. Arguments progress, thoughts move forward. *Argument* is active.

REHEARSAL TIME

Let's jump in with a superb example of Shakespeare's way with argument: the opening speech of *Richard III*.

The hunchbacked Richard, Duke of Gloucester, enters and talks about the changes that have taken place in England since his family (the house of York) prevailed in the recently ended civil war. He discusses how he fits in to the new world emerging under the leadership of his relative, the Yorkist King Edward IV, and what he's going to do to bend that new world to his will.

Try reading Richard's speech aloud:

> Now is the winter of our discontent
> Made glorious summer by this son of York;
> And all the clouds that loured upon our house
> In the deep bosom of the ocean buried.
> Now are our brows bound with victorious wreaths;   5
> Our bruised arms hung up for monuments;
> Our stern alarums changed to merry meetings;
> Our dreadful marches to delightful measures.
> Grim-visaged war hath smoothed his wrinkled front;
> And now, instead of mounting barbed steeds,   10
> To fright the souls of fearful adversaries,
> He capers nimbly in a lady's chamber
> To the lascivious pleasing of a lute.
> But I, that am not shaped for sportive tricks,
> Nor made to court an amorous looking-glass;   15
> I, that am rudely stamped, and want love's majesty
> To strut before a wanton ambling nymph;

I, that am curtailed of this fair proportion,

Cheated of feature by dissembling nature,

Deformed, unfinished, sent before my time   20

Into this breathing world, scarce half made up,

And that so lamely and unfashionable

That dogs bark at me as I halt by them;

Why, I, in this weak piping time of peace,

Have no delight to pass away the time,   25

Unless to see my shadow in the sun

And descant on mine own deformity.

And therefore, since I cannot prove a lover,

To entertain these fair well-spoken days,

I am determined to prove a villain,   30

And hate the idle pleasures of these days.

Plots have I laid, inductions dangerous,

By drunken prophecies, libels, and dreams,

To set my brother Clarence and the king

In deadly hate the one against the other.   35

And if King Edward be as true and just

As I am subtle, false, and treacherous,

This day should Clarence closely be mewed up,

About a prophecy, which says, that "G"

Of Edward's heirs the murderer shall be.   40

Dive, thoughts, down to my soul: here Clarence comes.

(1.1.1–41)

In Other Words: The Paraphrase

We begin rehearsal by making sure we understand what Richard is saying. A great way to do that—a great way to discover the argument of any Shakespeare speech—is to translate it into your own words, or to *paraphrase* it.

The paraphrase is the first step in the process of *Thinking Shakespeare*.

Paraphrase comes from the Greek for "to explain alongside," which is what a modern English paraphrase does for Shakespeare. *Translate* means "to transfer from one place to another," or "to move across," and that, too, is what paraphrasing does—moving Shakespeare from his place (England, 400 years ago) across to our place (America, today).

HOW DETAILED SHOULD THE PARAPHRASE BE?   Richard says that "the winter of our discontent," or the terrible times we've been through, have been transformed into happy times ("made glorious summer") by King Edward ("this son of York"—the pun is, of course, on the word *sun*), and that the bad luck that frowned ("loured," which rhymes with *flowered*, and which wonderfully has the same vowel sound as *clouds*, *our*, and *house*) for so long on his family has now gone away forever—it's buried undersea.

He then lists the ways in which the country has changed for the better. A paraphrase of that list might look something like this:

> Now we're wearing wreaths of victory on our heads, our
> damaged weapons are on display as mementos, our fearsome
> calls-to-arms are changed to pleasant gatherings, and our
> dramatic military marches are changed to happy music. Angry-
> faced War has smoothed out his screwed-up features, and
> now, instead of climbing onto armored horses and scaring the
> daylights out of terrifying enemies, he dances nimbly in a lady's
> bedroom to the sexy accompaniment of a guitar.

This paraphrase is highly detailed, rendering almost every word in the original into a modern equivalent. We could distill the passage into far fewer words, making it simpler and giving it a somewhat looser tone:

> Now the terrible times are changed to good times, and the misery that's plagued our family is over. Everyone's enjoying the York victory. Now we're wearing medals, our weapons are down, we're having parties, our music is upbeat, and even War himself, instead of fighting our vicious enemies, is now with the ladies, dancing to hot tunes.

Or, even more basically and freewheelingly:

> Now the bad times are over, now it's about music and fun, and now everyone's making love.

To what degree of detail should you go in your paraphrase? The maximum you can manage. Even if you have a pretty good idea of what a passage or a line means—"Now are our brows bound with victorious wreaths," for example, is not terribly hard to understand—a highly detailed modern translation is one of the best ways to get in touch with your character's thoughts. Careful paraphrases can be time consuming and intellectually challenging, but they are well worth the effort.[8]

---

[8] In preparing your paraphrase, it's very helpful to have access to some reference works. Dictionaries, and also good scholarly editions of the plays, which have explanatory notes, glosses of unfamiliar words, and, often, selected paraphrases of difficult passages, are good to have at hand. The SparkNotes editions of *No Fear Shakespeare* are also great resources. If you're lucky enough to be working on a play that's been published in this series, an excellent paraphrase is already done for you. See chapter 16 for a discussion of other useful resources.

You must understand everything you're saying before you can do anything else!

After all, you can't make an argument if you have no idea what you're arguing.

Let's continue our paraphrase:

> But I, who am not built for fun and games, nor designed to flirt with a lover's mirror; I who am poorly put together and lack the wooer's expertise at strutting my stuff in front of some sexy girl who's passing by; I who am just shy of well built—cheated of good looks by that fraud, Mother Nature—who am deformed, unfinished, born prematurely and not fully complete, indeed formed so miserably and unattractively that dogs bark at me as I limp past them—why I, in this wimpy peacetime, find myself with nothing better to do than look at my shadow and sing a little ditty about my deformity.

This paraphrase includes equivalents for all the thoughts behind Richard's lines and renders them in a jaunty tone that acknowledges an essential quality of Richard's voice. A good paraphrase of Shakespeare into modern English captures not only the sense of the original language but also its spirit. If the original language has wit and humor, the translation must as well. The loose, free feel of this paraphrase corresponds to the fun in Richard's language and thinking. His deformity may be an embarrassment to him, especially when others mock it, but he also seems to have a great sense of self-deprecating humor about it. His skeleton may not be fully developed, but his funny bone absolutely is. So "sing a little ditty" for "descant," and "wimpy" for "weak and piping," both of which capture some of Richard's surprising flippancy, are good paraphrases.

Paraphrasing can be tremendously freeing for an actor. Expressing Shakespearean thought in energetic, colloquial, modern terms is a great way to get over that intimidating feeling that the language is formal, remote, and even sacred. And it serves your broader goal, which is to own the language, making it yours, so that it feels like it's really you who's thinking and talking. Being a bit loosey-goosey in your paraphrase can only enhance your personal connection to the work.

As with the first chunk of the speech, it's possible to make a shorter paraphrase of this section:

> But I, who am not cut out for love; I, who am ugly and not
> much for wooing; I, who lack good looks and was short-changed
> by Mother Nature, who was born prematurely and with birth
> defects (I'm so ugly that dogs bark at me as I pass them);
> why, I have nothing to do in peacetime except look at my own
> shadow and hum a tune.

Or, to be even more concise:

> But I'm not made for wooing. I'm ugly, deformed, and so
> hideous that not even dogs can stand me. So during peacetime,
> there's nothing productive for me to do.

This leaves about a dozen lines of the passage still to paraphrase.

> Therefore, since I can't manage to be a lover and suit myself
> to this lovely and well-mannered time, I've made up my mind
> to be a villain, and hate this lazy, sensual time. I've put plans

in motion—dangerous prologues—based on drunken guesses, slanders, and fantasies. I've manipulated my brother Clarence and King Edward into intense hatred of each other. If the king turns out to be as trustworthy and upright as I am cunning, lying, and backstabbing, Clarence will be thrown in jail this very day, because of a prediction that someone whose name begins with "G" will murder the king's heirs. Thoughts, dive down into my soul. Here comes Clarence.[9]

The shorter version:

And so, since I can't be a lover and have all kinds of fun, I'm going to be a crook and make all kinds of trouble. I've already started, with lies, fantasies, and gobbledygook. I've made Clarence and the king hate each other. And if the king is as good a guy as I am a rotten one, Clarence will be thrown in jail today. It's all because of a prediction that someone with the initial "G" will kill Edward's sons. I'd better be quiet. Here's Clarence.

---

[9] About the "G" thing: Clarence's first name, as he says a few lines from now, is George, which is what Richard is referring to when he says that a "G" will murder the heirs. But it's Richard himself who murders the king's heirs later in the play, and his last name is Gloucester. Richard's trumped-up prophecy turns out to be correct, but not quite in the way he means it here.

The paraphrase's "someone whose name begins with 'G'" spells out what's understood in Richard's more condensed expression: "that 'G.'" Because Shakespeare is writing poetic drama, his language has the dense, compacted quality of good poetry. Modern translations often require many more words than the original to express exactly the same thought. Richard's most famous line, for example, "A horse! A horse! My kingdom for a horse!" in paraphrase might go, "Find me a horse! Get me a horse! I'll gladly exchange my entire kingdom for just one horse!" Shakespeare's nine words carry implied nuances and shades of meaning that require eighteen words to express fully in modern English.

And the shortest:

> So, since I'm no lover, I'm going to be a troublemaker. I'm already on it—getting Clarence and the king to hate each other. Clarence will be jailed today, because of a nutty idea that some "G" guy's gonna off his kids. Shh! Clarence!

It's important to begin with an attempt at the most detailed paraphrase possible. Don't just jump two steps to the shortest one. That final, fun, and free paraphrase is crucial—we'll see why in a moment—but it only has value if it evolves out of the highly detailed word-for-word paraphrase that builds the foundation of the rest of your work.

Certainly, it can be agonizing to work through every single word. But as the famous French director Antonin Artaud said, the actor is "an athlete of the soul." As every athlete knows, "No pain, no gain." Arduous preparation is a prerequisite of victory. Besides, the struggle to capture an equivalent for every detail in Shakespeare's text can be as inspiring as it is productive. For example, an actor working on Richard might paraphrase the first line of this speech by writing, "Now our terrible times, which were a kind of winter . . ." and find himself thinking deeply about the idea of winter, and then (*"Why am I using this word now?"*) wondering why "winter" is an apt image of "discontent." The actor might then ask himself why the line isn't about "the autumn of our discontent" or "the dreary December of our discontent." He'll remember some bleak winter from his childhood, or he'll see in his mind's eye news footage of a blizzard in Chicago, all blowing snow and bone-chilling cold. Discontent, indeed. Attempting to paraphrase this single line, he'll learn something about the particulars of Richard's mind, and about Shakespeare's writing. At the same time, he'll make his own thinking more specific. The more painstaking the paraphrase, the more the actor will force himself into the language's deep detail and specificity, and the more he will reveal—and revel in—the complexity of the thoughts behind that language.

A good, detailed paraphrase will spur a personal and valuable investigation.

The Argument Emerges

Look again at the various paraphrases of Gloucester's speech. As they get shorter and shorter, the central ideas of the speech become easier to see. As the flourishes and embellishments are pared away, what's left is a series of basic assertions. This is the scaffolding that underpins the character's thinking. These are the fundamental ideas the character is trying to express.

This is the speech's *argument*.

Here's Richard Gloucester again, in shorthand. Call him, "Dicky Glou":

Now it's peacetime. Everyone's stopped making war and started making love. But I can't be a lover because I'm nasty looking and deformed. So I'm going to be a bad guy and make as much trouble as I can. I've already started by setting King Edward against my brother Clarence. In fact, Clarence is going to jail today because of some cockamamie story I've spread about "G" killing Edward's kids. Quiet! Here's Clarence.

That's really all there is to this famous speech. A man walks on stage and takes forty-one lines of iambic pentameter to say that the war is over, everyone is happy, but he's miserable, so he's going to cause chaos, and he's starting with his brother.[10]

Finding the short chain of ideas, the series of basic thoughts that make up a speech's argument, is the indispensable first step in the actor's process.

Once that argument is found, the actor's next responsibility is making it clear, presenting it, putting it out there for the audience to hear. The audience has come to the theater to witness a story unfold. The actor's job is to tell it, and tell it well. Everything else comes later. Poetry, musicality, emotion, beauty, style—these are important, but they're the icing on the cake. The cake itself is the story. And a Shakespearean story is told through *argument*.

Directors will often say during rehearsal, "I'm not following your argument," or, "You're losing the thread of the argument about fifteen lines in." Others will congratulate an actor for doing a great job with a speech's "structure," its "main thrust," or its "story." They're all emphasizing the same idea: that it is the actor's responsibility to communicate her character's basic thoughts to the audience. These directors are telling their actors, "You've got to play the argument."

PLAYING THE ARGUMENT The actor playing Richard now understands the sense of his first big chunk of text. Unfortunately, he can't get on stage and deliver his modern-language précis. (Although doing so would certainly make Shakespeare's

....

10 It's a remarkable way to start a play: fast, direct, and straight to the action. Shakespeare does many things brilliantly, but starting a play with a bang is one of his greatest skills. It's worth sitting down with a *Complete Works* and simply reading the first few lines of each play. There's not a Hollywood screenwriter alive who wouldn't kill for Shakespeare's speed and economy in launching stories.

three-hour play a lot shorter.) As we discussed in chapter 1, people go to see Shakespeare for many reasons—larger-than-life characters, gorgeous costumes, exciting sword fights—but the reason of reasons is to hear the astonishing, transporting, mind-blowing language that only Shakespeare provides. No paraphrase can offer that.

The trick for the actor, therefore, is to return to Shakespeare's forty-one-line version, but to keep a tight mental hold on the speech's basic set of thoughts.

That is to say, when the actor plays the forty-one-line speech, he must be sure that no matter what else happens, he at least manages to communicate to the audience that simple group of ideas he identified in his shortest paraphrase.

It sounds harder to do than it is. Try reading the full speech again, and listen for the argument as you speak. See if you can hear those thoughts rise to the surface of what you're saying. Try to let the argument emerge as you work through the lines.

See if you can *play the argument.*

Whole = Part + Part + Part

As you worked through the speech that last time, you probably heard it very differently from the way you did when you first attempted it at the start of this chapter. That's progress. It's exactly what happens in a professional rehearsal. What you're saying begins to fall in line with what you're thinking. The words start to make sense. And best of all, that big chunk of complicated and unfamiliar verbiage begins to seem less daunting. It soon feels smaller, more manageable.

It does so in part because of the paraphrase-making process. While we were translating the speech into modern terms, we didn't work on it as one enormous block of words. Instead, we broke it down into smaller sections. Then we figured out what each section of the speech was about and how it contributed to Richard's overall argument.

Look again at the shorthand "Dicky Glou" paraphrase above. It reveals that the argument of the speech happens in five sections:

1. Now it's peacetime. Everyone's stopped making war and started making love.

2. But I can't be a lover because I'm nasty looking and deformed.

3. So I'm going to be a bad guy and make as much trouble as I can.

4. I've already started by setting King Edward against my brother Clarence. In fact, Clarence is going to jail today because of some cockamamie story I've spread about "G" killing Edward's kids.

5. Quiet! Here's Clarence.

In Shakespeare's text, those five basic thoughts occur as follows:

1. Lines 1–13
    "Now is the winter of our discontent" through "the lascivious pleasing of a lute"

2. Lines 14–27
    "But I" through "descant on mine own deformity"

3. Lines 28–31

   "And therefore" through "the idle pleasures of these days"

4. Lines 32–40

   "Plots have I laid" through "the murderer shall be"

5. Line 41

   "Dive, thoughts, down to my soul. Here Clarence comes."

These are the bricks that make up the building that is the speech, the chapters that make up the speech's book, the movements that make up the speech's symphony, the parts that make up the speech's whole.

....

THINKING SHAKESPEARE Rule: Always try to break a speech down into the smaller sections that constitute it.

....

ONE BEAT AT A TIME   You attack any formidable task (driving across the country, painting a house, climbing a mountain) by dividing it into smaller sub-tasks (ten days at three hundred miles a day, first the walls then the trim, get to base camp then gradually work higher). In the same way, you attack any speech in a Shakespeare play by breaking it down into more manageable sections. Think of one speech of forty-one lines as five smaller speeches of fewer lines. One chunk has thirteen lines, the next fourteen, then four, nine, and one. These chunks of text are far easier to deal with than some hulking monolith of a monologue. Assemble them together, one after another, and—*presto!*—you've made it through the speech.

Actors refer to these mini-speeches by any number of different terms. *Section, passage, unit,* even *chunk* are common. But in most rehearsal rooms, the word *beat* is heard the most. It's a great multipurpose theater word that encompasses many meanings. As a noun, *beat* means the rhythm of the material (as in, "the beat of the music," "the beat of your heart") or a pause that is shorter than a moment but longer than a breath ("wait a beat, then say the line"). As a verb, *to beat* is to count the meter or the time signature of a passage ("pounding the table, she beat out the pulsing iambic pentameter"). It's sometimes used as an adjective, describing physical exhaustion ("Boy, am I beat") or, rather rudely, dismissing lousy work ("that guy's performance is beat"). But it has a special additional sense in the theater. A *beat* of a scene is one small piece of it, one passage in which the subject or action is consistent. When the action changes, the next beat begins.[11]

So it is that in Shakespeare we talk of the beats of a speech. Every speech longer than a couple of lines is made up of shorter beats put together. Each of these beats makes its own contribution to the speech's larger argument.

Usually the subsections of the argument are fairly easy to identify. This is especially true in earlier Shakespeare plays like *Richard III* (written in 1591 or 1592, when Shakespeare was about twenty-five) which is why this play's opening speech is a great one to study.

....

11 No one knows for sure where this meaning of the word comes from, but many suspect that its roots are Russian. The story goes that the great early-twentieth-century director Constantin Stanislavski referred to sections of scenes as "bits," and that this was somehow misunderstood as "beat" when translated for American actors. The actual explanation is probably much more mundane, but it's fun to think about a bunch of passionate Russians and perplexed Americans struggling to make sense of each other.

Starting New Beats with *But* or *Yet*

Richard starts the speech with thirteen lines about what's happening in England now. The second beat tells in fourteen lines why these conditions are a problem for him. Notice the first word used in that beat: "But." Richard says, "But I, that am not shaped for sportive tricks." Or, in paraphrase, "Now there's peace and everyone is having fun. BUT I don't fit into this new way of doing things."

But and its cousin *yet* are very powerful words in Shakespeare. *But* and *yet* throw a wrench in the works and turn the argument in the opposite direction. You'll rarely go wrong if you really lean on *but* and *yet*.

....

THINKING SHAKESPEARE RULE: Use *but* and *yet* to give shape to your arguments.

....

In each of these examples, *but* or *yet* forces the argument to make a sharp turn.

From *Julius Caesar*:

ANTONY   He was my friend, faithful and just to me;
           But Brutus says he was ambitious,
           And Brutus is an honorable man. (3.2.82–85)

From *Macbeth*:

MACDUFF   What, all my pretty chickens and their dam
            At one fell swoop?

MALCOLM   Dispute it like a man.
MACDUFF   I shall do so; **but** I must also feel it as a man.

(4.3.219–223)

From *Twelfth Night*:

OLIVIA   Your lord does know my mind; I cannot love him:
          Yet I suppose him virtuous, know him noble . . .

(1.5.226–227)

In paraphrase:

Caesar was my friend, and he was good to me—**but** Brutus says
he was a climber, and Brutus is okay.

I will put a brave face on this horrible situation—**but** I will also
allow myself to feel the pain.

Your boss knows I don't love him—**yet** I don't think he's a bad guy.

Speak these three bits of Shakespeare aloud and you can
physically feel the arguments turning a corner when they come
to *but* or *yet*. Without those words, the sense of what is being said
in each passage would be lost. *But* and *yet* are necessary for the
thoughts to be clear and for the language to come alive.

TURNING THE ARGUMENT IN OTHER WAYS   Yet Shakespeare uses more
words than just *but* and *yet* to mark shifts in his characters' arguments. At the beginning of beat three of Richard's speech, on line
28, the words "and therefore" are like a neon sign announcing,

"Given all I've just laid out, here's what I conclude." *Therefore* is a signpost telling the actor that the argument is making a turn.

Shakespeare is actor-friendly. He gives clear indications that an argument is advancing, developing, making a turn, or reaching an end. It's generally true that the later a given play falls in Shakespeare's writing life, the more layered and less easy to spot are the signposts in its characters' arguments. Still, even the hyper-articulate Queen Katherine in *Henry VIII* (probably Shakespeare's last play) wraps up her lengthy and impassioned courtroom plea of innocence with an obvious "Wherefore," her version of Richard's "And therefore."

> . . . Wherefore I humbly
> Beseech you, Sir, to spare me till I may
> Be by my friends in Spain advised . . . (2.4.51–53)

(Paraphrase: And so, for all the reasons I've just given, I beg you to give me time to talk to my lawyers in Spain.)

Look carefully at each speech in Shakespeare, and you will see not only the beats that compose its argument but also the connections that join each beat to the ones before and after it.

Each Beat Has Its Own Structure

Every actor playing arguments must consider one more level of detail.

Once a speech has been broken down into its component sections, it is helpful to analyze the internal structure of those individual components.

Take a look at our paraphrases of the first section of Richard's speech. The long, detailed one; the shorter, more general one; and the quick, broad one, as different as they are, are all organized around the word *now*. This structural device comes directly from Shakespeare's text, where, in lines 1, 5, and 10, Gloucester uses that word.

Now is the winter . . .
Now are our brows . . .
    . . . and **now**, instead of mounting . . .

Our paraphrases render the thoughts as follows: "*Now* the bad times are turned to glorious ones . . . ," "*Now* we've put aside our military gear in favor of happier things . . . ," and "*now* War is dancing with cute girls instead of fighting against the enemy." Now this, now that, and now the other. Now . . . now . . . and now.

This simple device of three *now*s structures Gloucester's thinking. It organizes his thoughts. It gives this part of the speech a clear and distinctive shape.

Discovering the *shape* of an argument is a crucial step in acting it. Try these lines aloud, using the three *now*s to help carry you through the whole beat. Each *now* adds detail to Gloucester's description of the transformation that has taken place in England since the end of the war. The first *now* phrase is fairly general. Paraphrased, it says, "Now our discontent is changed to glory, and the problems that troubled our family are buried." The next *now* phrase explains how the specific equipment and attitudes of warfare have been turned to happier, peaceful uses. Paraphrased: "Now our heads have wreaths of victory, our battle marches are happy tunes, etc." The third *now* phrase introduces the notion that with peacetime comes romance. Paraphrased: "Now, that tough guy War is dancing in a girl's bedroom, and the lute's making lusty sounds." Together, the three ideas depict a new kind of England fit not for fighters but for lovers. This is the England that Richard—not a lover by any means—is bent on disturbing.

BUILDS As the phrases paint this picture, they develop a remarkable sense of momentum. Indeed, as you say the lines out loud, it's almost impossible not to sense how each new *now* phrase has a little more energy than the one before it. As the speech progresses, it gathers intensity. That is, this beat of the speech builds.

A *build* is a steady incremental increase in intensity, speed, force, volume, or all of the above. It's what musicians call a *crescendo*. It's exciting to hear and fun to do.

Shakespeare often shapes speeches by using builds. In particular, he loves to use builds made of three parts. There are countless such *three-part builds* in individual lines of Shakespeare, from "Friends, Romans, Countrymen, lend me your ears" to "The lunatic, the lover, and the poet" to "Tomorrow and tomorrow and tomorrow." As we continue through *Thinking Shakespeare*, we'll see many speeches in which a three-part build constitutes one beat of a longer argument. (In Things Further Thought On following chapter 7, we'll discuss these in more detail.)

Here's a great way to explore this build and to understand its power in the theater. Try to read Gloucester's speech as monotonously as you can. Keep it flat; don't let the momentum build. Then try it again, starting with great energy and then losing force as you go on. It stinks, right? It makes no sense. Worse, it just *feels* wrong. You simply must let the section build as it moves ahead, leaning on each "now" to give it form.

The build is there for a reason. Use it to give your thinking energy, edge, clarity, and passion.

Do you see a similar kind of structure binding together lines 14–26? Listen carefully as you work through those lines. Which word appears again and again? (A hint: it gives *now* a run for its money, making a four-part build rather than settling for a mere three.)

The word is *I*.

> But *I* who am not shaped . . . *I* that am rudely stamped . . . *I* that am curtailed . . . Why *I* have no delight . . .

Just as *Now . . . Now . . . And now . . .* holds together the first section of the speech, *But I . . . I . . . I . . . Why I . . .* unifies this beat. It provides an organizing structure, a roadmap through this part of the argument. Once again, the section starts with a general idea and then gets more specific, building in intensity as it does so. Richard's disappointment and desperation—some would say self-loathing—crest with the absurd and memorable image of him looking at his shadow and singing.

Try the lines aloud once again. Let the *I*'s pull you through the beat, accumulating vigor until, when you reach "descant on mine own deformity," the words become supercharged, shooting out of Richard's mouth like venom from the fangs of a snake. You will feel tangible proof of how the structure of Shakespeare's language contributes to its intensity.

OTHER SUB-STRUCTURES The next beat of the speech is very short—only four lines—but it too has a structure: the opposition of "lover" and "villain." These two contrasting personas are the remote boundaries of Richard's character, and he spends the rest of the play shuttling back and forth between them. Shakespeare uses strong opposites like "lover" and "villain" everywhere in his plays. (In fact, opposites are so important to his writing that they merit their very own chapter of *Thinking Shakespeare*. We'll explore them in detail next.) This powerful contrast is at the heart of this beat of Richard's speech. He says, in essence, "Since I can't be a *playboy*, I've decided to be a *thug*."

The structure underlying the argument of the last beat of the speech is perhaps the least obvious. This section has no governing device like *now* in the first beat or *I* in the second. Instead, it has two simple patterns that hold its two sentences together. The first pattern is a very straightforward account of Richard's nefarious plans. It's a list: "Plots . . . inductions . . . prophecies, libels, dreams." Lists are another of the devices Shakespeare loves to employ. (And see Things Further Thought On in chapter 9 for more on lists.)

The second structure at work in this beat is a little more complex. It depends on two sets of contrasting opposites, along the lines of "lover" and "villain" above. One is the contrast between "my brother Clarence" and "the king." The other is the contrast between "King Edward," who is "true and just," and Richard (*I*), who is "subtle, false, and treacherous." The sense of the section—its contribution to the argument—rests on these oppositions. As you say the lines, you simply must let the audience hear the contrasts. Without them, the lines make no sense. Richard is saying, essentially, "I've set *Clarence* against *the king*, and if *the king* is as decent as *I* am rotten, then *Clarence* will be jailed."

Summing Up the Speech

We now have a strong handle on the argument of this magnificent forty-one-line speech. We've broken it down into five beats, paraphrasing the sense of each, then identifying each beat's basic structure. The argument looks like this:

1. It's peacetime. Everyone has stopped making war and started making love.
    Structure: Three-part build using *now*.

But

2. I can't be a lover because I'm nasty looking and deformed.
    Structure: Four *I* phrases, also building.

Therefore

3. Since I'm no Casanova, I'm going to be an evildoer.
    Structure: Contrast between "lover" and "villain"

4. I've already started. I've set King Edward against my brother Clarence. He's headed up the river because of a bogus story about "G."
    Structure: List of evil plans, followed by oppositions between Edward and Clarence, and Edward and I.

5. Quiet! Here's Clarence.

Know that the particular devices that organize Richard's speech are just some of the many that Shakespeare uses in building his arguments. See if they are useful to your work on characters in other plays. Note every build; circle every *but* and every pair of contrasting ideas; highlight every list you come across. But also, follow your nose. Does the speech you're working on feature a multipart series of questions? Use them to trace the argument through. (See Falstaff's speech on the subject of honor in *Henry IV, Part One* [5.1.126–139].) Does it begin with a description of a past event, move into a discussion of the present, and then lay out a plan for the future? Let that progression organize your thinking. (See Hamlet's "O, what a rogue and peasant slave am I" speech [2.2.527–582].) Does it follow a logical formula, such as "if a leads to b, and b leads to c, then a leads to c?" Use that logic as the building block of your work. (See Shylock's great "Hath not a Jew eyes" speech [3.1.45–61].) Every speech has an architecture of argument. Make that architecture the core of your work.

Going Beyond the Paraphrase

There's much more to be said about the great and fascinating opening speech of *Richard III*. It uses verbs in a wonderful and vivid way. It's full of fantastically powerful contrasts. It features amazingly modern insights into the psychology of a man suffering from low self-esteem. We'll come back to it as we continue *Thinking Shakespeare*.

For now, it will stand as a great case study of how Shakespeare builds arguments. It shows us how crucial it is to dig and dig until we can bring the argument to the forefront of our work. And it demonstrates that the argument itself is the touchstone of the actor's process. On one hand, the argument leads the way. It pulls the actor through monsters of speeches even longer than Richard's forty-one lines and through shorter, though perhaps more linguistically complex, speeches. Many of Shakespeare's early history plays include speeches that are five and six dozen lines long. By distilling these long arguments into a handful of simple thoughts, actors can find footholds that lead them safely through that steep climb. Characters written later in Shakespeare's career, such as Prospero in *The Tempest*, speak in short bursts of dense, fervid language. By lifting basic arguments out of these thickets of poetic text, actors give themselves signposts by which to navigate, like blazes on some forest trail.

Then there are the speeches that are both long and also richly poetical and philosophical. Identifying their arguments will carry an actor through them too. Imagine taking a deep breath and then stepping onstage to deliver Hamlet's "To be or not to be" speech. Pretty intimidating. But if the primary goal is to lay out a simple argument . . .

> To live or to die, that's what I'm wondering. Is it better to end life's misery now, or to keep on fighting against it? Death: that would end all the pain and heartbreak. How great! *But* . . . Death, like sleep, might bring bad dreams. Problem! Because who would accept all the agony of being alive (the pain of getting old, meanness and arrogance, love affairs gone wrong, official corruption, the humiliations good people choose to accept rather than eliminating them with one thrust of a knife), who would put up with it if it weren't for the fact that we're all scared of dying? We don't know what happens to us after we die, so we choose the miseries we know over the terrors we don't. We're cowards. We think too much. And when we do that, we paralyze ourselves until we can't manage to do anything at all. Hold on a second. Here comes Ophelia.

. . . then it's not so terrifying.

Argument is a launching pad. Once the argument of a speech is clear in an actor's mind, he is free to lift off, to let the poetry soar. No one would mistake the paraphrase above for one of the most important pieces of poetic drama in the history of Western literature. Shakespeare's basic thoughts are there, but all the mystery, beauty, nuance, and elemental power are lost. Still, only after the actor has internalized this pedestrian version of the speech can he explore—and thrill to—all the richness and detail that makes Shakespearean speech so particular, expressive, and magnificent.

Paraphrase is necessary, but it has its limits. We may scribble this unmemorable sentence: "We're scared about what might happen to us after we die, and that's why we choose the miseries we know over the terrors we don't," but we must never regard it as equivalent to Hamlet's version of those same ideas:

> . . . the dread of something after death,
> The undiscovered country from whose bourn
> No traveler returns, puzzles the will,
> And makes us rather bear those ills we have
> Than fly to others that we know not of. (3.1.80–84)

Saying that the passage loses something in translation is the understatement of the century.

Making a paraphrase is crucial. Playing the argument is imperative. But they are only the first steps.

....

THINGS FURTHER THOUGHT ON

....

The Power of Now

Now is one of Shakespeare's favorite words, as we saw in *Richard III*. It has a special magic, particularly in the theater. It puts us smack-dab in the present. It makes action take place before our very eyes.

"Now could I drink hot blood," says Hamlet (3.2.360). Not two minutes ago, not yesterday; not later this afternoon or next month. *Now*, right this second, here, in this place, blood will be consumed.

"Now all the youth of England are on fire," the Chorus of *Henry V* tells us (2.0.1). Not once upon a time, not way back at some distant point in history; not after a while, not soon, not eventually. *Now*, today, at this instant, everywhere in the entire country, the young people are burning with excitement and anticipation.

Now drops us into the middle of the mix and gives us a ringside seat. Here's another example, from *The Winter's Tale*:

> . . . And many a man there is, even at this present,
> Now, while I speak this, holds his wife by the arm,
> That little thinks she has been sluiced in's absence . . .
>
> (1.2.193–195)

Leontes, unhinged by his belief that his wife has cheated on him, claims that at this precise moment there are countless men holding their wives' arms, blithely unaware that while they weren't looking, their wives have been "sluiced." (It's a nasty,

angry word, meaning literally "flushed with water," or, to use a
suitably edgy modern paraphrase, "hosed.")

Leontes's use of *now* is one of the slyest in Shakespeare. When
he says "now," what does he mean? What "many a man" is he
talking about? Men in his kingdom of Sicilia, or in the world at
large? Either is possible. But there is a group of men, their wives'
arms in hand, much closer to Leontes "at this present, / Now"
as he speaks these lines: the men in the audience. The thought is
shocking, awful, and funny. Leontes is referring to the men who
are watching this play, innocently holding their wives' cheating hands, blissfully unaware of their extracurricular activities.
In *The Winter's Tale*, *now* means, "even as I speak, in this very
theater, in rows D, F, and N, seats 101 through 109."

....

THINKING SHAKESPEARE RULE: Always stress the word *now*.
It's a simple rule that works every time.

....

Shakespeare the Schoolboy

During the English Renaissance, Latin was considered the essential component of a good education. The grammar schools that
provided the first year of that education were so named because
the core curriculum was Latin grammar. Latin was far from dead
400 years ago, when it was still the language of the Bible, the
church, and most important scientific and philosophical works,
not to mention the language of the great classical heritage of the
Western world. From the youngest ages, students were taught
Latin through rote exercises, sometimes administered by stern
taskmasters of the sort Shakespeare lampoons in both *The Merry*

Wives of Windsor and *The Taming of the Shrew*. Success in Latin grammar led to the study of Latin composition. Young students might start with texts from the Roman comedies of Plautus and Terence, then move onto Cicero or Ovid, and finally, at the most advanced levels, study Horace and Virgil. Everyone was encouraged to carry a notebook, called a "tablet," or "table book," at all times, and to write in it memorable sayings or excerpts they came across in their reading. (Hamlet takes a moment to jot something down in his: "My tables!—meet it is I set it down / That one may smile and smile and be a villain!") Students were given exercises in translation into and out of Latin. And expertise at translation led, finally, for the teenaged student, to the study of rhetoric.

In our culture, the word *rhetoric* has negative connotations. We associate it with fancy language devoid of real meaning. We might accuse a politician, for example, of spouting "empty rhetoric." But in Shakespeare's age, rhetoric was something else entirely. It was an art form, a noble field of study worthy of a lifetime's pursuit. In the context of Shakespeare's plays, rhetoric is, essentially, the art of using language to persuade. Rhetoric is also the study of that art.

Rhetoric was at the heart of Shakespeare's education. He would have been taught all its rules and technical devices. He would then have written compositions in which he argued one side or another of a question posed by his teacher. The best of these compositions would have been read aloud or sometimes dramatized in staged classroom debates that could resemble short plays. By the time he finished school, Shakespeare would have been skilled in the creation and execution of strong rhetorical arguments.

It's hard to imagine an educational system better suited to an aspiring dramatist than one built around the study of rhetoric. The centrality of argument to Shakespeare's education is something contemporary Shakespearean actors would do well to keep in mind.

ACT II

CHAPTER
—№—
5

THE WORD
AGAINST THE
WORD

ANTITHESIS, THE INDISPENSABLE TOOL

King Richard II is one of the most self-conscious talkers in all of Shakespeare. He relishes language and loves his own ability to turn a well-crafted phrase. One of his best lines just so happens to lay out a crucial principle of Shakespearean—and really, all—acting.

Once an all-powerful ruler, Richard is overthrown by his enemy Henry Bolingbroke and tossed into a dungeon jail. Sitting in his cell, waiting for Bolingbroke's henchmen to come and kill him, Richard meditates on "how I may compare / This prison where I live unto the world." He decides that his soul and his brain could be the father and mother of a new generation of thoughts that will "people this little world," his cell. Just as there are all sorts of folks in the real world outside the dungeon's walls, Richard's brain and soul will create all sorts of thoughts. There will be "thoughts tending to ambition" and "thoughts tending to content" (contentment, satisfaction). The best and richest will be "thoughts of things divine"—holy thoughts—but they won't be pure. They'll be "mixed with scruples," or doubts. And these scruples and thoughts divine will, like seminary students, spend their time in endless debate.

They will, Richard says, "set the word itself / Against the word." (5.5.13)

Set the word itself against the word.

There's no clearer definition in Shakespeare of the powerful rhetorical idea known as *antithesis*.

Mighty Opposites

The dictionary defines *antithesis* as "a figure of speech in which sharply contrasting ideas are juxtaposed in a balanced or parallel phrase or grammatical structure."

That is, *antithesis is the clash of opposites.*

Antithesis is everywhere in Shakespeare. It's difficult to get through even three lines of his text without running into it. And it is absolutely indispensable to making sense of Shakespeare on stage.

Look at these famous Shakespearean lines. The clash of opposites in them is impossible to miss.

That which hath made them drunk hath made me bold.

Macbeth (2.2.1)

The fault, dear Brutus, is not in our stars,
But in ourselves, that we are underlings.

Julius Caesar (1.2.140–141)

In peace, there's nothing so becomes a man
As modest stillness and humility,
But when the blast of war blows in our ears,
Then imitate the action of the tiger . . .

Henry V (3.1.3–6)

I come to bury Caesar, not to praise him.
The evil that men do lives after them,
The good is oft interred with their bones.

Julius Caesar (3.2.80–82)

The quality of mercy is not strained,
It droppeth as the gentle rain from heaven
Upon the place beneath. It is twice blessed;
It blesseth him that gives and him that takes.
'Tis mightiest in the mightiest . . .

The Merchant of Venice (4.1.179–183)

And one we've already seen:

Now is the winter of our discontent
Made glorious summer by this son of York.

In all these examples, the very sense of the passage depends on the thoughts that are opposed against one another. Therefore, for the audience to comprehend the lines, the actor saying them *must bring out the ideas that are opposites.*

EXACT AND INEXACT OPPOSITES   *Antithesis often takes the form of exact opposition.*

Here once again is one of Shakespeare's best known *antitheses* (the plural form of *antithesis*):

To be or not to be, that is the question.

"To be" is the opposite of "not to be." That's about as clear an antithesis as one can find. Any actor playing Hamlet needs to make the opposition between those ideas stand out, or his dilemma—"should I commit suicide or shouldn't I?"—won't be communicated. Antithesis is at the heart of this celebrated line.

Some more exact opposites appear as Richard II's jail cell speech continues:

Thus play I in one person many people . . .

"One" is the opposite of "many," so "one person" and "many people" are antithetical. The actor needs to bring out these opposing thoughts when he speaks these lines.

"Now is the winter of our discontent / Made glorious summer by this son of York" opens the speech we studied in the previous chapter. A "winter" of discontent has been turned into a glorious "summer." The key idea is that bad times have been transformed into their opposite: good times. Once again, that's antithesis. Any speaker of English who says these two lines will instinctively make the contrast between these words clear, and in so doing will make the passage understandable. Try it:

Now is the WINTER of our discontent
Made glorious SUMMER by this son of York.

"Winter" and "summer" are opposite by definition, like *dark* and *light*, or *boy* and *girl*, or "to be" and "not to be," or *one* and *many*.

But not all antitheses are strict opposites, as these same two lines demonstrate. Gloucester is contrasting more than the seasons. He's talking about a specific kind of winter, a winter of discontent, and a certain type of summer, a glorious one. *Discontent* and *glorious* are not direct opposites. The opposite of *discontent* might be *contentment, happiness,* or *satisfaction.* And the opposite of *glorious* might be *shameful, terrible,* or *ignominious.* Yet in these lines, "glorious" and "discontent" are clearly in an antithetical relationship to each other. To communicate the full idea, an actor playing Gloucester needs to contrast those two words. Try it:

Now is the WINTER of our *discontent*
Made *glorious* SUMMER by this son of York.

Or consider this line from Mark Antony's famous funeral oration in *Julius Caesar*:

I come to bury Caesar, not to praise him. (3.2.79)

"Bury" and "praise" are antithetical. But are they opposite? Not quite. The opposite of *bury* is, perhaps, *reveal, unearth,* or *exhume.* The opposite of *praise* might be *slander,* or *criticize,* or *mock.* But in this context, Mark Antony contrasts the two ideas, and so for an actor's purposes, this falls into the category of antithesis.

Antony's next two lines contain two antitheses:

The evil that men do lives after them,
The good is oft interred with their bones . . . [12]

One is a direct opposition: "evil" versus "good." The other is an abstract opposition: "lives after them" versus "is oft interred with their bones" (meaning, "is buried with their corpses"). It's clear that the two ideas are being contrasted, even though if we were asked to give the exact opposite of "lives after them," we might say "dies before them." What matters is that *in this context,* the two ideas are used in opposition. So we present the relationship between "lives after them" and "is oft interred with their bones" as an antithetical one. Try it:

I come to BURY Caesar, not to PRAISE him.
The <u>evil</u> that men do *lives after* them,
The <u>good</u> is *oft interred* with their bones . . .

Back to Richard II. He says:

I wasted time, and now doth time waste me.

---

12 Remember from working on scansion in chapter 3 that *interred* has three syllables, with the *-ed* ending pronounced: in-TER-red.

This is a powerful and wrenching antithesis. But again, strictly speaking, it's not a contrast between opposites. The opposite of "I wasted time" might be "I was efficient." Still, our instincts tell us exactly which words to emphasize to make Richard's sense clear. What makes the line so striking is that its second half, "time waste me," is such a surprise. We all waste time now and then, but very few of us imagine that time might somehow take revenge, as Richard imagines here. That the notion is so shocking is a testament to the power of antithesis.

One more. The aforementioned lines from *The Merchant of Venice* are worth examining closely.

> The quality of mercy is not strained,
> It droppeth as the gentle rain from heaven
> Upon the place beneath. It is twice blessed;
> It blesseth him that gives and him that takes.
> 'Tis mightiest in the mightiest; it becomes
> The throned monarch better than his crown . . .

When she speaks these lines, Portia, disguised as the young male lawyer Balthazar, has just told the vengeful Shylock that even though he may lawfully exact his infamous "pound of flesh" from his enemy Antonio's breast, he "must be merciful" in doing so. Shylock asks angrily, "On what compulsion must I? Tell me that." Shylock means, "Where does it say that I'm compelled to be merciful? Tell me." Portia's famous reply above begins, in paraphrase: "Mercy is never compelled.[13] Instead, it drops gently like

---

13 "Strained" is a shortened form of "constrained," meaning forced.

rain from heaven. It creates two blessings: it blesses both the person who acts with mercy and also the person who benefits from mercy. And it's most powerful when powerful people exercise it."

The lines are full of antitheses, such as "gives" versus "takes." "Not strained" and "droppeth" are antithetical too, even though they are hardly opposite ideas. The opposite of "not strained" would be "strained"; the opposite of "droppeth" might be—what?—"riseth." Yet *in this context*, Portia uses these two non-opposing ideas in contrast to each other. Mercy is never forced, she argues, it drops gently like rain.

In cases where the antithesis is created by a relationship that is not direct, as in the case of *winter* versus *summer*, but rather is abstract, as it is here, an actor can't merely stress individual words and expect the sense to be clear. Instead, an actor must bring out the two opposing *thoughts*.

An actor must work to clarify the thoughts rather than the individual words that express the thoughts.

This is true of Portia's next antithesis: "mightiest in the mightiest." Here, antithesis is created by the same word used in different ways. The first use of "mightiest" is as an adjective meaning "most effective"; the second is as a collective noun meaning "the ruling elite." Even though it's the very same word, *in this context* the different uses make it antithetical to itself.

Try it:

The quality of mercy is NOT STRAINED,
IT DROPPETH as the gentle rain from heaven
Upon the place beneath. It is twice blessed;
It blesseth him that <u>gives</u> and him that <u>takes</u>.
'Tis *mightiest* in the *mightiest* . . .

REHEARSAL TIME

The great "Molehill Speech" from *Henry VI, Part Three* is an excellent place to practice your skill with antithesis.

Some background: King Henry V, of the Lancaster family, led the English army in conquest of France. This "foreign quarrel" finally ended the bitter civil wars that had raged in England ever since the king's father, Henry Bolingbroke, had Richard II murdered (at the end of the jail cell speech we looked at earlier) and took his crown, becoming King Henry IV. But Henry V died very young and never got to enjoy the fruits of the peace he brought his country. His son was crowned King Henry VI while still an infant, so his uncle, Duke Humphrey of Gloucester, ruled the kingdom as the Lord Protector, in charge until the king reached maturity. Duke Humphrey's brutal murder by a member of the rival York family unleashed violent civil strife once again. The Lancaster family took as its symbol the red rose, while the Yorkists adopted the white rose as theirs, and the fight between them, dubbed the Wars of the Roses, raged for a generation. King Henry VI tried to follow in his father's footsteps and rule with a firm hand, but his inward-looking and scholarly personality, combined with the ruthlessness of Margaret, his wife and queen, rendered him all but useless. The bloody civil wars raged on.

As this scene begins, King Henry VI is wandering around the countryside and observing how his subjects are coping with the terrible national upheaval. He comes to a hillside overlooking a valley in which a horribly violent battle is taking place. Here's what he says:

This battle fares like to the morning's war,
When dying clouds contend with growing light,
What time the shepherd, blowing of his nails,
Can neither call it perfect day nor night.
Now sways it this way, like a mighty sea   5
Forced by the tide to combat with the wind;
Now sways it that way, like the selfsame sea
Forced to retire by fury of the wind.
Sometime the flood prevails, and then the wind;
Now one the better, then another best—   10
Both tugging to be victors, breast to breast,
Yet neither conqueror nor conquered.
So is the equal poise of this fell war.   (2.5.1–13)

As always, start by making sure you understand the argument. What's Henry saying? Here's a paraphrase:

The battle I'm watching is playing out like the one that takes place every morning between the fading clouds and the rising sun. At dawn, when shepherds blow on their hands to keep warm, it's impossible to tell if it's precisely day or night. Now one side seems to be gaining, just like the ocean, pushed in by the force of the tides against the opposing winds. And now the other side seems to be gaining, like the very same ocean receding again when the wind forces it away from shore. Sometimes the ocean gains, and then the wind gains. Now one seems to be winning, then the other does. They both struggle against each other in hand-to-hand combat. But neither one ever actually wins or loses. That's what this horrible war is like: balanced equally.

Next, ask the central *Thinking Shakespeare* question: *Why is he using these words now?* Henry is trying to make sense of what he is watching by defining it, by talking about it, by struggling to process it. To discuss it is to understand it.

Why does he begin with the image of the fight between the clouds and sun and then switch to the image of the fight between the wind and waves? Because every morning, the sun wins, so the battle at dawn is not a good comparison for this particular battle, which is one of "equal poise." Henry needs a metaphor that suggests an endless fight with no winner. He finds one: the ocean. Then he teases it out for eight lines.

Since Henry is talking about a battle, it's natural that the language he uses will be full of conflict. War is the clash of opposites, so antithesis is the perfect way to discuss it.

Let's list all the examples of antithesis in this speech.

- this battle / morning's war
- dying / growing
- clouds / light
- day / night
- this way / that way
- mighty sea / selfsame sea
- forced by the tide / forced to retire
- combat with the wind / fury of the wind
- sometime / then
- flood / wind
- now / then
- one / another
- better / best
- both / neither

- breast / breast
- conqueror / conquered (three syllables: CON-quer-ed)

That's sixteen distinct antitheses in thirteen lines of verse.

Many of these antitheses, like "day" versus "night," "dying" versus "growing," and "this way" versus "that way" are exact opposites, while others, like "one" versus "another," are more abstract oppositions. "Mighty sea" and "selfsame sea" are not opposite at all; in fact, they refer to the same body of water. But in the context of Henry's speech, they are antithetical. Similarly, the same word ("breast") is used as an antithesis of itself. In this context, it refers to two different breasts (one belongs to a soldier on one side of the battle and the other to his mortal enemy). Also note that "breast" and "breast" are right next to each other in these lines, as are "day" and "night." But other pairs of opposed terms, like "this way" and "that way," are separated by a few lines of verse. (We will discuss the significance of this shortly.)

All of this shows the many forms of antithesis Shakespeare uses. He varies the degree of opposition between antithetical terms, and he varies the proximity of the opposites to each other. He likes to mix things up, to keep his writing surprising.

The Dreaded Shatner Trap

One of the tricky lines in this speech is, "Now one the better, then another best." If you think of this line as three sets of antithetical words—now / then, one / another, better / best—here's how it will sound:

NOW. ONE. the BETTER. THEN. ANOTHER. BEST.

By stressing individual words you end up shouting. You start to bark. Everything becomes important. You begin to sound like Captain James T. Kirk. ("I. *Will*. *Not*. Kill. TODAY!!") You fall into what I like to call the "Shatner Trap."[14]

Try instead to think of this line as one antithesis made up of two sets of three conjoined pairs: "Now one the better" versus "then another best." Let the *thought itself,* not the individual words that express the thought, do the work of contrast and opposition. This will make the line sound smoother and flow better.

Now one the better, then another best.

The same applies to "dying clouds" and "growing light." It's true that the antitheses are "dying" / "growing" and "clouds" / "light," but really it's *the larger thoughts* that are being contrasted—dissipating clouds versus the rising sun—rather than the individual words.

Practice not *speaking* antithetically, but *thinking* antithetically. Leave Captain Kirk on the bridge of the *Enterprise* where he belongs. Shakespeare's loss is the Federation's gain.

---

14 An important disclaimer: I grew up watching *Star Trek* and I am a huge William Shatner fan. As such, I know that he began his career at the great Stratford Festival in Canada, doing Shakespeare. When he decamped for Hollywood and that famous five-year mission, he developed a signature acting style somehow better suited to lines like, "Scotty! Energize!" than to lines like Henry VI's here. Shatnerism works for Rodenberry, but it's not so great for Dogberry.

Rehearsal Continues

Here's the rest of the Molehill Speech:

Here on this molehill will I sit me down.

To whom God will, there be the victory.   15

For Margaret my queen, and Clifford, too,

Have chid me from the battle, swearing both

They prosper best of all when I am thence.

Would I were dead, if God's good will were so—

For what is in this world but grief and woe?   20

O God! Methinks it were a happy life

To be no better than a homely swain.

To sit upon a hill, as I do now;

To carve out dials quaintly, point by point,

Thereby to see the minutes how they run: 25

How many makes the hour full complete,

How many hours brings about the day,

How many days will finish up the year,

How many years a mortal man may live.

When this is known, then to divide the times: 30

So many hours must I tend my flock,

So many hours must I take my rest,

So many hours must I contemplate,

So many hours must I sport myself,

So many days my ewes have been with young,   35

So many weeks ere the poor fools will ean,

So many years ere I shall shear the fleece.

So minutes, hours, days, months, and years,

Passed over to the end they were created,

Would bring white hairs unto a quiet grave. (2.5.14–40)   40

Satisfied that he's found an apt image for the battle in front of him, King Henry decides simply to watch what happens. "Here on this molehill will I sit me down," he says, settling on the small mound that gives the speech its name. He declares that he doesn't care who wins or loses, and he laments that all he has left in his life is misery. Then he compares his kingly existence to the meager day-to-day routine of a lowly subject.[15] The king decides, surprisingly, that the shepherd has the better life: "Methinks it were a happy life / To be no better than a homely swain." For a dozen lines, Henry imagines the simple, pleasant times he would enjoy if only he could be an anonymous nobody. He sums up with an extended series of antitheses:

Ah, what a life were this! How sweet! How lovely!	41
Gives not the hawthorn bush a sweeter shade	
To shepherds looking on their seely sheep	
Than doth a rich embroidered canopy	
To kings that fear their subjects' treachery?	45
O yes, it doth—a thousandfold it doth.	
And to conclude, the shepherd's homely curds,	
His cold thin drink out of his leather bottle,	
His wonted sleep under a fresh tree's shade,	
All which secure and sweetly he enjoys,	50

....

15 In the second Shakespeare play that bears his name, King Henry IV, this King Henry's grandfather, makes a similar comparison, likening himself to a ship boy, whose job is to perch atop the mast and look out for other ships at night. The entire royal family is apparently obsessed with how much better the commoners live; King Henry V—son of IV and father of VI—also ruminates on the subject in his play.

Is far beyond a prince's delicates,

His viands sparkling in a golden cup,

His body couched in a curious bed,

When care, mistrust, and treason waits on him.[16]

(2.5.41–54)

Some explanations to help with a paraphrase: A "hawthorn bush" is a gnarled, scraggly thing, surely less comfortable to sleep under than is "a rich, embroidered canopy." The word "seely" is an old form of "silly," which evocatively describes helpless sheep. "Curds" are milk solids, similar to yogurt, and "delicates" are elaborate foods. "Viands" are fancy drinks, hardly "cold and thin." "Wonted" means "accustomed." "Curious," in this context, means "ornate." "Waits on him," means "attends him," or, roughly, "comes his way."[17]

Henry argues that even though the king has fancier stuff, the homely swain is happier and sleeps better. The shepherd may be impoverished, but at least his sheep aren't traitors trying to kill him.

These lines are superb examples of how Shakespeare's characters are capable of speaking extended and complex antitheses. The basic contrast underpinning the passage is between shepherds and kings. Everything else—where the shepherd sleeps versus where

---

16 As we saw in the previous chapter, it's very helpful to approach a giant speech like this one as a series of smaller beats. Henry first spends thirteen lines finding the right image to describe the battle. Next, he sits down, uncaring and wishing to die (lines 14–20). Then he imagines what he'd do as a shepherd (lines 21–40). Finally he pronounces that a shepherd is better off than a king (lines 41–54). (Some actors might suggest that lines 41–46 are a separate beat, and that the speech concludes, appropriately enough, with the four-line beat beginning on line 50, "And to conclude . . . ")

17 The verb "waits" is in the singular form even though the list of "care, mistrust, and treason" would seem to call for a plural, *wait*. This is not uncommon in Elizabethan English.

the king sleeps, what the king eats and drinks versus what the shepherd eats and drinks, the shepherd's peaceful state of mind versus the king's paranoia—elaborates on this central comparison. Let's once again list the antitheses:

- hawthorn bush / rich embroidered canopy
- shepherds / kings
- looking / fear
- their sheep / their subjects' treachery
- shepherd's / prince's
- curds / delicates
- cold thin drink / viands
- leather / golden
- bottle / cup
- wonted sleep / body couched[18]
- under / in
- fresh tree's shade / curious bed[19]
- secure and sweetly / care mistrust and treason
- he enjoys / waits on him

As before, it's important to defy Captain Kirk and find the contrasts between *thoughts* and not just between words. So we might prefer to group these antitheses in a different way:

- hawthorn bush / rich embroidered canopy
- shepherds looking on their seely sheep / kings that fear their subjects' treachery

---

18 Note the scansion here: "couched" has two syllables with an *-ed* ending
19 "Curious" is elided from three syllables to two "CURE-yus"

- shepherd's homely curds / prince's delicates
- cold thin drink out of a leather bottle / viands sparkling in a golden cup
- wonted sleep under a fresh tree's shade / body couched in a curious bed
- secure and sweetly he enjoys / care, mistrust, and treason waits on him

Distant Antitheses: Spinning Plates

One tricky aspect of this speech is that in some cases the first half of an antithesis is separated from the second by as many as four verse lines, perhaps thirty words, as in the contrast between "homely curds" and "delicates." It takes practice to bring out distantly separated antitheses like these. An actor has to invest the first half of the comparison with as much clarity and specificity as he can so that the audience will remember it when its opposite comes around so many words later.

Playing these lines, your task is similar to that of the circus performer who spins plates on top of sticks. He gets one plate spinning, then moves on to another and another and another, by which time the first plate has lost speed and needs to be spun more. But that first plate never falls to the ground, because the initial spin was strong enough to keep it going a good long time. In just this way, the first half of these comparisons need to be "spun" with lots of power so that they echo in the audience's ears until the second half approaches.

As you continue to hone your plate-spinning skills by working on Henry VI and his marvelous speech, you will find again and again that this mother lode of antithesis depends for its success on the energy of thought. *Think the thoughts that are in opposition*, and the words that express that opposition will be clear and strong.

THINGS FURTHER THOUGHT ON

Index Words

The phrase that starts the Molehill Speech, "this battle," refers to the actual battle that Henry is looking at, right in front of him, right now. Shakespeare doesn't put the battle on stage, but by giving Henry the word "this," he makes it real for the character, and for us too. "This" is what points us to the battle Henry sees. It *indicates* that battle, and so it's called an *index word*, just as your index finger is the one you use to point at things, to indicate.

This, *thus*, *that*, *these*, etc., function as index words. Almost always, index words are accompanied by gestures that point to things. Here, Henry might physically gesture toward the battleground or, at the very least, look over in its direction.

Hamlet contains a great example of index words in action. Polonius tells King Claudius that he believes the source of Hamlet's odd behavior is the prince's crush on Ophelia. Claudius asks if he's certain. Polonius replies, "Take this from this if this be otherwise." (2.2.157) Try saying it.

On its own, the line makes no sense. All those *this*'s mean nothing unless they indicate objects. Actors have fun figuring out to what objects Polonius refers. Most often, an actor will point to his head on the first "this" and his body on the second, and use the third to refer to his theory about Hamlet's behavior. He makes the index words and gestures express the thought, "Chop my head off if what I've said isn't true." Some actors wear a medallion or carry a staff of office indicating Polonius's high rank in the Danish court. They point to it on the first "this" and to themselves on the second, gestures that convey "Take away my high rank if what I've said isn't true." And some point first to themselves, then to the king, meaning "Get rid of me if what I've said isn't true." Whatever the choice, physical gestures are required to make the index words clear. Without indicating what it means, the line is gibberish. (We'll look more closely at physical actions in the text in chapter 12.)

The "Wooden O"

Three times in the Molehill Speech, Henry says words that are nothing but sound: "O God . . ." "Ah, what a life . . ." and "O yes." These words, "O" and "Ah," don't have any particular meaning in and of themselves, but they are tremendously expressive in context (the grammatical term for them is *interjection*). Many modern actors shy away from these words, preferring to make them naturalistic sighs or groans or grunts, or—heaven forbid!—throat-clearings. But it's always best to give these sounds full rein and see what happens. Big vowels like these do a great deal of work. They release emotion, often in a powerful surge.

Why does Henry use these words now? Because after he has fantasized himself as a carefree shepherd rather than a put-upon monarch, he feels thrilled, nearly ecstatic. So when he says, "Ah, what a life were this!" it comes from somewhere deep and powerful. The huge, open release of sound that comes on "Ah"— *Aaahhhhhhhhhh*—communicates more pleasure and joy than dozens of complex words ever could. To give "Ah" a casual once-over by saying something like, "*hrrmph*, what a life were this," is to turn a rich and resonant moment into clumsiness and mud. Such a stifled grunt, a stunted moan, a constipated, stillborn thought has a name, borrowed from the opening Chorus of *Henry V*: a "wooden O." Avoid it. Let O be *Ohhhhhhh*.

Not Only in Shakespeare

Once you start getting your eyes and ears accustomed to antithesis, you'll be amazed at how often you hear it all around you.

Watching a documentary on TV about the life of John F. Kennedy?

> Ask not what your country can do for you, ask what you can do for your country.

That's antithesis.

Happen to be browsing the self-help section at your local Barnes & Noble?

> *Men Are from Mars, Women Are from Venus.*

That's antithesis.

Listening to Bruce Springsteen on your iPod?

> In the day we sweat it out on the streets of a runaway American dream.
> At night we ride through mansions of glory in suicide machines.

"In the day" versus "at night"; "sweat it out" versus "ride"; "on the streets" versus "through mansions of glory." That's some hard-rocking antithesis.

And Finally . . .

MAN IN A RESTAURANT   Waiter, take back this orange juice.
                       It's like the quality of mercy.

WAITER   The orange juice is like the quality
                       of mercy?

MAN   Yup. (*spits out a pit*) Not strained.

ACT II

CHAPTER
—№—
6

DIFFERENT VOICES

THE CHANGING HEIGHT OF SHAKESPEAREAN LANGUAGE

Near the beginning of my career as a Shakespeare director, I staged a couple of productions at the wonderful Idaho Shakespeare Festival in Boise. A river ran behind the site of the outdoor amphitheater where the Festival produced its plays every summer. Most evenings, the cool water attracted scores of people, all looking for a place to escape from another scorching day in that high desert city. Some strolled the banks, others fished, and still others floated along the calm currents in inner tubes or on rafts. The actors in the Festival loved to sit by the river as well and relax a bit before the night's show.

It was quite a sight: a dozen thespians, wearing bits and pieces of theatrical costume, stretching, reviewing their lines, or warming up their voices with various hums and shouted tongue-twisters, while a flotilla of partying, bathing-suited tubers came bobbing past, literally just going with the flow. It was all very cordial—the two groups always greeted one another with a hello or friendly wave—and it was fun to see. I'm not sure there's another backstage scene quite like it anywhere in the world.

My favorite part of the whole scenario was that every night, with perfect inevitability, some guy on the river, well-lubricated by ample amounts of the beverage chilling in the Styrofoam box tethered to his tube, would see the actors on the bank and call out, loud, "Shakespeare! To be or not to be!" The guy was different each time, but amazingly the line was always the same, and oddly, so was the voice. It was always deep, full, and booming, and it always had a fake, overly formal, and very plummy British accent. It sounded like it belonged to the second runner-up in the Budweiser Patrick Stewart Sound-alike Contest.

Shakespeare! To be or not to be!

Although it could not have been further from their minds, these boisterous Boise river rats were acknowledging one of the central problems facing every American Shakespearean actor.

There is in our culture a deeply entrenched, preconceived idea of what Shakespearean acting sounds like. Ask any friend to imitate a typical Shakespearean actor and you're likely to hear a torrent of language that's big and loud, elevated and poetical, orotund and stentorian, and with a mailing address in one of the more aristocratic neighborhoods of the United Kingdom.

Shakespeare? It's grand, bombastic, and British.

This book will not attempt to get at the roots of this preconception, or to deconstruct the significance of Shakespeare in the

British crown's former colonies. Those sorts of fascinating and worthwhile studies are ably being pursued elsewhere.

Instead, *Thinking Shakespeare* will point out something the American actors on the Boise riverbank knew well: America's preconceived ideas about Shakespeare are a bit off the mark. "The Shouting Tuber's Error," as it might be called, is to suppose that all of Shakespeare's language is ornate and overly poeticized. Like so many received ideas about Shakespeare, this one is a misapprehension that collapses under scrutiny. In fact, only the smallest proportion of Shakespeare is flowery or fustian. The Shouting Tuber mistakenly assumes that the many passages in Shakespeare that sound complex to his modern ears—all that unusual grammar and complicated vocabulary, all those *-ed* endings, all the *thees* and *thous* and *doths* and *wilts*—represent everything in Shakespeare.

One of the most wonderful things to discover about Shakespeare as you work on his plays is that the vast majority of his language is not poetical at all. An enormous amount of it—one could even say the majority—is simple, straightforward, and unadorned. (My own favorite line in Shakespeare is a short phrase in *The Winter's Tale* that is as basic and un-Shakespearean as can be: "O! She's warm." [5.3.109] Nothing fancy there.) Shakespeare's characters use many different kinds of language, and Shakespeare sees to it that this language never stays in one place for long. If it's rich and literary for a little while, you can bet it's going to get plain and blunt soon. If a few lines consist of complicated, polysyllabic words strung together in long sentences, it's certain that the next lines will consist of short bursts of clipped, little words. *The language changes all the time.*

The actor's job is to recognize those changes, to ask why they're happening, and then to use them to make the character's thinking as surprising and fresh and spontaneous as real human thought always is.

We'll look at an example in a moment. First, let's examine some basic vocabulary.

The Height of Language

In chapter 1 we discussed two characters talking about the sunrise. Horatio in *Hamlet* used lofty terms:

> But look, the morn in russet mantle clad
> Walks o'er the dew of yon high eastward hill.

Duke Vincentio in *Measure for Measure* expressed himself in a much more down-to-earth manner:

> . . . it is almost clear dawn.

Notice that the words that best describe Horatio's language suggest height. We might call his description of the sunrise "elevated," "lofty," or "high toned." Or we might call it "lyrical" and "grand," words that suggest scale, scope, and stature. The words that describe the duke's language, on the other hand, imply lowness: "down-to-earth," "grounded," "prosaic," or "pedestrian" all suggest lack of height.

In discussing how Shakespearean characters express themselves, *Thinking Shakespeare* will talk about the *height of the language*. Some of Shakespeare's language, such as Horatio's, is *heightened*; some, such as the duke's, is *lower*.

Many Shakespeareans make this distinction in terms of *poetic* language versus *naturalistic* language. That's not a bad way to go, although it can get imprecise quickly. My favorite line, "O! She's warm," is simple and naturalistic, but it wouldn't be correct to say it is not poetic. I would argue that this succinct expression of joy, wonder, and faith is among the most beautiful poetry Shakespeare ever wrote. Then there's one of Hamlet's most amazing utterances:

> There's a divinity that shapes our ends,
> Rough hew them how we will. (5.2.10)

This is as brilliant an example of Shakespearean poetry as one can find, yet in form it's quite naturalistic. Paraphrased, it means, "God creates an orderly outcome for our lives regardless of the mess we make of them." The sentiment is poetic, but the language is plain and straightforward. Indeed, the imagery derives from everyday life. "Ends" refers to the tidy eaves on a thatched roof line; "end" thatches are chopped roughly from their stalks, then "shaped" neatly by the roofer who installs them. Thatching as a metaphor for our destinies: only Shakespeare—and perhaps extreme devotees of Home Depot—would talk about Divine Providence in terms of roofing materials. Is it poetry? Yes. But is the language itself poetic? Not exactly.

It's more precise, more descriptive, and finally more helpful to give poetry a rest, and to talk instead about Shakespearean language that is heightened versus language that is not.

Finding and Using Changes in Height

What follows is the first line in Act One, Scene Four of *Hamlet*. The given circumstances: Horatio has reported to Hamlet that the ghost of his father, old King Hamlet, appeared last night on the castle ramparts (we rehearsed this beat in chapter 2). It's now the night after Horatio's report, and Hamlet has gone outside to await the ghost's return. Horatio and the soldier Marcellus are along to keep him company. Christmas is a few weeks away, and the temperature in Denmark is as low as the young prince's spirits. Hamlet opens the scene by saying:

The air bites shrewdly. It is very cold. (1.4.1)

That's one line of iambic pentameter, with a regular, masculine ending.

the AIR bites SHREWD-ly IT is VE-ry COLD

The line has two halves. The first is a complete sentence: "The air bites shrewdly." So is the second: "It is very cold."

Paraphrase the line to make sure you're clear about Hamlet's argument. The second half of the line, "It is very cold," couldn't be clearer. There's nothing Shakespearean about it at all, nothing poetic or heightened. It's just a simple expression of a meteorological fact. You might say it at Christmastime, or on your next ice fishing expedition, or in the frozen food aisle of your local supermarket. "It's cold." No big deal.

The first half of the line is a bit trickier. The air is biting something, presumably Hamlet's skin, and it's doing so "shrewdly," which means "cunningly," "trickily," or, literally, "in the manner of a shrew." A shrew is a tiny rodent with a long snout known for insinuating itself into even tightly sealed places. So the sense of Hamlet's first sentence is, "The air is a shrew that's biting my skin." This is a wonderfully vivid metaphor for coldness. You could paraphrase it succinctly as, "It's cold."

Put the two halves of the paraphrase together, and this is what the line says:

It's cold. It's cold.

The same thing, said twice. The first half says it in metaphoric, complex, and heightened language; the second, in language that is flat and simple.

Why?

Why would Hamlet say the same thing in two different ways? Some ideas:

Hamlet, like Horatio, is a student at the University of Wittenberg. As the play makes amply clear, the two young men are comfortable with heightened language and complex thought. Marcellus, however, is a simple soldier. His language bears no resemblance to the dense, lush speech of the prince and his friend. So perhaps Hamlet says the complex first half of the line to Horatio, and the second, simpler half to Marcellus.

Or perhaps he says the first half of the line to Marcellus, but the stolid soldier looks blank and confused, so Hamlet repeats the idea in simpler terms.

Or perhaps Hamlet says the first half of the line to himself, standing off to one side, and then turns to his companions and says the second half loud enough for them to hear.

Or the other way around. Maybe Hamlet says the first half to his companions, and then turns aside and mutters the second half to himself.

Try all of these.

You've now rehearsed the scene. Answering the question "Why?" has led to four possible interpretations. Trying different approaches is exactly what happens in a professional Shakespeare rehearsal session. Is one way "right" and another "wrong"? Hardly. These are just choices, options from which the director will select, and there may well be others. Each team of director and actors will find their own best path.

This is the important part: *all the choices arise from the simple observation that the first half of the line is heightened and the second half is not.* The changing height of the language is the key that unlocks what is happening onstage.

The only so-called wrong approach to the line is one that ignores or doesn't even notice the change in height between the first and second halves.

Try giving the line the old *"Beverly Hills 90210* Once-over." That is, treat both halves as though they are the naturalistic mumblings of some disaffected heartthrob on your favorite cheesy TV melodrama. Deny the first half of the line its height.

hmm. (*pause.*) the air . . . bites . . . um . . . shrewdly. (*sigh.*) itisvery . . . um . . . cold.

Wrong.

Now turn it over to the Shouting Tuber, and lay into it with a blast of phony, nineteenth-century, BBC lung power, ignoring the fact that the second half of the line is plain and artless.

The AIIR BIIIITES shRRRRReeeewdly. 'Tis VEEERRRY *Cooooooooold!!!*

Wrong again.

One half of the line is one thing, and the other half is another. The actor must first discern the difference, then think about why the change between halves exists, and then say the line in a manner that uses the change in height to make the underlying thought sharp and clear.

Height in the Language of Real Life

The key is to keep in mind the lesson of chapter 1, and to regard the language, no matter how high or low, as *the expression of living thought*. Even when the words are heightened and their form is sophisticated, approach them as the spontaneous thoughts of a person who is trying to communicate something to someone else. That is, the actor's first task is to think of the text as off-the-cuff human speech. Then, whenever the actor notices a jump from simple to elevated or elevated to simple—*whenever the height changes*—the next job is to ask *Why?*

It's helpful to listen to your own speech, noticing its changes in height. Suppose you're hungry in two different situations: first, while walking around New York City, and second, at your grandmother's house. The language you use to ask a street vendor for a hot dog ("Hey, gimme one with mustard and 'kraut!") is a long way from the language you use to ask your grandmother for more chicken soup ("It's delicious, Grandma. May I please have another bowl?"). In both cases, your objective is the same (to eat), and the reason you're using words now is the same (to communicate your hunger to someone who can help you satiate it), but the words you use are very different. Similarly, you would greet a good friend ("Yo, dude! 'Sup?!") with different language than you'd use to greet a government official

("Good afternoon, Mr. Ambassador. How are you, sir?"). In both situations, you are the same person. Your character doesn't change. Yet the language you use does.

Listen for height changes in the world at large. Take specific note of the language your friends, family, and coworkers use. You'll be astounded by how frequently it changes height. Watch the evening news and listen to how regular people (not politicians, who are practiced at speaking in public) describe things to interviewers. These spontaneous speeches often shift between plain language and extraordinary turns of phrase, which, when written down, would look remarkably like poetry.

Shakespeare writes people in this way. His characters use different language for different circumstances. They speak plainly the majority of the time, but when circumstances warrant, they have access to language of real complexity.

Language changes height all the time, all around you. Tune into it and take your Shakespearean acting a giant leap forward.

REHEARSAL TIME

This is the opening of *The Merchant of Venice*. We'll use it to focus on the question at the center of this chapter: the changing height of Shakespeare's language.

ANTONIO   In sooth, I know not why I am so sad.
            It wearies me, you say it wearies you;
            But how I caught it, found it, or came by it,
            What stuff 'tis made of, whereof it is born,

                 I am to learn.   5

And such a want-wit sadness makes of me,

That I have much ado to know myself.

SALERIO   Your mind is tossing on the ocean,

There where your argosies with portly sail

Like signiors and rich burghers on the flood,   10

Or as it were the pageants of the sea,

Do overpeer the petty traffickers

That curtsey to them, do them reverence,

As they fly by them with their woven wings.

SOLANIO   Believe me, sir, had I such venture forth,   15

The better part of my affections would

Be with my hopes abroad. I should be still

Plucking the grass to know where sits the wind,

Peering in maps for ports, and piers, and roads;

And every object that might make me fear   20

Misfortune to my ventures, out of doubt

Would make me sad.

SALERIO   My wind cooling my broth

Would blow me to an ague when I thought

What harm a wind too great might do at sea.

I should not see the sandy hour-glass run   25

But I should think of shallows and of flats,

And see my wealthy Andrew docked in sand,

Vailing her high top lower than her ribs

To kiss her burial. Should I go to church

And see the holy edifice of stone   30

And not bethink me straight of dangerous rocks,

> Which touching but my gentle vessel's side
> Would scatter all her spices on the stream,
> Enrobe the roaring waters with my silks,
> And (in a word) but even now worth this,   35
> And now worth nothing? Shall I have the thought
> To think on this, and shall I lack the thought
> That such a thing bechanced would make me sad?
> But tell not me: I know Antonio
> Is sad to think upon his merchandise.   40

ANTONIO   Believe me, no. I thank my fortune for it,
             My ventures are not in one bottom trusted,
             Nor to one place; nor is my whole estate
             Upon the fortune of this present year.
             Therefore my merchandise makes me not sad.   45

SOLANIO   Why, then you are in love.

ANTONIO   Fie, fie!

SOLANIO   Not in love neither? Then let us say you are sad
             Because you are not merry; and 'twere as easy
             For you to laugh and leap and say you are merry, 50
             Because you are not sad. (1.1.1–51)

Simple Words from a Sad Man

Let's begin at the beginning, with Antonio, the first speaker. Since this is the very first scene of the play, all we know about him is what we can gather from his physical appearance. His age, for example, is easy to discern, and his clothing and bearing tell us about his social status. We can determine, therefore, that Antonio is middle-aged and rich. Everything else we learn about him comes from what he says and how he says it.

As always, let's start with his argument. This time, we notice immediately that it hardly seems necessary to paraphrase. Most of Antonio's language is simple and straightforward. Now and then we encounter an unfamiliar word or turn of phrase, as in the first and last lines of the speech: "sooth" is an archaic word meaning "truth"; a "want-wit" is someone who is mentally dim (*want* = lack, *wit* = intelligence). Paraphrased, Antonio's argument sounds like this:

> I'm telling you, I'm sad and I don't know why. I'm tired of it, and you say you are too. But I have no idea (*or*, I have yet to discover) where this sadness came from, where I picked it up, what it is, or what brought it on. And I feel so dulled by it that I don't even know who I am anymore (*or*, it's hard work to figure out who I am).[20]

Try to describe Antonio's language. Is it heightened? Not really. Indeed, the language is so plain that most of the words have just one syllable—they are *monosyllabic*. Only "wearies," "whereof," "sadness," "ado," and "myself" have more than one

---

20 Notice how many aspects of this language are familiar from previous chapters. There is antithesis ("wearies me" versus "wearies you"); there is the "But" at the beginning of line 3 that turns the argument's direction. The scansion is regular except for line 3, the feminine ending of which points to the stress falling on "by" (came BY it); and line 5, which only has four syllables, or two iambic feet, meaning that there is a short pause where the missing six syllables should be. (More on that in Things Further Thought On at the end of this chapter.) *Thinking Shakespeare* is cumulative, and each technique of analysis is relevant to every new piece of text.

syllable, but even their two syllables hardly qualify these words as elevated. Are there any metaphors or similes or other sorts of figurative or poetic language here? Again, not really. Once or twice there's an old-fashioned word, such as "sooth" or "ado." And Antonio uses slightly unusual verb placements ("know not" instead of "do not know" and "such a want-wit sadness makes of me" instead of "and sadness makes me such a want-wit"), but that's about it for complexity. Antonio's language is not at all heightened.

Why not?

Antonio answers the question himself: because he is sad. When you're sad, you feel low and tired ("weary," as Antonio describes himself), and you don't have the energy to use fancy-schmancy language. A sad man does not put on a dazzling display of Gilbert and Sullivan–like linguistic acrobatics; doing that requires too much effort. Antonio's simple, flat, monosyllabic language reflects perfectly his mood and temperament.[21]

Changes in Attitude and Changes in Altitude

Salerio speaks next. Before paraphrasing his speech, take a moment to describe the language. It's complicated and much more difficult to understand than Antonio's. Is it fair to call it heightened? You bet. Whereas Antonio's words are almost entirely monosyllabic, Salerio's are *polysyllabic*—"argosies," "overpeer," "traffickers," "reverence." He uses metaphor immediately, comparing Antonio's mind to a storm-tossed ship at sea. He uses

---

[21] Like the opening speech of *Richard III*, this is another extraordinary and surprising way to start a play. A man walks on stage and announces, "I'm sad and I don't know why." Immediately, we in the audience want to know more. Who is this man? Why is he sad? Will he ever be happy again?

simile; Antonio's big cargo ships (argosies) are "like signiors" (aristocratic gentlemen, lords) and "rich burghers" (wealthy citizens). The words sound fancy and musical. He uses *alliteration* (the repetition of initial consonant sounds, as in "woven wings") and *assonance* (the repetition of similar vowel sounds, as in "fly by"). Salerio even calls attention to how exotic his own speech is, using "as it were" in line 11 to put verbal quotation marks around the image that follows: "the pageants of the sea."[22]

Take a look at his first line. "Your mind is tossing on the ocean." The scansion is odd. The line has only nine syllables and is missing one:

your MIND is TOSS-ing ON the O-cean _____

The line sounds fine when spoken naturally—your MIND is TOSS-ing on the O-cean—and the audience won't particularly notice any rhythmic hitch as they listen. But remember, actors and directors have an obligation to ask *Why?* even when something seems fine enough as is.

Why is this line one beat too short? Think about the word *ocean*. If you gave it three syllables instead of two—O-ce-AN—the line would scan normally. *O-shee-un.* "Your mind is tossing on the o-shee-un."

So far, so good. Except for one problem. "O-shee-un" is just plain bizarre. After all, the word scans in its usual way, with two

---

22 This term refers to ceremonial processions of decorated barges held on water. In Shakespeare's London, the river Thames hosted many of these "pageants of the sea," and in Venice, where the play takes place, such water parades are still held during various public celebrations today. The idea survives in our culture: we persist in using the word *float* to describe an ornamental vehicle in a parade held not on water but on land.

syllables, elsewhere in Shakespeare. (We saw it in *Richard III* in chapter 3—"In the deep bosom of the ocean buried.") Then why would anyone deliberately say "o-shee-un"?

Answer: Because that's the kind of guy Salerio is. "O-shee-un" is a mannered, affected way of pronouncing an ordinary word, and the rest of Salerio's self-conscious, ornate, heightened speech suggests that he is a mannered, affected person. Antonio speaks low and simple; Salerio speaks wild and crazy. They're in the same play, they're in the same scene, and they're standing right next to one another on the same stage. They're both Shakespearean characters. But they're using *different heights of language*.

Mismatched Heights Energize Scenes

A man walks on stage and says, exhaustedly, "I'm sad and I don't know why." Another guy says, "I do. You're thinking about your great ships at sea." But he says it with an energy that is completely different from the first man's. Here's a paraphrase:

> Your thoughts are bouncing around on the billowing main! That's where your cargo ships with their fat sails (they look like aristocrats or wealthy bankers on the water—or, if I may say so, like a floating version of the Macy's Thanksgiving Day Parade) stare down at the little ferry boats that bow to them as they blast past with their stunning silken sails!

Suddenly, a scene is taking place in front of us. We get conflict. We get two contrasting energies, two vastly different voices, and two distinct perspectives on the question of why the first guy is sad. In addition, we get some important plot information—the second man seems to know a lot about the first man, who is a wealthy ship owner. (Antonio is the titular merchant of Venice, not Shylock—a common misapprehension.) All this is accomplished in just fourteen lines, and it is all communicated through the simple fact that one man speaks a very plain kind of language, while the other speaks with huge complexity, ornament, and imaginative energy.

The difference in the height of the language is *the engine that makes the scene run.* Antonio talks like Clint Eastwood, and Salerio talks like Carson Kressley. The contrast between sounds and energies, not to mention the unlikely pairing of these men in the first place, is what compels the audience's attention. If you see a production of *The Merchant of Venice* in which the actors get it backward, and Antonio sounds like he's left over from last season's Oscar Wilde play, while Salerio sounds like a grunting cowpoke out of some old Western, get up from your seat and head for the door. It's not going to get any better from there. Mozart has his sound, and Jimmy Hendrix has his. Salerio's heightened language must sound like what it is, and Antonio's simple language needs to do what it does.

Language Between High and Low

Let's return to the scene. The third character, Solanio, is easier to understand than Salerio, but harder to follow than Antonio. Put another way, his language is higher than Antonio's—polysyllabic, full of alliteration and assonance, and complex—but not as over-the-top as Salerio's.[23] The actor playing Solanio has the

---

23 Most directors take a cue from this height clue and cast Solanio younger than Salerio, adding an interesting age dynamic to the relationship between this pair of guys who show up throughout the play like a Venetian version of Tweedledee and Tweedledum.

hardest job of the three men now onstage. He must play word music that is heightened, but not wildly so. It's a delicate balance. His argument:

> Believe me, if I had that kind of money invested, the majority of my emotions would be with my stake at sea. All I would do all day is throw grass in the air to see which way the wind's blowing. I'd look in maps for ports and piers and places to drop anchor. And every single thing that might make me think something bad could happen to my ships would, without any doubt, make me sad.

A noteworthy detail in Solanio's speech is what happens with his last seven words: "out of doubt / Would make me sad." His high-flown speech suddenly becomes blunt and monosyllabic. These thudding words sound much more Antonio-like than Salerio-esque. Their weight makes them sound as if they are underlined, which makes sense, because they express the key point Solanio wants to make to Antonio: "If I had as much at risk as you do, I'd be sad too." This is why it's so crucial to study variations in the height of the language. *The changes actually tell you where the key thoughts are.*

The basic arguments of the scene so far:

ANTONIO	I'm sad and I don't know why.
SALERIO	You're preoccupied with your expensive ships at sea.
SOLANIO	If I had as much cash at stake as you do, everything I thought about would make me sad too.

Changes of Height Within Speeches

Now comes the tricky stuff. After Solanio says that if he were Antonio he'd be sad too, Salerio leaps in and takes that notion to a new level with a long list of objects that would drive him to utter despair. Here's a paraphrase:

> When I blew on my soup to cool it, I'd have a nervous breakdown thinking about the damage a blowing wind could do to my ships. I couldn't look at the sand in an hourglass without thinking of sandbars. I'd imagine my great ship *SS Andrew* run aground, the top of its mast bent over to the bottom of its hull, kissing the shallow ocean floor. Could I go to church, and see that great stone building, and not think immediately of horrible rocks? If they merely touched my ship's side, they'd scatter her cargo of spices on the water, covering the raging waves with her freight of silks. And—to put it briefly—in an instant, the ship would go from being worth a lot to being worth zilch. Am I capable of imagining such things, and not capable of being certain these things would make me sad? But don't tell me. I know Antonio's sad from thinking about his investments.[24]

As in Solanio's speech above, the height of the language changes to help underline the point. In line 40, Salerio's spectacular display of giddy linguistic invention crashes way, way down into a blast of four strong monosyllables: "But tell not me," and

---

[24] Once again, all the features of Shakespearean text we've seen thus far appear in these lines. There is a clear argument, which in this case is developed from an idea introduced by Solanio. There are lots of antitheses ("high top" versus "ribs"; "worth this" versus "worth nothing"; "have the thought" versus "lack the thought"). The meter is powerfully audible too—you can hear those iambs driving Salerio forward to his conclusion.

continues from there with plain-spoken and forthright talk: "I know Antonio / Is sad to think upon his merchandise."

This drastic shift in the height of Salerio's speech leads us to a key point:

Height changes occur not only between the characters speaking in a scene, but also within those characters' speeches.

Before Salerio gets to that emphatic drop in height at line 40, he speaks 16 lines full of high-flown rhetoric. Why?

Your friend tells you he is sad. What do you do? You probably sympathize with him and speculate about the reasons for his melancholy, both of which Salerio and Solanio do. But you might also try to cheer him up. That's the action of this beat. Salerio's objective is to snap Antonio out of his bad mood. His wild suggestion that blowing on his soup would make him go insane thinking about a hurricane at sea is amusing, designed to make Antonio smile. It's also gently mocking. Salerio is sending up his friend. He is saying, in modern terms, "Oh, you're a shipping magnate who's depressed? Well, if I had your problems, I couldn't look at an ice cube in my soda without thinking about the iceberg that sank the *Titanic*." Salerio uses high, complex, decorative language to express his arch and humorous thoughts.

Stay with it long enough, take it apart in sufficient detail, keep asking *Why am I using this word now?* and any scene's depths will reveal themselves.

In the few lines that are left Antonio denies Salerio's theory, telling him, in paraphrase, "No, thank goodness, I don't have all my money tied up in one ship or invested this year. So it's not my merchandise that's making me sad." Again, his language is crisp, clear, straightforward, and not particularly heightened. Only Solanio's next provocative suggestion elicits something other than a even-tempered response from Antonio: "Then you're in love." Antonio shoots back two acid syllables that are hard to paraphrase without resorting to profanity. "Fie" is a type of interjection (the technical term, I'm afraid, is "ejaculation") that here represents a short burst of disapproval. "Pshaw!" is the nineteenth century's version; "Bull!" or something less family-friendly, is about the closest modern equivalent. The suggestion that love has caused Antonio's sadness disturbs the man so powerfully that he can't find any language to express his outrage beyond a forceful release of angry sound. Nothing in Antonio's language to this point would suggest that he is capable of such a heated response; he has been low energy and taciturn throughout the scene. Now, he's practically screaming curses. Why?

You don't have to be Dr. Freud to guess the answer. Antonio is protesting too much. He *is* in love. Salerio and Solanio know this, and they are desperate to get Antonio to admit it, which is why they have been mocking the idea that their friend is sad over his ships. About 100 lines from now, the play reveals exactly what is happening in Antonio's life: he is in love with a dashing young Lord named Bassanio, but Bassanio is in love with a beautiful heiress named Portia. And that is why Antonio is sad.

It's All about the Language

For our purposes, the central point is that a change in the height of Antonio's speech—from laconic and plain to angry and profane—points to the emotional issue at play in the scene. *The height of the language tells us what is going on.*

The words' texture, their character, directs the scene.

The first time you read through these fifty lines, they were likely a sludge of impenetrable gobbledygook. Now work through the scene again. Listen carefully to the changes in the language. Watch how they signal shifts of power and emotion among the three speakers. This time through, the scene is a rich portrait of three friends jousting, prodding, and parrying one another about an intense and private emotional matter. Each of the three has his own clear personality. Each deploys his own highly individual kind of language. This forbidding bulk of dense language has now become just a scene in a play, and an exciting scene at that.

That transformation comes from one insight, and one alone: Shakespeare's language is never on a single level for long. It changes. It varies. It dances around from comic to dramatic, from heavy to light, from high to low.

Learning to hear those changes, to decode what they reveal of their speakers' minds, and then to let the audience hear them, is the center of the Shakespearean actor's art.

THINGS FURTHER THOUGHT ON

Partial Verse Lines

Look again at the opening speech from *Merchant*. Antonio has an odd line in the middle: "I am to learn." It's printed in the text on its own, with a big blank space to its right. Why?

This is Shakespeare's way of telling the actor to *pause*.

The actor playing Antonio needs to let some time pass before continuing to speak. How much time? The exact amount of time it would have taken him to say those missing three iambs—six syllables—of text? No. The actor, along with the director, has to decide how long to wait before he continues with his speech. (He will also have to decide whether the pause comes before or after the partial line in the text. It is not always as clear as it is in this case.)

How does he decide how long to wait? By figuring out *why* he pauses. In this case, there are many possible reasons.

Perhaps Antonio feels that he has said his fill on the matter, but then notices that Salerio and Solanio don't look satisfied, and chooses to go on.

Perhaps he takes a moment to let his first statements hang in the air, to make sure they have been heard, before wrapping up with the next two lines.

Perhaps he moves from his original position on stage to a place closer to his friends for the more intimate revelation of the last two lines.

Or perhaps he does what I saw an Antonio do in one memorable production. The three men were revealed sitting in an outdoor café in some Venetian piazza. Their table had an umbrella that said "Cinzano" and some newspapers and coffee cups strewn about. After saying, "I am to learn," Antonio stirred some sugar into his espresso, sipped, and then continued. That's probably not the pause Shakespeare had in mind, but it worked, and even got a nice laugh. So why not?

....

THINKING SHAKESPEARE RULE: Partial verse lines
indicate pauses.

....

Monosyllables

Antonio's speech, as we've already noted, is full of monosyllables. Try to scan his first line. According to iambic pentameter, it goes:

in SOOTH i KNOW not WHY i AM so SAD

"Sooth," "know," "why," "am" and "sad" are the words that get stress. But isn't "I" an important word in this line, both times it's used? And isn't "not" crucial to understanding Antonio's point? And isn't the issue not that he is sad, but that he is "so" sad?

The natural way of saying the line requires emphasis on every word in this declaration:

In sooth. I. Know not. **WHY**. I. Am. SO. **SAD**.

That's what tends to happen when Shakespeare's characters speak in monosyllables. The stress spreads out across the line. The iambic pulse recedes, and each word gets weight and import. *The consequence is that the actor must slow down.*

Try saying Antonio's first line fast. It makes no sense. He has to be even, purposeful, and emphatic when he says it. Try saying, "To be or not to be, that is the question" fast. Again, it makes no sense. Or try speaking what are perhaps the most astonishing monosyllables in the entire canon, King Lear's lament over the corpse of his daughter Cordelia:

> . . . No, no, no life!
> Why should a dog, a horse, a rat, have life,
> And thou no breath at all? (5.3.304–306)

No actor in his right mind would rattle through that amazing language quickly. The monosyllables demand space, time, and care. This is not to say that there is a fixed monosyllable speed limit. But *relative to the pace at which you had been talking*, the monosyllables almost always go a bit slower (as we saw in both Solanio's "out of doubt would make me sad" and Salerio's "but tell not me"). The actor and director will decide what pace is best.

Take care to avoid the Shatner Trap by keeping your speech natural. But be sure to follow this:

THINKING SHAKESPEARE RULE: Monosyllables mean *slow down*. Spread the stress across the whole line, giving each word weight.

The Fallacy of the Brilliant Elizabethan

When early in this chapter we analyzed Hamlet's discussion of the cold weather, we surmised that one reason he might switch from the heightened language of "the air bites shrewdly" to the simple language of "it is very cold" is to translate a complicated metaphor into something more comprehensible to the simple soldier Marcellus who is with him.

Bear in mind that Marcellus may not be the only person in the theater who might have trouble understanding what Hamlet means when he utters his fancy phrases. Related to the Shouting Tuber's Error is another mistake we might call "The Fallacy of the Brilliant Elizabethan." It holds that everyone in Shakespeare's England spoke the way Shakespearean characters do. According to everything historians have discovered about the period, that is simply not true.

From the ample correspondence, business documents, diaries, and other so-called ephemera that survive from the period, we know that people spoke in a simple, unadorned way. Besides, Elizabethan and Jacobean England were overwhelmingly illiterate societies. Only the wealthiest and most educated people knew how to read or could afford to buy books (and these would almost all be men—the illiteracy rate for women was far higher). Shakespeare at his most elevated would have been every bit as difficult for the average Elizabethan to understand as he is to many of us 400 years later. This is comforting to anyone who finds Shakespeare a bit of an uphill climb now and then. But it's not surprising. For all his discussion of "holding a mirror up to nature," Shakespeare was not attempting to put real life on stage. He was interpreting real life in artistic terms. He was writing poetic fiction, creating works that are highly crafted, full of artifice, and constructed with deliberation and premeditation. The language he uses is a heightened version of the language of real life.

That doesn't mean that the language is always highly literary. Sometimes Shakespeare brilliantly renders the simple, everyday speech he heard around him. (We'll see some Shakespearean language that closely resembles Elizabethan street speech in chapter 14.) But even this language, though not heightened, has been artfully arranged to sound plain and recognizable.

Folio and Quarto

If you look at your own copy of *Merchant*, you might be surprised to see that it does not precisely match the text we analyzed. Here, line 19 begins "Peering in maps," but in your edition it might read, "Piring" or "Prying." This kind of difference between editions is common.

Thinking Shakespeare is not the place for a review of how Shakespeare's plays got from his quill pen in the sixteenth century to Barnes & Noble in the twenty-first. But it is useful to know a couple of facts.

First, about half of Shakespeare's plays were printed more than once during his lifetime. When a play was a hit, audiences wanted not just to see it but to read it as well. Publishers would therefore rush it into print in small, paper-bound volumes called "Quartos." (The word refers to the number of pages the printer could get out of one folded sheet of paper—four, in this case.) If the first printing eventually sold out, the printer might make a second run, perhaps years after the first. This required starting from scratch: newly typesetting each individual page by hand, a labor-intensive and error-prone task. Spelling, punctuation, single words, and even entire lines could be changed by typesetters rushing to meet a deadline or choosing for some reason to alter the text. (Printing usually took place with next to no authorial participation. Once produced, plays were the property of the playhouse, not the playwright.) In some cases, as with *Richard III*, there were *thirteen* separate Quartos printed over many decades. There are countless textual differences among these many printings of the play. In 1623, the first leather-bound *Complete Works of Shakespeare* was printed: the famous *First Folio*. The plays that had already reached print in Quarto now were reproduced in yet another version with yet more imperfections and variations in the text. Shakespeare had been dead for seven years, so, as with the Quartos, he had nothing to do with what was printed in Folio.

Second, in the 400 years since those first publications, an industry of Shakespeare scholarship has come into existence. Editors, specialists in Shakespeare's text, have the important job of looking at all the period printings of the plays, analyzing the differences of wording among them, and then choosing which one is the most appropriate for the modern edition being prepared. The scholarship is so sophisticated that for each Shakespeare play, editors can discern which text—one of the Quartos, the Folio, or some combination—is the most "authentic" representation of what the Bard actually wrote.

What all this means is that the volume on your bookshelf is in many ways the product not of William Shakespeare, but of William Shakespeare and others. These others include the theater professionals who brought the manuscripts to the publishers 400 years ago, the typesetters who arranged the lines for their first printings, and the scholars who collated all of those into a modern volume for sale in the nearest mall. The bad news is that Shakespeare's actual writing can sometimes end up hidden behind layers of filters whose quality may be questionable. The good news is that there are alternate choices for actors working on roles.

Solanio may well be "peering" into maps. That's what the Folio says. But this does create an awkward echo with "piers" later in the line. So maybe he's "piring," as Q1 has it. *Piring* is an archaic word meaning *examining in detail*, and it is the reading in 1987's

New Cambridge Shakespeare edition of the play (although it seems regrettable that the Cambridge editors chose a word whose sense practically no one in a contemporary audience would know). Maybe Solanio is "prying," per Q3. This is unlikely, unless his map is a huge one that requires a crowbar to open. So perhaps "peering" is best after all, despite the proximity of "piers." An actor playing the role can try all three words and decide for himself.

Reproductions of the Folio and the Quartos are available in any good library and online. And good scholarly editions like the New Cambridge include a listing of the major textual variations in each play. Don't feel uncomfortable about consulting the alternatives for every word you're saying, and don't hesitate to try one on for size if you think it will be clearer or better. The Shakespeare Police won't arrest you. Just be sensible about it. Follow Hamlet's advice, and let your own discretion be your tutor.

Other Writers Change Altitude

Shakespeare is not the only dramatist to exploit the power of the changing height of language. Every one of the world's greats does precisely the same thing. To cite just one example: in Arthur Miller's masterpiece, *Death of a Salesman*, Willy Loman's long-suffering wife Linda spends most of the play speaking very plainly, in the not-quite-grammatical Brooklynese of a working-class woman of the 1940s. Then, late in the play, she gives this speech:

> Willy Loman never made a lot of money. His name was never in the paper. He's not the finest character that ever lived. But he's a human being and a terrible thing is happening to him. So attention must be paid. He's not to be allowed to fall into his grave like an old dog. Attention, attention must finally be paid to such a person.

Critics have picked on this speech, claiming that Linda's sudden leap from banal talk such as "I'll make a sandwich" to the rhetorical heights of "Attention, attention must finally be paid" is simply not believable, or worse, is a classic example of a playwright shoehorning his own views into the mouth of one of his creations. But both critiques miss the point of this moving and eloquent speech, because they fail to ask what is, as we know by now, the actor's key question: "Why is she using these words now?"

This speech comes at a moment of crisis in Linda's life, and the life of her family. Under terrible duress—her husband's threat of suicide and her sons' neglect of their father's wellbeing—Linda's expressive capacity somehow increases. Like the parent who, after a car accident, suddenly possesses the superhuman strength to lift an automobile off her crushed child, Linda makes a leap into language that is passionate, forceful, and searing. In extraordinary circumstances, the human mind can do extraordinary things. Such is the case with Linda Loman.

That's why this speech simply kills in the theater. It hits the audience square in the solar plexus. It is a surprise blow, a sucker punch of stunning language.

The same sudden leap inspires Hamlet's "There's a divinity that shapes our ends," and Macbeth's "Tomorrow and tomorrow and tomorrow," and Othello's "It is the cause, it is the cause my soul." The language bounds upward, hurtling toward previously unknown heights and giving form to rare air. That is called poetry.

It's made when language changes height. Actors need to watch for it.

Attention must be paid.

CHAPTER
—№—
7

ONE LINE AT A TIME

PHRASING WITH THE VERSE LINE

We've already seen that Shakespeare's characters speak in ten-syllable bursts. We've also seen that they always choose the language that best expresses their thoughts.

These two concepts fuse together to imply a third, more surprising idea:

Shakespeare's characters think ten syllables at a time.

Actors playing Shakespeare's characters must do the same. They must *think* ten syllables, then *say* them.

They must learn to phrase with the verse line.

Old Hamlet's New Lesson: Finding the Best Words

The lines we rehearsed and analyzed in chapter 3 have a few more secrets still to yield:

> Let not the royal bed of Denmark be
> A couch for luxury and damned incest.

Take a look at how both lines end. The first line has no punctuation of any kind, and the second has a period. This poses a challenge for the actor playing Old Hamlet. Should he read the lines together as one unit or treat them as two smaller units? Should he take some kind of break at the end of the first line or keep going straight into the second?

Let's answer those questions by asking another (see if you can guess what it will be):

Why is he using these words now?

Remember that Old Hamlet is speaking spontaneously. He has a series of important thoughts that he is trying to communicate to his son in a limited time, and he is choosing his words right now, in the moment. So when he tells the prince not to let the "royal bed of Denmark"—a noble, exalted, and dignified place—get corrupted by Queen Gertrude and the usurper Claudius having incestuous sex on it, Old Hamlet has to find exactly the right image to convey how disgusting the bed could become. He might call it any one of a million things:

> Let not the royal bed of Denmark be . . .
> . . . some filthy futon on a lava-lamped dorm-room floor!
> . . . a heart-shaped platform number at the Vegas Honeymoon Lodge!
> . . . the back seat of some Cadillac Casanova's car!

But he settles on this vivid word-picture: "A couch for luxury and damned incest."

The Lightning Flash of Thought

The moment in which Old Hamlet does his thinking, that lightning-fast instant when he searches his mental hard drive for precisely the right idea, *comes at the end of the first line.*

Old Hamlet is not the only character in the plays who thinks in this way. Throughout Shakespeare, characters do their thinking at line endings. These endings carve out space for the briefest interval of thought—a trick, a trice, a jiffy, a flash, a twinkle—in which the character's brain comes up with the next chunk of language the character will use.

The microscopic interval of thought created by the line ending *is not a pause.*

The microscopic interval of thought created by the line ending *is not a pause.*

You read that right. The previous sentence is printed in this book twice. If I could, I'd have it printed 100 more times—emblazoned on *Thinking Shakespeare* T-shirts, even—because this is one of the most important concepts to grasp for any actor serious about exploring what it means to speak verse.

It does not mean taking a long moment to ponder, cogitate, ruminate, and decide. A Shakespeare play is not the late-night shift at the college FM radio station: "And now . . . here comes a beautiful tune by . . . . John Coltrane."

It does not mean rattling through every five-iamb line at a clip and then stopping short at each line ending as though someone in the room had just shouted, "Red light!"

It does not mean falling into a mechanical, metronomic rhythm in which artful hesitations at the end of each line come so regularly that every audience member could set his watch by them.

No. The microscopic interval of thought created by the line ending **is not a pause.**

(Got it in there a third time!)

THE SHAKESPEAREAN DIVING BOARD   Think of the line ending as a springboard. Imagine yourself as a diver heading out for your big five-meter leap. You stride along the board—*step, step, stepstep stepstep*—get to the end, plant your feet—*steppy-step!*—do a vertical lift, and then . . . into the pool you go. In Shakespeare it's the same. The line impels you forward, and at the end, you take a little mini-lift—that microscopic interval of thought—and then dive into the beginning of the next line.

The line ending is an opportunity for thought.

The great British Shakespeare director Sir Peter Hall, a cofounder of the Royal Shakespeare Company, calls himself, only half-jokingly, an "iambic fundamentalist." In his productions, he insists that every actor observe every single line ending in the play. *Thinking Shakespeare* is not quite as doctrinaire on the issue, as this chapter will go on to discuss. But Hall offers every Shakespearean actor a wonderful way of thinking about what the line ending is. He calls it an "energy point." That's a superb image and a great description.

The line ending doesn't stop thought; it launches thought forward. It doesn't arrest momentum; it creates it. It doesn't point down; it points up. The line ending is a point of possibility, a point of thought, a point of energy.

And on the most practical level, it poses the question, "What word comes next?"

Two Types of Line Endings

Look one more time at Old Hamlet's two lines.

Let not the royal bed of Denmark be
A couch for luxury and damned incest.

That period that ends the second line is there because the idea being expressed comes to an end. The syntax of the sentence and the thought behind it demand a full stop, and that's what the period delivers. The thought stops exactly where the line does. This kind of line is called *end-stopped*.

Lines can be end-stopped without periods. Commas, semicolons, dashes, colons, question marks, exclamation points—any punctuation at the end of the line that's there to mark the close of a thought or part of a thought—signals an *end-stopped line*.

The first line, conversely, is not end-stopped. The thought it expresses doesn't end at the end of the line but keeps going. That's why there's no punctuation mark. The sense of the line is

Don't let the bed in which the monarchy of Denmark sleeps turn into

Because the thought is not finished, we don't find out precisely *what* the royal bed shouldn't turn into until the beginning of the next line. The first line runs on to the second line.

This kind of line is called *run-on* (or, sometimes, more technically, *enjambed*).[25]

---

25 *Enjambed* comes from the French (note that the *b* is silent). *En-* is a prefix meaning "to put into or onto," and *jambe* is the French for "leg." *Enjambed* means, literally, "on leg." The line has legs that run it onto the next line.

The complete thought is "be a couch," but the *enjambment* at the end of the first line splits it: "be / A couch."

Mr. Shakespeare, Meet Mr. Mamet

Shakespeare was aware of what he was doing when he split lines. As he wrote, he made an endless series of choices about how to deploy iambic pentameter, the form he chose for the overwhelming majority of his output. It's possible to read his plays in the order he wrote them and actually trace his increasing facility with the architecture of the verse line. His skill grows with each new play, until, by about the midpoint of his career, he becomes a kind of sculptor, carving exceptional and lissome word art out of the iambic marble.

Contemporary actors working on modern stage writing and on TV and film can't be expected to have the kind of skill with verse lines that Shakespeare's own company surely had. But today's actors know plenty about how our own playwrights structure language. The modern master David Mamet, revered and studied by countless actors, uses a device that provides an exceptionally useful way for a Shakespearean to begin phrasing with the verse line.

Here are three speeches from Mamet's controversial play *Oleanna*. They are all spoken by Carol, a university student, to her professor:

You are to be disciplined. For facts. For *facts*. Not "alleged," what is the word? But *proved*. Do you see?

No. No. There are *people* out there. People who came *here*. To know something they didn't *know*. Who *came* here. To be *helped*.

To be *helped*. So someone would *help* them. To *do* something. To *know* something. To get, what do they say? "To get on in the world."

I speak, yes, not for myself. But for the group; for those who suffer what I suffer. On behalf of whom, even if I were inclined, to what, forgive? Forget?

Midway through all three speeches, Carol takes the briefest moment to ask herself how she's going to continue to articulate her thought. "What is the word?" she wonders in the first excerpt, before finding it: "proved." "To get, what do they say?" she asks herself in the second, then answers, "'To get on in the world.'" And in the third, she simply interrupts her own line with "what" before continuing, "forgive?"

Mamet, like Shakespeare, knows that people speak spontaneously. They do not recite prewritten speeches. They think in the moment and then find language to say what's on their minds. So Mamet *writes Carol's thinking into her lines*. Her questions—"what is the word?" "what do they say?" "to what?"—give Carol the space to find her next piece of language as she goes along.

Here is another Mametian gem, from the wonderful *A Life in the Theatre*. John and Robert, two actors in a dressing room after a performance, discuss the night's audience:

JOHN   An intelligent house. Didn't you feel?
ROBERT   I did.
JOHN   They were very attentive.
ROBERT   Yes. (*Pause.*) They were acute.
JOHN   Mmm.
ROBERT   Yes. (*Pause.*) They were discerning.

JOHN	I thought they were.
ROBERT	Perhaps they saw the show tonight (*pause*) on
	another level. Another, what? another . . . plane,
	eh? On another level of meaning.

Robert searches for exactly the right way to describe the special attentiveness of the night's audience. He asks himself, "Another, what?" and finds the word he's been looking for: another "plane." Again, Mamet has woven the character's thinking right into the fabric of the line.

This is exactly what Shakespeare does at his line endings.

Let not the royal bed of Denmark be   *(what?)*
A couch for luxury and damned incest.

The line ending provides the actor a brief opportunity to figure out what he will say next. By emulating Mamet, we can ask our own questions—let's call them Mamet Magic Moments—and turn every Shakespearean line ending into a springboard for thought.

THE MAMET MAGIC MOMENT   Let's return to some material we've analyzed in previous chapters. Try it again, but this time ask the questions in parentheses below—the Mamet Magic Moments (MMM)—to yourself as you encounter them. Better yet, ask someone to cue you with them as you read through the lines. In Richard of Gloucester's famous speech, here are the MMMs you might encounter.

Now is the winter of our discontent   *(what?)*
Made glorious summer by this sun of York;   *(okay, so?)*
And all the clouds that loured upon our house *(what about them?)*

In the deep bosom of the ocean buried.   *(anything else?)*
Now are our brows bound with victorious wreaths;   *(fine, and?)*
Our bruised arms hung up for monuments;   *(what else?)*
Our stern alarums changed to merry meetings;   *(what else?)*
Our dreadful marches to delightful measures.   *(got any more?)*
Grim-visaged war hath smoothed his wrinkled front;   *(so what?)*
And now, instead of mounting barbed steeds,   *(why?)*
To fright the souls of fearful adversaries,   *(yeah?)*
He capers nimbly in a lady's chamber   *(how?)*
To the lascivious pleasing of a lute.

Next, Salerio. The MMMs in his speech might sound like this:

Your mind is tossing on the ocean,   *(where?)*
There where your argosies with portly sail   *(what about them?)*
Like signiors and rich burghers on the flood,   *(what else?)*
Or as it were the pageants of the sea,   *(yes . . . ?)*
Do overpeer the petty traffickers   *(which ones?)*
That curtsey to them, do them reverence,   *(when?)*
As they fly by them with their woven wings.

The particular questions used in the MMMs aren't that important. Even if every question were *what?* it would still do the job. The questions are simply cues to get the actor to think—in that moment, right then and there—about what he's going to say next. I've used the MMM in my own rehearsal room countless times. Every once in a while I will ask the actors to run a scene, and I'll sit there with the script shouting WHAT?! at the ends of lines. They usually want to strangle me, but they get the point I'm making. *The line ending creates an opportunity for thought.*

REHEARSAL TIME

One of the best speeches I know for practicing how to phrase with the verse line is this one of Portia's in *The Merchant of Venice*.

Because she is young, ready for marriage, beautiful, and fabulously wealthy, Portia has many, many suitors from all over the world. One of her admirers is Lord Bassanio. His refusal to love Antonio (whom we've previously met) is the reason the merchant is "so sad." Portia's father is dead, but before he passed away, he devised a plan to control Portia's choice of husband. In one of the rooms of the family manor at Belmont, he set up three boxes (Shakespeare calls them "caskets"). One is made of gold, one of silver, and one of lead. A picture of Portia is in one of them, but nobody, including Portia, knows which. Every suitor must agree to go into this room and "hazard" which box has the picture. If he gets it right, he gets to marry Portia. If he gets it wrong, he must swear "never to speak with lady afterward / In way of marriage." Not surprisingly, this caveat discourages most men from even trying. Two brave souls hazard guesses that turn out to be wrong: a Moroccan prince picks the gold box (he learns that "all that glisters is not gold"); a Spaniard guesses silver. Now Portia, her household, and the audience all know that lead is the winning box.

At long last, Bassanio, flush with 3,000 ducats borrowed from Shylock on his behalf by Antonio, goes to the casket room to hazard his choice. Portia has already admitted that ever since they met years ago, she has dreamed of marrying Bassanio, so she—and we—root for him. While he looks over the three boxes, Portia's companion Nerissa sings a sweet song, the lyrics of which all happen to rhyme with "lead" ("Tell me, where is fancy bred? / Or in the heart or in the head?" etc.), which some directors interpret as a not-too-subtle hint to Bassanio, who isn't the sharpest tool in the, well, shed. Whether he catches on or figures it out on his own, Bassanio delivers a long and beautiful speech of deliberation and then points to the lead box, hoping that "Joy be the consequence!"

He opens it and finds the picture of Portia, and general celebration erupts. A message left inside tells him, "Turn you where your lady is / And claim her with a loving kiss." But before Bassanio plants one on his wife-to-be, Portia makes an extraordinary speech of love, devotion, and prenuptial agreement. Here it is:

PORTIA   You see me, Lord Bassanio, where I stand,
Such as I am. Though for myself alone
I would not be ambitious in my wish
To wish myself much better, yet for you
I would be trebled twenty times myself,   5
A thousand times more fair, ten thousand times
    more rich,
That only to stand high in your account
I might in virtues, beauties, livings, friends,
Exceed account. But the full sum of me
Is sum of something: which to term in gross   10
Is an unlessoned girl, unschooled, unpractised;
Happy in this, she is not yet so old
But she may learn; happier than this,
She is not bred so dull but she can learn;
Happiest of all, is that her gentle spirit   15
Commits itself to yours to be directed

> As from her lord, her governor, her king.
> Myself, and what is mine, to you and yours
> Is now converted. But now I was the lord
> Of this fair mansion, master of my servants,   20
> Queen o'er myself; and even now, but now,
> This house, these servants, and this same myself
> Are yours—my Lord's.—I give them with this ring,
> Which when you part from, lose, or give away,
> Let it presage the ruin of your love,   25
> And be my vantage to exclaim on you.
>
> (3.2.149–176)

It's a tough but gorgeous speech, rich with rhetorical devices and heightened language. Before we work through it, let's give it a second read, this time using one of the most powerful aids to good Shakespearean acting ever invented: a blank piece of paper.

The Paper Trick

Grab a blank sheet of paper and cover the entire speech except for the first line. Read that line, and when you get to its end ("stand"), move the paper down just enough to expose the next line. Read that, then move the paper again, repeating this process until you've reached the end of the speech. Don't cheat; it's important that you only reveal one line at a time and that you don't move the paper until you have reached the very end of the line you're on. Listen as you read, and see if this Paper Trick changes the sound of the speech.

Many actors find that this exercise revolutionizes their approach to Shakespeare. They notice that, thanks to a simple piece of paper, material that was all but incomprehensible on first reading suddenly undergoes a total transformation in terms of clarity, sense, and understandability. I've even seen the Paper Trick change the way some very smart and talented non-theater folk read Shakespeare and other poets.

If you've never read a certain piece of Shakespeare's verse before, one of the best first things to do is cover it with a piece of paper and work through it one line at a time. It's a revelation. I'm almost tempted to say it's a miracle, except it's not really, because that's the way the stuff was written in the first place: to be phrased one line at a time.

The Speech in Beats

Now let's look at some of the details of Portia's speech. We'll start with the argument, breaking it down into its constituent sections and looking at each one individually, using all the tools of the previous five chapters, plus some new tricks we'll pick up as we go.

The argument can be given this quick paraphrase:

Well, Bassanio, here I am. I wish I were better than this. But I'm not so bad. I hereby turn over to you myself and everything I have. A second ago I was in charge, but now you are. Here's my ring. If you lose it, I'll kill you.

Portia develops this argument in a number of beats.

Beat One is "Well, Bassanio, here I am. I wish I were better than this," which runs from the first line through the first half of line 9. (Some might consider "Well, Bassanio, here I am" its own beat, and "I wish I were better than this" a second beat.)

There's a lot going on here. Portia uses antithesis ("I stand" versus "I am"; "for myself alone" versus "for you"; "I would not be" versus "I would be"; "stand high in your account" versus "exceed account"). There are a couple of builds of the sort we saw in *Richard III*—lists that increase in intensity as they move forward ("trebled twenty . . . a thousand . . . ten thousand"; and "virtues, beauties, livings, friends"). There's some strange scansion. Line 6 has twelve syllables. Some editors put "more rich" at the beginning of line 7, giving that line twelve syllables, while others put those two words on their own line 6.5, giving lines six and seven ten syllables apiece. Each solution has its own problems. Sometimes it's best to let Shakespeare have the occasional long line. Why would Portia speak with too many words for the meter? Certainly her enthusiasm and boundless happiness help explain her excess.

Beat Two, "But I'm not so bad," starts midway through line 9 and runs through line 17. The beat starts with a "but" that turns Portia's first idea around. More antitheses follow ("sum of me" versus "sum of something"). So do builds, this time all in threes ("unlessoned . . . unschooled . . . unpractised"; "happy . . . happier . . . happiest"; "lord . . . governor . . . king"). There's another strange scansion problem in line 13. "Happier" elides into two syllables, *HAPP-yer*, which leaves the line one iamb short. Editors, seizing on some odd discrepancies in the printed texts from the period, have proposed all sorts of additions and rewrites, but again, it's sometimes best to chalk up metric strangeness to Shakespeare's idiosyncrasies, and in this case, Portia's turbulent emotions.

Beat Three, lines 18 through the first half of line 23, is the center of the speech and the whole reason it is in the play. An enormous dramatic action takes place at this point: Portia gives herself to Bassanio. This is, essentially, their wedding. The antitheses in this beat ("myself . . . mine" versus "you . . . yours") reflect the larger antithesis in what Portia is saying—*I* used to be the boss and now *you* are. The thick accumulation of three-part builds here reflects the enormousness of this transaction: "lord . . . master . . . queen"; "mansion . . . servants . . . myself"; "house . . . servants . . . same myself." The last and most extraordinary three-part build harnesses the Power of Now: "but now . . . even now . . . but now." These builds express the energy of Portia's thinking—that particular swirl of fear, anxiety, and excitement that envelops a bride in the moment she says, "I do."

Beat Four starts with the second half of line 23 and goes through the end of the speech. In this beat Portia says, in essence, "Here's my ring. If you lose it, I'll kill you." This beat offers a textbook example of the potency of the changing height of language. Suddenly, after a euphoric rush of language so intense that at times it shatters even the rigid framework of iambic pentameter, so sweeping and heady that it piles build upon build upon build, Portia slams in the clutch and downshifts to thumping monosyllables and hard, straight talk.

It's typical of Shakespeare to undercut an outpouring of emotion in this way. The instant after Portia proclaims her exhilarated happiness (and remember, Bassanio predicted "joy"), she turns immediately to talk of "ruin," and declares that her privilege will be to "exclaim," a dense word meaning both *scream* and *break a legal contract* (similar to *quitclaim*, a word still in use in legal transactions today). She pulls the rug out from under the speech. Those insistent monosyllables—*I. Give. Them. With. This. Ring.*—function almost like a smash cut to close-up in the movies. They focus the audience on this ring and endow it with immense significance, a significance Shakespeare won't fully unpack until late in Act V of the play. An actress playing Portia must execute the change in linguistic height at this moment, dizzying though it is, for the over-all design of Shakespeare's play to function. She must explore this change, think it, so that she will really understand what it means to Portia to give all her authority, wealth, and love to a young man who, after all, won her heart by winning a raffle.

Verse Versus Punctuation

So far, so good. We've gone over the speech a couple of times, digging through layer after layer of detail, analyzing Portia's thinking as we scrutinized the words that express what is on her mind. But this chapter is about *phrasing with the verse line*, and that's where this speech gets really interesting.

Look again at Beat Three, which we have already identified as the meat of the speech. Let's apply the MMM.

```
Myself, and what is mine, to you and yours        (what?)
Is now converted. But now I was the lord          (where?)
Of this fair mansion, master of my servants,      (anything else?)
Queen o'er myself; and even now, but now,         (Yes . . . ?)
This house, these servants, and this same myself  (What??!!)
Are yours—my Lord's.—I give them with this ring,
```

The MMMs get more forceful as they progress, right in line with Portia's own language, which builds as it continues.

Notice the enjambed line ending between lines 18 and 19. Try to say those lines with no regard at all to the enjambment there. "Myself, and what is mine, to you and yours is now converted." It's a simple statement, clear and concise.

Reading the line this way—*phrasing with the punctuation*, as opposed to phrasing with the verse—is absolutely fine. Portia can ignore the line endings to her heart's content and still make perfect sense, move the audience, and convince them of her passion.

But consider what you lose by disregarding this line ending. At this moment, Portia is becoming more than Bassanio's wife; she is becoming his property. She and everything she owns are being "converted" (great word) from what they were—Portia's— to what they will be—Bassanio's. This formidable change in status happens *now*. Not later, not once a priest pronounces them man and wife, not once the clerk at City Hall grants them their marriage license, but *now*. Now, in front of each other, in front of everyone else on stage, and, most important of all, in front of the audience. Portia knows all this. "Now" is a momentous, almost overwhelming word for her to say.

That's why she needs a tiny interval of thought before she says it. She has to find it, think it, let it sink in, pronounce it, deliver it. And that's why there's a line ending before she speaks the word.

Myself, and what is mine, to you and yours   (*omigod can this*
                                                be happening can
                                                i really do this yes
                                                i can i love him i
                                                really want this i've
                                                been waiting for it all
                                                my life here goes)

Is now converted.

This is a breathtaking moment. It's suspenseful. Will Portia go through with it? Won't she? Is she about to kiss the boy or faint dead away? It's the kind of thrilling flash that makes Shakespeare in the theater so incredible. I've seen Portias hold that line ending for what seemed like an eternity. It's a great bit of stagecraft.

Let's be clear. To ignore that line ending wouldn't be "wrong." But it would be a shame. There is gold in these line endings. To disregard them is to make your production less interesting, less dramatic, less dynamic.

Look at the enjambment between lines 22 and 23. Once again, it's perfectly legitimate to phrase the lines according to the punctuation: "This house, these servants, and this same myself are yours." That works. It's clear, it makes sense, we get it. But it sacrifices a nuance in Portia's thinking.

Portia restates, giddily and disbelievingly, what she has just done. She says, in paraphrase, "Only a second ago, I was the boss of this beautiful house, in charge of my servants, mistress of my whole soul. And now—*now!*—this house, these servants, and my very soul—*line ending*—(*oh my god i really did it i gave myself to him i'm not my own anymore i belong to him it feels great i love him i'm happy*)—**are yours. My Lord's**." Once again, the line ending forges that electric moment of emotion. It carves out room for the specific personality of the character to resonate. It creates the space in which the actor's art can flourish.

More: it syncopates the music of the text. That rushing build of, "my house . . . my servants . . . myself" soars up in a crescendo of love and pleasure, then flutters down to a soft and graceful landing on the monosyllables "are yours—my Lord's." Without the microscopic interval for thought in the line ending after "myself," the rhythm is pedestrian, clumsy. With it, it's amazing, surprising.

Not every line ending in Shakespeare delivers the goods like these do. Most simply organize thought and language into manageable building blocks. But even this is an invaluable service.

Try the first beat of the speech with MMMs doing their helpful work.

You see me, Lord Bassanio, where I stand,	*(how?)*
Such as I am. Though for myself alone	*(what?)*
I would not be ambitious in my wish	*(what wish?)*
To wish myself much better, yet for you	*(yes . . . ?)*
I would be trebled twenty times myself,	*(what else?)*
A thousand times more fair, ten thousand times more rich,	*(why?)*
That only to stand high in your account	*(yes?)*
I might in virtues, beauties, livings, friends,	*(WHAT?)*
Exceed account.	

The text simply *wants* to be spoken one line at a time.

Notice that when lines are end-stopped and have strong punctuation (such as lines 1, 5, 6, and 8 here), you will almost automatically phrase at the line endings. It's natural to take a micro-break after "where I stand," because the syntax of the language and the shape of the thought being expressed have a break right at that point. That's why the comma is there. Of the remaining enjambed line endings (2, 3, 4, and 7), perhaps only the one at the end of line 4, with its "myself alone" set in antithesis to "yet for *you*," is interesting enough to spend time with. "Yet for you *(what?)* I would be twenty times myself." Portia needs that moment to think about what she would like to be for her lover, rather than what she already is. The line ending provides that opportunity.

Lines 2, 3, and 7 are not as rich. That's why it's fine to phrase with the punctuation when there is no special reason not to. Only

Peter Hall and other iambic fundamentalists would be disappointed in a Portia who ran some lines together.

But this poses an even more interesting question.

Inspiration: Breathing the Verse

Try playing Beat One ("You see me" through "exceed account") to the punctuation. You may get through two lines, maybe more, before you simply run out of air. Sooner or later, you're going to need to take a breath. Perhaps you'll sneak one near the end of line 2 or the middle of line 3. Most likely you'll take a big breath after line 2's "such as I am," where the period ends one sentence and starts another. By the time you get into line 9, you'll have gulped air at so many punctuation marks, and sliced the language into so many small bits and pieces, that it will hardly resemble iambic pentameter at all.

This is what directors mean when they tell actors that they're "breaking it up." Pauses created by fitful gasps for air break up the flow of the lines, giving the language a herky-jerky, stop-and-start quality. It may resemble the studied inarticulacy of much of our best contemporary stage writing, but it's not appropriate to the skillfully wrought iambic verse structure and long, arcing thoughts of Shakespeare.

This is where the line endings once again assert their value. Paying attention to them will help you avoid choppiness. Line endings not only create an opportunity for thought, but *they also create an opportunity for breath.*

Spiritually inclined Shakespeareans will be quick to point out the happy coincidence that the word *inspiration*, which means "the inhalation of a breath of air," also means "a stimulation of the intellect and emotions, especially to an act of creativity." *To inspire* is to fill with arousing or enlivening energy. It is also, literally, to breathe in. Anyone who has looked into Eastern spiritual practices, taken a yoga class, or read the story of the Garden of Eden in *Genesis* knows that an intimate connection exists between creativity and breath. This connection is present in Shakespeare's verse.

Inspiration happens at Shakespeare's line endings. Characters draw breath, and as that new breath rushes into their lungs, it carries a new idea into their minds.

Not every end-of-line breath is the same, of course. Portia's breath after "Myself, and what is mine, to you and yours" in line 18 is longer and fuller than her breath after "Though for myself alone" in line 2. The latter is really more of a quick inhalation, or *catch-breath*, as voice teachers call it. It doesn't take time or stop the flow of the speech; it just sounds like the natural, unconscious breath a person takes while doing a lot of talking. Singers use catch-breaths in places where the music in songs allows for a quick, quiet grab of sustaining air. Shakespearean actors, especially those facing a long bomber of a speech, use the same technique.

One of the side benefits of breathing at the ends of lines is that you will only ever need enough breath to get through ten syllables of language at a time. There is never any reason to run out of gas.

AN EXERCISE IN BREATHING THE VERSE   Here's another piece of Portia, marked up with MMMs and indications of where the breaths fall. Slap a piece of paper over it and see what happens.

> The quality of mercy is not strained.   *breath—(what is it?)*
> It droppeth as the gentle rain from heaven *catch-breath—(where?)*
> Upon the place beneath. It is twice blest: *breath—(what*
> *do you mean?)*

It blesseth him that gives, and him that takes.   *breath—(what else?)*

'Tis mightiest in the mightiest. It becomes *catch-breath—(what?)*
The throned monarch better than his crown.   *big breath— (Okay, and?)*

His sceptre shows the force of temporal power,   *breath—(what?)*
The attribute to awe and majesty,   *catch-breath—(what about it?)*

Wherein doth sit the dread and fear of kings;   *nice breath— (so what's your point?)*

But mercy is above this sceptred sway.   *breath—(what else?)*
It is enthroned in the hearts of kings;   *breath—(what else?)*
It is an attribute to God himself,   *breath—(what else?)*
And earthly power doth then show likest God's   *long breath—(when?)*
When mercy seasons justice.

(4.1.179–192)

The phrasing of this famous speech is not especially difficult to begin with. Most of the verse is regular and end-stopped, and there are only three enjambed lines: 2, 5, and 13. In each of those cases, the sense would be perfectly clear and the argument undamaged were Portia to phrase with the punctuation:

It droppeth as the gentle rain from heaven upon the place beneath.

It becomes the throned monarch better than his crown.

And earthly power doth then show likest God's when mercy seasons justice.

But there are consequences to phrasing the text in this way. For the actor who disregards the verse structure and plays to the punctuation, every piece of punctuation has an equal claim to importance. This actor finds herself observing all of it, creating breaks or pauses throughout the text, at every comma, semicolon, dash, and period. Line 3 gets a pause at the period between "the place beneath" and "It is twice blest." Line 5 gets one at the period before "It becomes." And line 14 gets one at the period after "seasons justice." The speech turns into a series of full sentences of different lengths, broken up by periods.[26] Try it.

The quality of mercy is not strained.

It droppeth as the gentle rain from heaven upon the place beneath.

It is twice blest: it blesseth him that gives, and him that takes.

'Tis mightiest in the mightiest.

It becomes the throned monarch better than his crown.

His sceptre shows the force of temporal power, the attribute to awe and majesty, wherein doth sit the dread and fear of kings; but mercy is above this sceptred sway.

---

26 Just as he constantly varies the height of the language, Shakespeare constantly varies the rhythm as well, writing sentences of various lengths—some long, some short, some medium. We'll explore the ramifications of all this in chapter 9.

It is enthroned in the hearts of kings; it is an attribute to God himself, and earthly power doth then show likest God's when mercy seasons justice.

This version of the speech may be many things, but the one thing it isn't is verse. It might as well be printed like this:

The quality of mercy is not strained. It droppeth as the gentle rain from heaven upon the place beneath. It is twice blest: it blesseth him that gives, and him that takes. 'Tis mightiest in the mightiest. It becomes the throned monarch better than his crown. His sceptre shows the force of temporal power, the attribute to awe and majesty, wherein doth sit the dread and fear of kings; but mercy is above this sceptred sway. It is enthroned in the hearts of kings; it is an attribute to God himself, and earthly power doth then show likest God's when mercy seasons justice.

The occasional choice to run past a line ending works fine and may even in some cases be advisable. But in general, *phrasing with the punctuation transforms verse into prose.* Had Shakespeare wanted to write Portia in prose, he would have. He wrote Beatrice in prose, and much of Rosalind, so he certainly knew how to do it.[27] But he wrote Portia in verse, and so she should speak in verse.

Try to keep the verse lines together. Try to breathe at the ends of those lines and let whole thoughts flow out in units of iambic pentameter.

That's what this writing demands.

---

27 We'll look at the special texture of Shakespeare's prose in chapter 14.

Get to the End of the Line

As you practice phrasing with the verse line on more speeches, you'll begin to make all sorts of discoveries about the particular textures and qualities of Shakespeare's writing.

Over the years, I've found that all actors have a big *Eureka!* moment when they realize that Shakespeare's characters think with a special kind of energy. Their thoughts have motion. They grow. They progress from where they start to someplace else.

Shakespearean thinking never stands still but always moves *forward*. This insight leads to a technique that goes hand in hand with phrasing with the verse line. To really understand how it feels inside your brain and inside your mouth to speak Shakespeare a line at a time, you also need to understand how to *drive through to the end of the line.*

Once again, consider Richard of Gloucester's opening lines, paying particular attention to the ideas at their ends.

Now is the winter of our discontent
Made glorious summer by this son of York.

If Richard fails to state the idea of *discontent* clearly, then the fact that discontent has been transformed to glory by the Yorkists won't make any sense. And if he fails to establish that the new Yorkist king is the agent of this great transformation, the rest of the play won't make any sense.

These failures would make the line sound like this:

Now   is the winter   of our   discontent
Made glorious summer by this son of York.

The language peters out, ebbs toward nothingness, and the thoughts it exists to express evaporate into the ether.

But if Richard drives through to *discontent* and *York*, the sense of the lines etches itself into the air like neon light.

Now is the winter of our **discontent**
Made glorious summer *by this son of* **York**.

The energy of the lines builds toward their ends.

Once you catch a breath at that microscopic moment of thought after the fifth iamb in a line of verse, you must begin again at the start of the next line and let your thinking carry you through its five iambs until you reach its end. Then breathe again, and spring forward onto the next line. And repeat. And repeat. And repeat. And repeat.

After dozens, hundreds of lines of practice of getting to the ends of lines, another discovery will start to make its way into your brain and into your bones. This is one of the most uncanny and downright striking features of Shakespeare's verse.

The important words tend to gravitate toward the ends of lines.

Take another look at *Henry VI* from chapter 4.

When this is known, then to divide the times: 30
So many hours must I tend my flock,
So many hours must I take my rest,
So many hours must I contemplate,
So many hours must I sport myself,
So many days my ewes have been with young,   35
So many weeks ere the poor fools will ean,
So many years ere I shall shear the fleece.

In lines 31 through 34, the new information comes at the end of each line. "So many hours must I" is only important the first time it's said. After that, the audience understands the idea and is more interested in what Henry would do in all those hours: tend his flock, take his rest, contemplate, and so on.

The good stuff clusters at the line endings. You've got to drive through toward them.

AN EXERCISE IN THE WORDS AT THE ENDS   Here's a fast and easy exercise that will illustrate the importance of driving toward the line endings. Take the speech you're working on and write down the last word (or, if it's a preposition or other tiny word, the last thought) in every line. Then say them out loud, slowly. Portia's speech to Bassanio would go like this:

> stand
>
> alone
>
> wish
>
> you
>
> myself
>
> rich
>
> account
>
> friends
>
> me
>
> gross
>
> unpractised
>
> old
>
> this
>
> learn
>
> spirit

directed

king

yours

lord

servants

now

myself

ring

away

love

you

Listen again to this sequence: "yours . . . lord . . . servants . . . now . . . myself . . . ring . . . away . . . love . . . you." It lays out Portia's thinking so clearly and concisely that she hardly needs to bother doing the rest of the speech! This remarkable exercise not only helps train actors to keep their thinking moving forward toward the end of the line, but it also, mysteriously and almost spookily, *reveals the very argument of the speech itself.*

Here's what Richard's opening speech looks like. Again, read it out, deliberately.

discontent

York

house

buried

wreaths

monuments

meetings

measures

front

steeds

adversaries

chamber

lute

tricks

looking-glass

majesty

nymph

proportion

nature

time

half made up

unfashionable

halt by them

peace

time

sun

deformity

lover

days

villain

days

dangerous

dreams

king

other

just

treacherous

mewed up

> "G"
> shall be
> Clarence comes

Once again, it's possible to hear the speech's entire argument through these forty-odd words. "Deformity . . . lover . . . days . . . villain . . . days . . . dangerous . . . dreams . . . king . . . other . . . just . . . treacherous . . . mewed up . . . "G" . . . shall be . . . Clarence comes." This sequence tells the speech's entire story. And once again, the exercise of listing the words will help make the actor drive toward them when he returns to do the full speech.

Here's one more example, from one of Shakespeare's best-known speeches. See if you can hear the rest of the text simply by saying the last word in every line.

> tomorrow
> day
> time
> fools
> candle
> player
> stage
> tale
> fury
> nothing

That, of course, is Macbeth's extraordinary "Tomorrow and tomorrow and tomorrow" speech (5.5.18–27). Distilled down to the words each line drives toward, the speech reveals its essential nature as a kind of tone poem of disbelief, despair, regret, and withdrawal in the face of the relentless and destructive force of time.

Write out the words at the ends of the lines. Speak the list. Returning to the speech, press onward through the lines until you get to those words you wrote. Then inspire the next set of words and do it all over again.

Thoughts That Don't End at the End

"Okay," you're thinking. "I'll try to keep the lines together, drive toward their final words, and breathe at the line endings."

But . . .

"What about lines with a punctuation mark in the middle, where the thought ends midway through?"

Good question. What you're asking about—that break midway through the line—has a name: *caesura*.

A caesura (plural: caesurae) is a break in a line of verse created not by the meter but by the sense of what is being said, or by the syntax. (It has a non-Latin name too: "medial pause." Caesura, from the Latin for "a cutting off," is much lovelier.)

Caesurae are one of the trickiest challenges in all of Shakespearean acting. Look at these Portia lines:

Such as I am. Though for myself alone

Exceed account. But the full sum of me

Is sum of something: which to term in gross,

Is now converted. But now I was the lord

and

Are yours—my Lord's.—I give them with this ring,

In these examples, if you land on the caesura in the middle of the line, creating a pause there, and if you then also breathe at the end of the line, you'll have made two breaks within ten syllables, and you'll be guilty of the sin of fragmentation—you'll fall into the Shatner Trap.

But if you race right past the caesura on your way to the end of the line, you'll risk obscuring the thought. The audience won't hear the first thought end and the next one begin, and they will lose track of the sense of the speech.

The best approach is to strike a balance between both extremes. Try to let the line carry you through toward the end, yet see if you can let the punctuation mark in the middle have its weight *without letting it stop you entirely*. And if you find that that's just too difficult, or if it sounds weird or hard to follow, then by all means take the caesura and also the line ending. The Shakespeare Police are forgiving, as long as they don't have to deal with repeat offenders.

Coping with caesurae requires a certain confidence; you must be in complete command of the thought that the whole line expresses. It requires a good breath; you need to have taken in enough air at the end of the previous line to allow some maneuvering room in this one. And most of all, *it requires an ability to keep your thinking moving forward* even as the words you are speaking take a momentary break.

Always remember that you are *thinking* Shakespeare. You're not reciting it. If your thinking is alive and energetic and always progressing ahead onto the next thought and the next one and the next, the language will sound real and spontaneous and believable.

The form of the words sculpts the thoughts they express. Let the thoughts *lead you through* the form.

···

THINGS FURTHER THOUGHT ON

···

Trick Consonants Sound Difficult

Sometimes Shakespeare will write an adjoining pair of words connected by the same consonant sound. Portia has some in the speech we examined in this chapter:

more rich

these servants

this same

same myself

These are called *abutted consonants*. In each pair, the first word ends with the same consonant sound that begins the second word. The consonants butt up against each other—they "abut" each other. Even those pairs that are separated by another letter, such as a silent *e*, still end and begin with the same consonant sound.

There are two schools of thought about abutted consonants. One holds that actors *should always split* abutted consonants, making sure that the consonant sounds do not blend into each other. Separating the consonants, this theory maintains, sets off the second word and makes it special:

A thousand times mo<u>re</u>— <u>R</u>ICH

This house, the<u>se</u>—<u>S</u>ERVANTS, and thi<u>s</u>—**SAME**—*MYSELF* [28]

Somewhat exasperatingly, though not surprisingly, there is another school that says *never split* abutted consonants, but instead connect them together, using the power of the doubled consonant sound to make the second word—and to a certain extent, the first word too—special.

Give each approach a try with these examples, and see which one you prefer.

KING LEAR   No rescue? What, a prisoner? I am even
                     The natural fool o<u>f f</u>ortune. Use me well.
                                              (4.6.184–185)

KING HENRY V   But tell the Dauphin I will keep my state,
                     Be like a king, and show my sail of greatness
                     When I do rouse me in my throne o<u>f F</u>rance.
                                              (1.2.273–275)

KING RICHARD II   For God'<u>s s</u>ake, let u<u>s s</u>it upon the ground
                     And tell sad stories of the death of kings.
                                              (3.2.151–152)

---

28 One of the great advocates of the "always split them" school—its dean, as it were—is the great British Shakespeare director Michael Langham. He directed Canada's Stratford Festival during its glory days in the mid-twentieth century (and hired as his leading man our very own William Shatner) and afterward staged sterling productions of Shakespeare all over the world. Given that his own name has abutted consonants, it is perhaps no surprise that when he ran the Juilliard Drama Division in the 1970s and 1980s, he taught his students to split every abutted consonant they found. They in turn took to calling the school the "Juillia<u>rd</u>—<u>D</u>RAMA Division."

More on Three-Part Builds

We touched briefly on the power of the amazing rush of builds in Portia's speech.

lord . . . master . . . queen
mansion . . . servants . . . myself
house . . . servants . . . same myself
but now . . . even now . . . but now

As every comedian will attest, there is a rule of three in comedy. A punch line always works best if it's the third item in a list, for example, and a gag is funniest on its third repetition. Shakespeare also relies on the rule of three, as in this prose bit of stand-up comedy in *The Two Gentlemen of Verona*. In it, Launce describes an emotional family farewell by recreating it with his dog and pieces of his clothing:

This hat is Nan our maid; I am the dog. No—the dog is himself, and I am the dog. O!—The dog is me, and I am myself!

(2.3.18–19)

But most of the time, Shakespeare uses the three-part build not for comic effect but simply to get momentum going, as he does with Portia's speech. It's an exciting rhythm that sweeps the audience along on a dynamic ride.

Here are some examples. Try to lift out the three-part builds and feel how they carry the language forward:

Friends,[1] Romans,[2] countrymen,[3] lend me your ears.

Julius Caesar (3.2.70)

Inch thick,[1] knee-deep,[2] o'er head and ears [3] a forked one!

> *The Winter's Tale* (1.2.187)

Tell me, sweet lord, what is't that takes from thee
Thy stomach,[1] pleasure,[2] and thy golden sleep? [3]

> *Henry IV, Part One* (2.4.34–35)

Rumor is a pipe
Blown by surmises,[1] jealousies,[2] conjectures [3] . . .

> *Henry IV, Part Two* (Ind.15–16)

Grapple your minds to sternage of this navy,
And leave your England, as dead midnight, still,
Guarded with grandsires,[1] babies,[2] and old women [3] . . .

> *Henry V* (3.0.18–20)

Fie, fie, unknit that threatening unkind brow,
And dart not scornful glances from those eyes
To wound thy lord,[1] thy king,[2] thy governor. [3]

> *The Taming of the Shrew* (5.2.140–142)

Thy due from me
Is tears and heavy sorrows of the blood,
Which nature,[1] love,[2] and filial tenderness [3]
Shall, O dear father, pay thee plenteously.

> *Henry IV, Part Two* (4.3.167–170)

The courtier's,[1] soldier's,[2] scholar's [3] eye,[1] tongue,[2] sword [3] . . .

> *Hamlet* (3.1.150)

And here are a couple of examples in which the three parts of the build are made up of groups of words or longer clauses that build over the course of a number of lines:

Tomorrow [1] and tomorrow [2] and tomorrow [3]
Creeps in this petty pace from day [1] to day [2]
To the last syllable [3] of recorded time.

Macbeth (5.5.18–20)

O, if I wake, shall I not be distraught,
Environed with all these hideous fears,
And madly play with my forefather's joints, [1]
And pluck the mangled Tybalt from his shroud, [2]
And, in this rage, with some great kinsman's bone
As with a club dash out my desperate brains? [3]

Romeo and Juliet (4.3.48–53)

How will this fadge? My master loves her dearly, [1]
And I, poor monster, fond as much on him [2]
And she, mistaken, seems to dote on me. [3]
What will become of this?

Twelfth Night (2.2.31–34)

What will become of this, indeed. Excitement, that's what. The three-part build is a great tool for ratcheting up the tension of a scene and winding the audience into a dizzying, delightful swirl. Use the three-part build every time you see it.

When Did He Write It?

Over the course of more than twenty years, Shakespeare wrote thirty-six (some argue thirty-seven or even thirty-eight) plays, a sequence of 154 sonnets, two long narrative poems, and other scattered material, some, alas, now lost.

Like any artist, he matured over the course of his career and his style evolved. His plays grew increasingly complex as he aged. It is difficult to believe *The Two Gentlemen of Verona*, an early play, and *The Tempest*, a late one, were written by the same man, so vastly more dense, rich, and sophisticated in structure, theme, incident, and characterization is the latter play.

Shakespeare's verse also bears proof of his artistic evolution. His early iambic pentameter is very regular, with the words that take natural stress placed in the lines exactly where the meter says the stress ought to be. By the end of his writing life, though, the verse becomes so choppy, irregular, turbulent, and syncopated that it barely holds together as verse at all. The midpoint between regular and more freewheeling verse seems to come around 1598 or 1599, with the composition of the two plays on the reign of King Henry IV, and, not coincidentally, the opening of the Globe Theater on the south bank of the river Thames.

Thus far in *Thinking Shakespeare*, we've seen very early Shakespeare (as with King Henry VI in chapter 4) and mid-career Shakespeare (as with Portia, in this chapter). Let's take a brief look at what late Shakespearean verse looks like, with this bit of *The Winter's Tale*:

LEONTES   How blest am I
              In my just censure, in my true opinion!
              Alack, for lesser knowledge! How accursed
              In being so blest! There may be in the cup
              A spider steeped, and one may drink, depart,   5
              And yet partake no venom, for his knowledge
              Is not infected; but if one present
              Th'abhorred ingredient to his eye, make known
              How he hath drunk, he cracks his gorge, his sides,
              With violent hefts. I have drunk, and seen the spider.   10
                                              (2.1.38–47)

There is much syncopation, there are lines that are too long and too short to be regular iambic pentameter, there is enjambment, there are key words in positions where there is no stress, there are a zillion caesurae, there are thoughts colliding with one another all over the place . . . this stuff is a mess!

But for all that, it's still built according to all the principles we've been observing.

Leontes has convinced himself that his wife has been cheating on him and that he was right to lock her away in jail. But the knowledge that she betrayed him gnaws at him. Leontes compares that knowledge to a folk belief about how the poisoned bite of certain spiders is only effective if the victim knows the spider has bitten him. A paraphrase:

I'm blessed that my punishment of her is just and that my conclusions on the matter are so truthful. Oh, how I wish I knew less! I'm cursed in being so blessed! There might be a poisonous spider lurking in the cup some guy is about to drink from, and yet he can drink, go home, and not be affected by the venom, because he had no knowledge it was there. *But*—if you shove that spider in the guy's face and tell him what he drank, then he'll bust open his throat and guts with hardcore vomiting. I drank, and I saw the spider.

As the paraphrase reveals, there is a vigorous argument, and it even has a "but" in the middle to help give it shape. There is antithesis: the speech is built on the contrast between *knowing* about the spider and *not knowing*, and the text has at least one specific antithesis, as well: "accursed" versus "blest." The language undergoes a huge change of height when it crashes from the Grand Guignol description of poison and its effects down to the stark, horrifying admission, "I have drunk, and seen the spider."

But for all its similarities to the way Shakespeare writes elsewhere, when it comes to *phrasing with the verse line*, this passage is completely different from everything we've looked at thus far. Try the Paper Trick. Try putting MMMs at the end of each line. Try grabbing a breath every ten syllables. It's challenging. This speech is a toughie! Though the techniques we've learned certainly help, they also reveal a passage with a halting, constipated rhythm that's sure to induce hyperventilation in any actor who attempts it.

And yet . . .

Perhaps that's the very point! Why is Leontes using these words now—these fitful, lurching, staccato spasms of language, now? Because they reflect the wretched, tortured, twisted state of his thinking. This is a man in total psychological meltdown whose every waking moment is suffused with images of adultery, cuckoldry, and even—God help him!—poisonous spiders. Would anyone expect such a man to speak with the fluidity and élan of Portia? No way. To phrase this language with the verse line is to capture exactly what's happening in Leontes' head. It's just devilishly hard to play it.

It's good to know when the verse you're working on was composed, and where in Shakespeare's career your play falls. That knowledge will help you understand what will be required to make the verse take flight. The introduction in the edition you're working from will tell you your play's date of composition and may even have a chronology of all of Shakespeare's plays.

A rough guideline to verse complexity would look like this:

1591–1598	Early period. Verse is simple and straightforward.
1598–1603	Middle period. Verse is nuanced, supple, and muscular.
1603–1609	Mature period. Verse is getting complex but is still elastic and accessible.
1609–1612	Late period. *Fuhgeddaboudit*.

The Period in the Period

Punctuation didn't even begin to be standardized in the English language until more than 100 years after Shakespeare's death. There were no rules governing when to use a comma, a semicolon, a dash, a period, and so forth. People just winged it.

The chaos was multiplied in the printing house. As we've seen, the playwrights in Shakespeare's day had little or no involvement in the publication of their works. Punctuation was left largely to people who came into the process long after the writer. First, copyists—called *scribes*—wrote out clean versions of the authors' manuscripts called "fair copies" that were then submitted to the printing houses. (Sometimes *prompters*, Renaissance versions of today's stage managers, made *promptbooks*, which recorded the version of the text used in the theater, and these became the bases of printed texts.) Next, the typesetters at the publishing house—they were called *compositors*—set out the thousands of individual letters of the text, one page at a time, into frames that were then smeared with ink as paper was pressed down upon them. Each one of these intermediaries had his own views about punctuation and had total license to implement those views as he saw fit.

Today's textual scholarship is so good, especially where the First Folio of 1623 is concerned, that it can actually discern which page of a printed text was set up by which compositor. It can then tell us things about his habits in punctuation and spelling: compositor A liked semicolons; compositor E introduced a lot of parentheses, etc. Armed with this information, modern editors can undo the compositors' supposed improvements and substitute their own punctuation in their best attempt to retrieve what Shakespeare wrote, this time according to the standard rules of contemporary English grammar and composition. The result is a text whose punctuation is the product of many, many hands, only one pair of which belongs to William Shakespeare.

This is yet one more reason to use the verse line, rather than the punctuation, as a guide to Shakespeare's original phrasing. After all, scribes, compositors, prompters, and editors can make whatever tossed salad they wish out of commas and periods, but they can't change the fact that "O what a rouge and peasant slave am I" is a line of regular iambic pentameter.

We'll see in chapter 9 that punctuation, whether it belongs to Shakespeare or compositor C, can be extremely helpful in discovering the rhythm of a complex passage of text. So don't disregard it altogether. But note this interesting development: many of today's best Shakespeare directors follow Sir Peter Hall and, on the first day of rehearsal, issue to their casts specially prepared texts that include only the bare minimum of punctuation. Or, using the Internet as their ally, they download a text from any number of websites that post them, and make their own edition of the play, cutting lines, choosing textual variants from among the many options that have come down from the period printings, and re-punctuating the whole play according to their own sense of what works best.

INTERMISSION

Gwyneth Paltrow as Rosalind and Alessandro Nivola as Orlando in *As You Like It*, directed by Barry Edelstein at the Williamstown Theater Festival, 1999. Photo © Richard Feldman, 1999.

CHAPTER
№
8

PUTTING IT TOGETHER

THE FUNDAMENTALS IN ACTION: A REVIEW

Most major American theater companies that mount Shakespeare plays follow a similar production schedule. Weeks one through four, and sometimes five, are spent in the rehearsal studio. Another week, called the "tech period," is spent on stage, when costumes, lights, scenery, and sound are added. Then, depending on the company's resources and producing philosophy, another week or more is spent in previews, when the show is performed for audiences at night and further rehearsed and refined during the day.

Phase one of the process, those heady, creative weeks in the rehearsal room, also unfolds according to a fairly standard plan. Most directors prefer to spend a number of days, perhaps a week or more, "at the table." The cast sits down and works through the text slowly and methodically, so that everyone in the play understands exactly what is happening in each scene and where his or her character fits in the scheme of things.

This is the time when the text is gone over with a fine-tooth comb. This is the time when, together with the director, each actor will expand on the homework she has done before the first day of rehearsal and look hard at the nuts and bolts of her lines. This is the time when the rubber of the techniques covered in chapters 3–7 of this book meets the road of the script in action.

Scansion. Argument. Antithesis. Heightened language. Phrasing. Now they really get to work.

Hands drum on tabletops like Mighty Max Weinberg on an E-Street tear—*dee DUM dee DUM dee DUM dee DUM dee DUM*. Highlighters swoosh across lines, draping Ophelia and Gertrude in not-terribly-flattering fluorescent yellow (but they don't mind). Pencils scratch underlines, circles, arrows, and squiggles until script pages start to look like hieroglyphics worthy of some Egyptian monument. The director asks, *"What?"* at the line endings and *"Why?!"* everywhere else. "The thought changes at 'but'!" one actor discovers. Another interjects, "This line's a pick-up, no?" The vocal coach declaims, "If you don't take a breath at 'villain,' you're going to faint!" And at the very moment "contumely" threatens to stop the whole thing cold, the dramaturg bounds in with her two-volume *Oxford English Dictionary*, magnifying glass at the ready. "It means 'rudeness,' 'arrogance,'" she humbly offers in the nick of time, adding, "The stress is on the first syllable." As Hamlet gets ready to continue, the director coaches him, helpfully, "Remember—he *really loved* his father."

Now that we've covered the fundamental building blocks of *Thinking Shakespeare*, we can do some table work of our own.

REHEARSAL TIME

Here's a terrific short scene from a hidden corner of *Henry V*, one of Shakespeare's mid-period masterpieces. The critics call this "The Bees' Commonwealth Scene," for reasons we'll soon see. I like it not only because it's fun and interesting, but because in its fifty-five lines, Shakespeare deploys every arrow in his verse-writing quiver. It's as good a laboratory as any I know for reviewing the basics of *Thinking Shakespeare*.

The given circumstances: King Henry V is considering a preemptive invasion of England's long-standing nemesis, France, the kingdom a few dozen miles, and one treacherous body of water, to the south. He summons his key advisers to an emergency strategy session to hear their views on the issue. Henry worries that were England to invade France, Scotland might take advantage of the opportunity and launch an invasion of its own from the north. Canterbury reassures him that the last time England went to war with France, three generations ago, Scotland wasn't an issue, so there's no reason to worry now. Westmoreland responds to Canterbury's point, and it's with him we'll jump in. Grab your blank piece of paper and give it a go.

WESTMORELAND   But there's a saying very old and true:
                         "If that you will France win,
                         Then with Scotland first begin."
                    For once the eagle England being in prey,
                    To her unguarded nest the weasel Scot   5
                    Comes sneaking, and so sucks her princely eggs,
                    Playing the mouse in absence of the cat,
                    To 'tame and havoc more than she can eat.

EXETER   It follows then the cat must stay at home.
              Yet that is but a crushed necessity,   10
              Since we have locks to safeguard necessaries,
              And pretty traps to catch the petty thieves.
              While that the armed hand doth fight abroad,
              Th'advised head defends itself at home.
              For government, though high and low and lower,   15
              Put into parts, doth keep in one consent,
              Congreeing in a full and natural close,
              Like music.

CANTERBURY   True. Therefore doth heaven divide
              The state of man in divers functions,
              Setting endeavor in continual motion;   20
              To which is fixed, as an aim or butt,
              Obedience. For so work the honey-bees,
              Creatures that by a rule in nature teach
              The act of order to a peopled kingdom.
              They have a king, and officers of sorts,   25
              Where some like magistrates correct at home;
              Others like merchants venture trade abroad;
              Others like soldiers, armed in their stings,
              Make boot upon the summer's velvet buds,
              Which pillage they with merry march bring home   30
              To the tent royal of their emperor,
              Who busied in his majesty surveys
              The singing masons building roofs of gold,
              The civil citizens lading up the honey,
              The poor mechanic porters crowding in   35
              Their heavy burdens at his narrow gate,

The sad-eyed justice with his surly hum
Delivering o'er to executors pale
The lazy yawning drone. I this infer:
That many things, having full reference   40
To one consent, may work contrariously.
As many arrows, loosed several ways,
Come to one mark, as many ways meet in one town,
As many fresh streams meet in one salt sea,
As many lines close in the dial's center,   45
So may a thousand actions once afoot
End in one purpose, and be all well borne
Without defeat. Therefore to France, my liege.
Divide your happy England into four,
Whereof take you one quarter into France,   50
And you withal shall make all Gallia shake.
If we with thrice such powers left at home
Cannot defend our own doors from the dog,
Let us be worried, and our nation lose
The name of hardiness and policy.   55

(1.2.166–220)

You might be thinking, *"Huh?! That's one big mouthful of text, especially that long Canterbury speech! What the heck are they talking about??!!"*

Fair enough. It's complicated material, and exasperation is a perfectly valid initial response. But let's take a deep breath, open the toolkit we've worked hard to assemble, and start *Thinking Shakespeare*.

Identify the Argument

This scene is particularly productive to work on because its dramatic context is a debate. Each of the king's advisers makes an argument, using language to convince someone (in this case, the king) to see things his way (for or against the invasion). The conflict between views and words is the heart of what's happening. Argument *is* this scene.

Let's look at the gist of what's being said. Westmoreland trots out the "old and true" saying that if you want to win France, you have to start with Scotland. Exeter seems at first to agree but then goes in a different direction, suggesting that the Scottish threat need not be a serious concern because governments are capable of undertaking more than one project at a time. Canterbury elaborates on this idea with a long spiel about honeybees and their society. He concludes that since, as the bees demonstrate, it is possible to do many things at once, the king ought to invade France with one quarter of his army, and leave three quarters at home to defend against the Scots.

In the broadest sense, then, Westmoreland argues, "Don't invade France because of the Scottish threat." Exeter argues, "The Scots are not a problem because we can deal with more than one thing at a time." Canterbury agrees with Exeter and argues, "Honeybees can do many things at once; we should follow their example, putting one part of the army on the offensive and the rest on defense against Scotland." The first man is against the invasion and the other two are gung-ho in favor of it.

With that general sense of the arguments established, read through the scene again. This time the three divergent points of view should start to emerge more clearly. You're on your way to having a piece of theater on your hands.

Make a Paraphrase

As you read the scene a second time, listen for the details of each man's case. Here is a paraphrase of Westmoreland's argument:

> But there's an old, true saying: "If France is your goal, then Scotland's the toll." England is an eagle. When she's on the hunt, she leaves her nest unprotected. That's when Scotland will sneak up like a weasel and ransack the place. Scotland will be like a mouse when the cat's away, breaking in and causing chaos just for the sake of it.

Like the paraphrases we made in chapter 4, this one strikes a balance between capturing every idea and staying nice and loose.

For example, Westmoreland says that the "weasel Scot" will sneak into England's nest and "suck her princely eggs." Weasels were notorious for that nasty behavior (in *As You Like It*, the chronically depressed Jaques manages to get a laugh out of it: "I can suck melancholy from a song as a weasel sucks eggs" [2.5.11]). But is it necessary to include that detail in your paraphrase? Not really. Your goal is to paraphrase *the thought behind the language*. Hence, "ransack the place." Alternate paraphrases such as "destroy everything," "do untold damage," or "cause the kingdom great pain" would do the job just as well.

The paraphrase of Westmoreland's last line is also worth a closer look. His word "'tame"—note the apostrophe—is an elided form of *attame*, a military term meaning "to break into using force," as a medieval army would a castle wall. (The word is elided because of the line's scansion, as we'll see shortly.) "Havoc" is also a military term. Today we use it as a noun, as in, "Those drunken frat boys caused havoc in the basement." But it started its life as a verb meaning "to devastate utterly." A commander who called out "Havoc!" to his troops was instructing them to pillage, plunder, and burn. (That's what Mark Anthony means in *Julius Caesar* when he says that Ate, goddess of violence, will "Cry 'Havoc!' and let slip the dogs of war.") To paraphrase Westmoreland's line as, "Scotland will be like a mouse when the cat's away, making huge mischief," would be too general, because it fails to capture the escalation from *break in* ("attame") to *do damage* ("havoc") and ignores the fact that the weasel is sucking more eggs "than she can eat." Hence, my paraphrase, "breaking in and causing chaos just for the sake of it."

On to Exeter. He starts by agreeing with Westmoreland. In paraphrase, he says, "According to your logic, then, the cat should stay home." Then he says the word that, as we have seen, causes an argument to change direction: *yet*, the cousin of *but*. Paraphrased: "But that has already been taken care of." (The Scottish issue is a "crushed necessity"; that is, the need to worry about it has been crushed.) He continues, in paraphrase:

> England has locks to guard valuables and traps to catch crooks. While the hand takes up weapons and fights overseas, the head stays smart and home to defend itself. Government, at all levels, divides into many smaller units that all share a common goal. These units come together totally and effortlessly, like harmony in music.

Once again, it is *the sense of the thoughts* that matters in the paraphrase, not every last detail of the text.

We'll discuss the height of Exeter's language in more detail, but note that the paraphrase fails miserably at capturing the humor of his speech, in particular his puns. An "armed hand" is an amusing turn of phrase because every hand has an arm attached, and a military hand has not only its human arm, but its firearm, its weapon too. The singsong antithesis between "pretty traps" and "petty thieves" is also terrific and nimble—and absent from the paraphrase. And the paraphrase only manages one of the dual senses of the words "full" and "natural," which, in addition to meaning "total" and "effortless," are also terms from music. (A *full close* is a musical cadence that is perfectly complete in its form, and a *natural* note is neither sharp nor flat.)

The bottom line: paraphrases are lousy substitutes for Shakespeare's erudite and delicious wordplay. Paraphrases are of great value to the actor because they whittle heightened language down to the *basic thoughts* underpinning it. *But that doesn't mean that the other shades and layers of meaning aren't there or aren't important.* Even if the audience takes away only the surface meaning of a line, the actor must know the echoes, resonances, and subterranean senses that make it poetic and rich.[29] In a sense, "Shakespeare" is a measure of the distance between the banality of the basic thought and the high artistry of the words that express it. The paraphrase needn't reflect this, but the actor's sensibility and mind and heart and soul truly must.

Canterbury speaks next. Here's a paraphrase:

That's right. And that's why God divvied up man's situation into various pursuits. He set man's activities in constant motion, and their upshot—their goal, their target—is obedience to His wishes.

---

[29] For a list of resources that shed light on all those additional layers, see the Epilogue.

Bees work this way. They are creatures whose instinctive behavior teaches organization to the world of mankind. They have a king, and officers, sort of. They have cops who keep order at home and businessmen who make deals abroad. They've got soldiers, whose weapons are their stingers. They conquer the summer flowers and then, marching happily, they bring the spoils of war back to the king's tent. His Majesty is busy looking out at his kingdom. He sees stonemasons building golden roofs. He sees government workers measuring honey. He sees manual laborers schlepping their heavy stuff into the loading dock. He sees the serious-looking judge, hemming and hawing as he sentences lazy bees to death at the hands of the white-faced hangman.

Here's what I conclude from all this: many beings work in opposite directions while still sharing a common goal. Just as arrows shot from different spots arrive at the same target, just as lots of roads lead to one town, just as countless streams flow to the ocean, and just as the lines on a sundial come together in the middle, so a thousand different acts can share one purpose, and all turn out great and victorious.

Go to France, your highness. Divide England into four parts. Take one quarter into France and you'll make that whole country shudder. If the three quarters left at home can't protect us against those Scottish dogs, then we should really worry. We should lose our reputation for machismo and smarts.

Okay, so this paraphrase lacks Shakespeare's panache. So what? At this point in rehearsal, the goal is to capture the basic thoughts of the speech. Reaching that goal may sometimes require you to take significant liberties.

For example, first this paraphrase makes the structure of Canterbury's speech easier to see by breaking it into four paragraphs that correspond to the four sections of his argument. The final paragraph, for instance, shows Canterbury's deliberate decision to end his argument by returning to the issue of Scotland. His canine slur ("Scottish dogs," in this paraphrase) dismisses the king's major strategic concern out of hand and closes once and for all the worrisome discussion opened by Westmoreland. Our structure makes details like this much more apparent.

Second, this paraphrase cuts Shakespeare's longer sentences down into shorter ones. Breaking up long sentences comprising lists of small clauses, such as lines 25 through 39, makes them more comprehensible.

Third, in this paraphrase, the order of the thoughts is slightly altered in the interest of making the overall argument easier to grasp. In paraphrasing line 30, for example, it is important to capture the detail that the returning forces do a "merry march," because Canterbury's argument depends on depicting the happiness of life in the super-obedient, militaristic Commonwealth of Bees. The paraphrase includes this thought but places it somewhere different from its spot in Shakespeare's text. No matter. As long as the thought is there, the paraphrase is a good and useful one.

Fourth, this paraphrase spells out some ideas that Shakespeare only implies. For example, Canterbury suggests that "heaven" has ordained "obedience" as the "aim or butt" of all human activity. He doesn't need to specify that he means obedience *to God*, because in Elizabethan England, an authoritarian society obsessed with hierarchy, everyone knew that God was at the pinnacle and that even monarchs were one step beneath Him. Modern readers might miss what was obvious to Shakespeare's audience and assume that Canterbury means obedience in general: the obedience of a subject to her king, or a servant to his employer, or a child to his parent. The paraphrase makes the point explicit. Similarly, this paraphrase of lines 32–39 spells out the implied suggestion of what the Bee King "surveys" (he is "looking out at his kingdom") before detailing his view. [30] This small expansion helps make the thought crystal clear and does not damage the shape of the argument. That's the privilege, and the value, of the paraphrase.

Once again, the arguments:

WESTMORELAND	Don't invade France; the Scottish threat is too dangerous.
EXETER	That's not a problem, because we can deal with more than one issue at a time.
CANTERBURY	Exactly. Honeybees teach people to do many tasks at once, so we should do precisely that, putting one part of the army on the offense, and the rest on the defense against Scotland.

Now that we understand what the characters are saying, let's turn our attention to how they are saying it.

---

30 The fact that the king bee was actually a *queen* bee had been discovered a few decades before Shakespeare wrote this play. But the all-male scientific establishment wasn't comfortable with the notion of female authority, even in bee hives, so this "rule of nature" wasn't unanimously accepted until well into the eighteenth century—nearly 100 years after a queen (Elizabeth I) led England to one of its most prosperous eras.

Start the Meter

Scansion is a major touchstone of *Thinking Shakespeare*, so we'll begin with the meter.

WESTMORELAND'S PROVERB Westmoreland's meter is interesting right off the bat. His first line is routine iambic pentameter. But lines 2 and 3, the "saying very old and true," are something else entirely. Say them naturally:

IF that YOU will FRANCE WIN,
THEN with SCOT-land FIRST be-GIN.

DUM-dee DUM-dee DUM DUM
DUM-dee DUM-dee DUM-dee DUM

The pattern is STRESSED-unstressed. Recall from chapter 3 that feet like these are called *trochees*. And note that Westmoreland's lines have four stresses, not five. They are not iambic pentameter; they are *trochaic tetrameter*. Diagrammed, they look like this:

```
 ´    ˇ     ´    ˇ       ´      ´   (ˇ)
If that | you will | France | win,
```

```
 ´    ˇ      ´    ˇ      ´    ˇ     ´   (ˇ)
Then with | Scotland | first be | gin.
```

"Now wait a minute," you're saying. "The first line has only six syllables and the second, seven. Trochaic tetrameter—four two-syllable trochees—is supposed to have *eight* beats. What's the deal?"

The deal is this. First, the final foot in each line—which, like all trochees, is a falling meter that ends on an unstressed syllable—needn't actually appear in the text for its presence to be felt. It's as though the line ending, that magical little moment for breath that we explored in the previous chapter, becomes the final unstressed syllable. Think of it as a rest in music. It's there, even though, in a sense, it's not. That's why these syllables are marked in parentheses in the diagram.

Second, in Elizabethan English, the final, silent *e* on some words was actually pronounced. Sometimes it would even get an accent mark or *umlaut* (that German mark with two dots above the letter: ë). In *Henry VI, Part Two*, we find, "Erect his statuë and worship it"—STAT-u-AY. Similarly, the actor playing Westmoreland in the first production of *Henry V* would have said, "If that you will Francë win." FRAN-seh. Not that *France* has two syllables anywhere else in the play. It doesn't. In these lines Westmoreland is punning on an old proverb that went, "He that would the daughter win, must with mother first begin." That proverb is in trochaic tetrameter, and so here we get "Francë."

Should a modern actor say FRAN-seh? Won't that sound off-putting and odd? If you really lay into the intentional jog-trot bounciness of the *DUM-dee DUM-dee* meter, these lines can work wonderfully and not seem at all self-conscious or weird. On the other hand, I've seen some productions avoid even the risk of sounding strange with a rewrite to "French land," which is a pretty neat solution. I've also heard actors simply extend the vowel—"Fraaance"—to make up for the missing beat. Try all these, see what works for you, and, if nothing does, then just say *France*. No problem. As long as you make it work, the Shakespeare Police will be too busy enjoying the scene to bother arresting you.

Notwithstanding the technical details and metrical nuances of Westmoreland's old saying, what really matters is the basic observation that it is in a different meter from everything else in the scene.

Why is that? *Why is he using these words now?*

Westmoreland is trying hard to convince the king to see things his way. Making reference to a piece of plain common sense enshrined in an "old and true" saying is a forceful tactic, proving the time-tested wisdom of his anti-invasion stance.

His use of this odd old saying is also surprising, funny, and entirely original. It grabs his listeners' attention. It's the equivalent of the secretary of defense standing up in the middle of a cabinet meeting about the best date for a military strike and saying to the president, "Thirty days hath September, April, June, and November." Many playwrights in the Elizabethan theater wrote plays about the reign of King Henry V. Shakespeare's is the only one still produced. In part, its longevity is due to quirky, human moments like this. No one but Shakespeare would have a government dignitary wheel out a nursery rhyme in the middle of a national security debate.

That is why the actor *must be sure* the audience hears the line's oddball rhyming music. If they don't, he's simply not doing his job. Observing the different rhythm of Westmoreland's saying is merely the first step. *Saying it that way* is what counts.

The scansion of the remainder of Westmoreland's speech is fairly straightforward. The lines are regular iambic pentameter, and the natural stresses fall right where the metric stresses do. There are two exceptions. According to the meter, "unguarded" in line 5 gets stressed on the second syllable, "guard." But

Westmoreland's point is that when the eagle is away, nobody is home to safeguard the eggs. That is, the nest is *unguarded*. Without the syllable "un," the sense of the line isn't clear. The natural stress pattern, then, looks like this:

To her | unguar | ded nest | the weas | el Scot

dee-dee DUM-DUM dee-DUM dee-DUM dee-DUM. The first foot is pyrrhic, the second, spondaic, and the rest, iambic.

In line 7, the meter says that the first word should be pronounced "play-ING"; the iamb puts the stress on the second syllable. But that's clearly not right. Nobody says "play-ING." Westmoreland should say "PLAY-ing," a trochee, then continue with the rest of the iambic line.

We've already touched on his final line, which includes the unusual verb "to 'tame," the elided combination of *to* and *attame*.[31] Had Westmoreland said the word in full, the line would scan, "to AT-tame AND hav-OC more THAN she CAN eat," which is gibberish. Elision shifts the stresses to where they naturally belong and makes the line work. The audience will probably hear "to tame" (no apostrophe), meaning "to subdue," "to forcibly becalm." That meaning isn't the one Westmoreland intends, but it still makes a kind of sense in context. Welcome to the wonderful world of weird words!

---

31 In case you're not boggling at all this, consider that some editors chose to spell this elided infinitive verb as "t'attame," which is metrically the same, just spelled differently!

EXETER'S ELISION   Now on to the scansion of Exeter's speech. Lines 13 and 14 are interesting:

> While that the armed hand doth fight abroad,
> Th'advised head defends itself at home.

For these lines to scan, the *-ed* endings on both "armed" and "advised" need to be pronounced. Without *-ed*, line 13 has only nine syllables. The tenth beat, which should be stressed, is empty and just sits there. Plus, you have to stress "DOTH," and also say "A-broad." The line doesn't sound right at all: "while THAT the ARM'D hand DOTH fight A-broad (*clunk*)." Crazy.

With *-ed*, all's well: "While that the ARM-ed HAND doth FIGHT a-BROAD."

Line 14 contains the antithesis of "arméd," namely, "adviséd." But because *-ed* is there, "the" at the beginning of the line can't be left on its own. "The" and "advised" are elided into "Th'adviséd." If they weren't, we would have "the AD-vis'd HEAD de-FENDS it-SELF at HOME," which is regular iambic pentameter but makes "advised" sound strange and fails to provide the antithesis to "arméd."

The elided line goes, "th'ad-VIS-ed HEAD de-FENDS it-SELF at HOME."

Exeter likes elision. Line 17's "natural" scans with only two syllables, "NATCH-rul," which is so close to how the word is naturally pronounced that many dictionaries regard the three-syllable pronunciation, "NATCH-ur-ul," as secondary. The feminine ending on line 11 ("NEC-es-SAR-ies") might just as well be the masculine "NEC-e-SRIES," which elides the word's four syllables into three: "necess'ries." Same with line 15, where "lower" makes a feminine ending and might be elided into one stressed syllable, "LOW'R."

Good so far? Great. Now let's take a breather before we turn to Canterbury's long speech.

WEIGHING SCANSION AND INSTINCT   Twice in the last paragraph, I've suggested that certain words *might* be elided. The implication is that, on the other hand, they might not. And in the discussion of Westmoreland's speech, we found two places where the iambic pentameter isn't iambic pentameter at all but is peppered with trochees, spondees, and pyrrhics. Canterbury's speech will reveal the same thing. The scansion of the text is full of departures from what it's "supposed to be."

These departures demonstrate an idea we touched on briefly in chapter 3. To Shakespeare, iambic pentameter is not set in stone. It's not some rigid formula that must be obeyed at all costs. Instead, it is a framework, an organizing principle, around which to improvise.

Like a good musician, Shakespeare loves to set up a rhythm and then vary it to keep things from getting predictable. A little bebop now and again, some syncopation here and there, keeps the audience on its toes and gives the ears some relief. (For example, one of Shakespeare's favorite tricks is starting a line of iambic pentameter with a trochee, as he does here in line 7.)

And as if all this syncopation didn't mix things up enough, sometimes Shakespeare simply leaves the rhythm in the actor's hands. For instance, the actor playing Exeter must look at the elision in lines 11 and 15 and decide whether to give each word its full number of syllables and create a feminine ending or say the word in its shorter, elided form to keep the verse regular and risk sounding precious, British, or just odd. Shakespeare doesn't specify.

There is no definitive right or wrong way to do this stuff. There is only informed decision making, taste, and instinct. *You must always weigh what the scansion says against what your instincts say.* Try it, listen to it, see how it feels, then go with your gut.

But note this: balancing scansion and instinct is different than ignoring the technical information completely. Step one: master the technique. Step two: decide whether to adhere to it. Don't skip step one!

CANTERBURY'S RHYTHMS   Let's approach Canterbury a little differently, looking at each line in isolation:

True. Therefore doth heaven divide
- The line is a pickup, as we saw in Things Further Thought On after chapter 6. Canterbury's half line completes the full verse line begun by Exeter. He jumps right in, agreeing with his colleague.
- "Heaven" is elided into one syllable, "heav'n," as it is almost every time it appears in Shakespeare.

The state of man in divers functions,
- "Divers" is a separate word from "diverse," even though their meanings are the same; but unlike that word, it gets stress on the first syllable.
- "Functions" technically has three syllables: "FUNC-shee-uns," like Cressida's "moderation" in chapter 3 and Salerio's "ocean" in chapter 6. Try it on for size, and if it sounds too mannered, don't worry about it.

Setting endeavor in continual motion;
- The line starts with a trochee—a bit of syncopation to keep the rhythm lively.

To which is fixed, as an aim or butt,

- The *-ed* is pronounced—fixéd—making this the only word in the line that's not monosyllabic.

Obedience. For so work the honey-bees,

- Technically, it's "o-BEED-yence"—three syllables instead of four. But the word is so important to Canterbury's argument that it may be worth adding the extra beat to the line.

Creatures that by a rule in nature teach

- Another first-foot trochee.

The act of order to a peopled kingdom.

- Feminine ending, giving special weight to "kingdom." This is clever of Canterbury, who is, after all, speaking to a king.

They have a king, and officers of sorts,
Where some like magistrates correct at home;

- The first two regular lines of iambic pentameter in the speech!

Others like merchants venture trade abroad;
Others like soldiers, armed in their stings,

- "Others" is trochaic in both lines.
- The *-ed* ending in "armed" is pronounced, as in Exeter's speech

Make boot upon the summer's velvet buds,
Which pillage they with merry march bring home

- Two more regular lines, though some might argue that "Make boot" is a spondee.

To the tent royal of their emperor,

- The natural stress wants "to the | TENT ROY | al of | their EM | per-or." *dee-dee DUM-DUM dee-dee dee-DUM dee-dee.* There's only one iamb in the line!

Who busied in his majesty surveys
The singing masons building roofs of gold,

- Two more regular lines. This return to regularity sets off the odd line above even more.

The civil citizens lading up the honey,

- A syllable drops out of "citizens," eliding the word into "CIT-zens."

The poor mechanic porters crowding in
Their heavy burdens at his narrow gate,

- Back to regular iambic pentameter. The first line places stress on "in" because the word is part of the compound verb. The delivery bees are crowding in their huge loads through a very small gate.

The sad-eyed justice with his surly hum

- The monosyllables in "sad-eyed" make the scansion look like this:
  the SAD | EYED JUST | ice with | his SUR | ly HUM

Delivering o'er to executors pale

- Shakespeare wrote the elision into the line: "o'er."
- "EX-e-CUT-ors" is stressed on the first syllable. The word was a synonym for "executioners" and so is different from our modern word *executors*, which is accented on the second syllable and refers to those who execute a will or some other formal or legal process.

The lazy yawning drone. I this infer:

- Regular iambic pentameter.

That many things, having full reference

- Another heavily syncopated line:
  iamb-iamb-trochee-spondee-pyrrhic.
  that MA | ny THINGS | HA-ving | FULL REF | er-ence

To one consent, may work contrariously.

- con-TRAR-yus-ly, five syllables elided into four. Or, even though it would create a feminine ending, use all five syllables, and really give this unique word tremendous weight and force.

As many arrows, loosed several ways,

- Looséd.

Come to one mark, as many ways meet in one town,

- A trochee starts the line, but the monosyllables do a great job of spreading the stress out across the rest of it, slowing Canterbury down and underlining his point as he approaches the climax of the speech.

As many fresh streams meet in one salt sea,
As many lines close in the dial's center,
So may a thousand actions once afoot
End in one purpose, and be all well borne

- More powerful monosyllables:
  fresh. streams. meet. in. one. salt. sea
  lines. close. in. the. dial's. cent(er)—feminine ending
  end. in. one . . . and. be. all. well. borne
  The polysyllabic words ("thousand," "actions," "afoot," "purpose") contrast against these monosyllables and gain special prominence as a result.

Without defeat. Therefore to France, my liege.
Divide your happy England into four,
Whereof take you one quarter into France,

- Three regular iambic pentameter lines restore the so-called normal rhythm of the speech.

And you withal shall make all Gallia shake.

- "All" gets no stress according to the meter, but it calls for huge stress when the line is spoken: Henry is going to rattle *the entire country of France*. The spondee near the end of the line does a great deal of work, making Canterbury's point with real power and nicely echoing the second syllable of "withal" in a clever verbal reinforcement.

and YOU | with-AL | shall MAKE | ALL GALL | ia SHAKE

If we with thrice such powers left at home
Cannot defend our own doors from the dog,
Let us be worried, and our nation lose

- More monosyllables make each word count. Canterbury is overwhelmingly forceful as he boldly issues a command to the King of England.

  if. we. with. thrice. such . . . left. at. home
  our. own. doors. from. the. dog

The name of hardiness and policy.

- The speech ends on a nice, regular line of iambic pentameter.

SCANNING ON YOUR OWN TIME   There are over three thousand lines in *Henry V*. That's about average for Shakespeare. *Hamlet* is longer; *Macbeth* is shorter. Were the director of one of these plays to devote rehearsal time to the scansion of every single line, there would be no time left to do anything else. For this reason, actors must take extra time on their own to do the kind of close analysis conducted in the previous section. The director will usually mention scansion only if she hears something that sounds odd, or if she feels a meter matter will help the actor with the scene. Rarely will you hear the terms *trochee, spondee, elision,* or *feminine ending* spoken in rehearsal.

Yet, as our analysis of Canterbury's speech shows, every time one of those words does come up, it's because the meter is doing something unusual. And when the meter does something unusual, *it's because the thought being expressed demands something unusual.* As with every other technique in *Thinking Shakespeare*, that is the crucial link. *The thought drives the language.*

Those five syllables of "contrariously," those monosyllables in the long "as many" versus "one" sequence, the way in which "all Gallia" jumps out of the meter after three highly regular lines—these quirks of scansion underline particularly compelling ideas in Canterbury's argument. The rhythmic organization of the words he uses—their very music—helps him persuade the king to see things his way.

The bottom line: scansion is not an end in itself. Its value, its interest, its reason for being, is to help the actor communicate thought through language.

Word Against Word

Now let's turn to the next *Thinking Shakespeare* fundamental: antithesis.

Break out those pencils or markers and circle, underline, highlight, or just list the antitheses you find in these three speeches. Then compare your list to the one below. Notice that the antitheses are listed by *thought*, not by individual word.

WESTMORELAND
- If France win / then Scotland begin
- eagle England / weasel Scot
- in prey / Comes sneaking
- mouse / cat

EXETER

- pretty traps / petty thieves
- armed hand / advised head
- fight abroad / defends at home
- put into parts / keep in one consent

CANTERBURY

- heaven / man
- Creatures / peopled
- some / Others
- magistrates / merchants
- correct at home / venture trade abroad
- many things / one consent
- many arrows / one mark
- many ways / one town
- many streams / one sea
- many lines / dial's center
- a thousand actions / one purpose
- well borne / defeat
- France / England
- one quarter into France / three such powers left at home

There's a lot that's remarkable about this list. First, note how much antithesis appears in these few dozen lines. It really is everywhere.

Second, it's plain to see how central antithesis is to the way these characters express themselves. Read through this list and you will hear the scene in miniature. All the antitheses carry the thread of each character's argument forward. Consider Canterbury's peroration, the formal recapitulation that ends his speech. It's as rousing in its way as any of the great speeches Henry gives during the battle scenes later in the play. What accounts for its arresting power? Antithesis. Canterbury builds through a list of "many versus one" phrases that bring vividly to life the central contrast on which his argument is based: the virtue of doing many things at one time. Those phrases climax in one more antithesis: the ringing opposition between "well borne" and "defeat." This is Canterbury's slam dunk. [32]

Once again, *the technical features of the text support the actor's ability to communicate his thoughts clearly and passionately.*

High and Low and Lower

The next item in our table work is the height of the language.

We've already discussed Westmoreland's incongruous nursery rhyme, an old saying he uses to bolster his argument to King Henry. Throughout Shakespeare's plays, characters resort to quotations when their own powers of language will not do the trick. Sometimes they quote the Bible, sometimes a proverb or other "old and true" saying, sometimes a line from ancient Greek or Roman literature, and sometimes a snippet from something in Elizabethan or Jacobean popular culture such as a ballad (the rough equivalent of a pop song), a pamphlet, or even a recent play by another author.

In each case, the character doing the linguistic borrowing *knows* he is referring to some recognizable piece of language. This self-consciousness gives the language a certain height that differentiates it from what surrounds it. Actors need to recognize

....

32 The Quarto reads "defect" rather than "defeat." Perhaps the former word makes a better opposite to "well borne," but in the context of a military operation, "defeat," the Folio reading, seems more appropriate.

that difference and make it heard, putting verbal quotation marks around the phrase in question.

Westmoreland's rhyme is a textbook case of intentional quoting. He introduces the saying as a familiar chestnut, so the actor playing Westmoreland must speak the words with a sense of quaintness and familiarity. Not to do so is to neglect something essential about Westmoreland's thinking, the stakes at issue in the scene, and Shakespeare's writing.

After the quotation, Westmoreland speaks in a more conversational register. But even within it there are some interesting word choices. In addition to his use of military terms such as "attame" and "havoc," which we have discussed, he also uses animal imagery: "eagle," "nest," "weasel," "eggs," "mouse," and "cat." What's all this about? *Why does he use these words now?*

Westmoreland's background helps answer these questions. He is a high-ranking official in the king's inner circle. His familiarity with government and military matters explains his knowledge of "attame" and "havoc." As for the animal imagery: he is from Westmoreland (today known as Cumbria) in the north of England, close to the Scottish border. Like anyone from that area, which was largely farmland, Westmoreland would have been familiar with preying eagles, egg-sucking weasels, and the damage caused by Scotland's frequent incursions across the frontier. Westmoreland's place of origin informs his choices of language.

In contrast, Exeter's language is tough and lean: "crushed," "locks," "safeguard," "traps," "catch," "arméd," "fight," "advised," and "defends." There are no weasels or eggs here, just harsh consonant sounds. Even Exeter's name sounds action packed and macho. Why? Because he is a military man, a soldier, a general. The texture of his language reflects his decisiveness and firmness. Then his language changes in a surprising way, and this military man reveals that he knows something about music. Exeter is an exemplar of that guy in every war movie ever made, the hard-as-nails butt-kicker with a soft side, the pugilistic Patton who listens to Chopin in his tent.

If Exeter is the military man and Westmoreland is the civilian expert, who is Canterbury? And why is his language so different from the other men's?

Canterbury is the town in England whose great cathedral is the seat of the Anglican Church. The man speaking in this scene is the head of that church, the Archbishop of Canterbury. He has been delivering a sermon every Sunday for the past fifty years, which explains his long and literary speech. In Shakespeare's day, churchmen gave homilies every week, discoursing on matters both religious and secular. The pastor would use a passage from the Bible or a current event as a point of departure, explicating it and gleaning from it a lesson that could be applied to everyday life. (One famous one called "A Homily Against Disobedience and Rebellion" is not far from Shakespeare's mind here.) Canterbury builds his homily around honeybees. He introduces them, explores the way they organize themselves, and then, as he puts it, "infers" a lesson applicable to a vexing life question. Canterbury's speech marks a third major change of height in the scene. We have already had the language of the countryside and the language of the military. Now we get the language of the church.

And just as Westmoreland's and Exeter's language changed height within their own speeches, there are height changes within in Canterbury's lines too. Look at line 25: "They have a king." Like Hamlet's "It is very cold," this line is as simple and flat as can be. Now look at lines 37 through 39:

The sad-eyed justice with his surly hum
Delivering o'er to executors pale
The lazy yawning drone.

This language is ornate, musical, and intricate. The thought behind it is complicated. You can hear the buzzing of the beehive in the justice's "surly hum" and in those *z* sounds of the "executors" and the "lazy" drone. The vowel sounds get long and drawn out. These lines feel and sound very different than the clipped simplicity of "They have a king." The fourteen lines from 25 to 39 see a gradual increase in the language's height. By the end, it is in the stratosphere.

Then, abruptly, there is yet another big gear change: "I this infer." From the dizzy heights of the humming justice and the beheaded drone, Canterbury crashes down to three terse words. *Why?*

Directors have a field day with this moment. In Kenneth Branagh's memorable film of the play, the other noblemen in the room, eager to get on with this urgent discussion, start to fidget as Canterbury rambles on. Finally, one shoots a look to another, as if to say, "Is this guy ever going to shut up?" Canterbury catches it out of the corner of his eye, and decides to wrap it up: "I this infer." Branagh observed the sudden change in the language, and he invented a fun piece of business to make sense of the change within the dramatic context of the scene. I've seen Canterbury catch someone looking at his watch, and I've seen the king yawn like one of the lazy drones. I've also seen the simpler choice of Canterbury deciding for himself that it's time to draw the speech to its conclusion. All these choices come from the simple fact that someone noticed *a change in the language's height*.

We've already looked at Canterbury's peroration—that building series of antitheses between "many" and "one." From its climax, "without defeat," his language changes height one more time, to the striking direct order he issues to the king—"Therefore to France, my liege"—and onto the harsh alliteration of those many *d* words: "defend . . . doors . . . dog."

This poses an interesting question. Why is the churchman the person arguing most passionately for a preemptive invasion? Why isn't he arguing for peace instead, as we would expect the clergy to do?

The answer lies in the first scene of *Henry V*, which immediately precedes this one. In it, Canterbury and another clergyman, the Bishop of Ely, discuss pending legislation that, if passed by Parliament, would levy an enormous new tax on the church. Canterbury's objective is to defeat this measure by getting the king to focus on something else—namely, his interest in ruling France. Canterbury has information that will help the king legitimize his claim to the French throne, and, what's more, he has secretly arranged for the church to make a donation to the war effort on condition that the new tax bill doesn't pass. Enlightened self-interest explains Canterbury's support of the invasion. As often happens in Shakespeare, selfishness trumps idealism, even in the church.

There is always a reason the language takes the form it does. It may be a function of who the character is (his profession, his class, his background, his hometown). It may be some dramatic circumstance hidden far underneath the present scene. It may be in response to something another character says. But it's *always* based in the character's need to communicate his specific thoughts.

Thought comes first in argument, scansion, antithesis, and the level of height of the language itself. Thinking gives the text its very warp and woof.

Line Endings

Thought shapes the verse lines too.

The Paper Trick you used when you first read this scene will have revealed that each character constructs his argument a line at a time. The majority of these fifty-five lines are end-stopped, so the phrasing will jibe with the lines almost automatically. Let's look at just a few of the more interesting line endings to understand their special contribution.

Exeter ends his speech with a two-word simile, "Like music," which captures his complex notion of harmony among different areas of government. Notice that the simile falls at the beginning of a line, or, to look at it from the other end of the telescope, after a line ending.

The actor playing Exeter could phrase this to the punctuation and turn the verse to prose without doing too much damage:

For government, though high and low and lower, put into parts doth keep in one consent, congreeing in a full and natural close, like music.

Read this way, it's clear that Exeter plans to end with the image of music before he even begins to speak. That works. You could even argue that the presence in his language of the musical terms "full" and "natural" prove that Exeter has music in mind from the start.

But look at what happens if a Mamet Magic Moment helps him phrase with the verse line:

Congreeing in a full and natural close   *(what do you mean?)*
Like music.

In this reading, Exeter doesn't have a simile in mind when he starts out. Instead, it occurs to him as he is speaking. *He has to discover it.* He has to rifle through the files in the back of his mind to find an image that will capture his big, sophisticated idea. When he finds it, he lays it out prominently, at the start of its very own line.

Approaching the verse in this way makes Exeter *think right now*, right in front of the audience, right in this moment. It creates an opportunity to see a living, breathing human being *use his mind* before our very eyes. Phrasing with the punctuation is well and good, but what could be more interesting than watching human thought in action? That's where phrasing with the verse line really pays off.

Canterbury's verse lines yield similar dividends. Try the "last word in the line" exercise with his speech. You'll find some gems:

> France
> shake
> home
> dog
> lose
> policy

Drive toward those line endings and the argument makes itself.

Notice how the enjambment in Canterbury's speech clusters near its end. Contrast the enjambment in lines 40, 46, 47, 52, and 54 with the end-stopped line 21 and what follows at the beginning of line 22. Notice how the phrasing break at the end of the earlier line, signaled by the comma after "butt," serves to underline the significant word "Obedience." The enjambed lines do the same thing, differently. As Canterbury works toward his point, he uses those bursts of inspiration—of breath, of thought—to hammer home his thesis.

I this infer:	
That many things, having full reference	*(to what?)*
To one consent, may work contrariously.	
So may a thousand actions once afoot	*(do what?)*
End in one purpose, and be all well borne	*(how?)*
Without defeat.	
If we with thrice such powers left at home	*(what?)*
Cannot defend our own doors from the dog,	
Let us be worried, and our nation lose	*(what?)*
The name of hardiness and policy.	

The ideas given special weight are the ones following those enjambed line endings: "one consent," "end in one purpose," "defend our doors," and "the name of hardiness." These are the crucial notions that Canterbury needs to plant in the king's mind to get him to launch the invasion of France and block the pending tax bill. Thanks to the line endings, Canterbury scores.

Once again, the verse structure makes the argument. And once again, you may choose to ignore this and phrase with the punctuation. Just know that to do so is to lose some of the uncanny subtlety in the way Shakespeare presents ideas, and to deny the characters the chance to do their thinking in front of us, to find the terms of their arguments under the pressure of real time and in the heat of the here and now.

To ignore the verse structure is to take the thinking out of Shakespeare. That's no fun at all.

After the Table Work

Every time I work on a Shakespeare play, I'm amazed at the sheer volume of detail in every single line. We have attacked these fifty-five lines from every direction, prying them open with the full array of technical tools in our *Thinking Shakespeare* kit. Like archeologists on a dig, we've found a vast trove of fascinating and valuable material.

So now we're ready for opening night, right?

Not quite. An archeologist has no real use for a pile of clay shards. Shards only become interesting when they are reassembled into a beautiful vase and when they reveal something about the house they were kept in and the life of the ancient who lived there. Similarly, an actor has no use for a particular foot of meter or run-on line or insight about a change in the language. These details become meaningful only when they are put together in the context of the entire play. That's what comes next. That is the real meat of the rehearsal process.

Besides, the audience doesn't care a whit about anapestic hexameter or enjambment or any other technical this or that. They don't want to know where in the line the actors breathe; they just want to believe that they are the people they are pretending to be, in the situations they are pretending to experience.

The technical work on the text is only a part of the job. The fundamentals of *Thinking Shakespeare* are means to an end, not the end itself.

Still—and this is the essential heart of the actor's project—*everything that happens in rehearsals arises from of the fundamental work on the text.*

That week around the table lays the groundwork for the rest of the process. The production is founded on what the characters are thinking and how that informs what they are saying. Actors and directors can and will—and should—explore every nook and cranny of each play. What is Hamlet's relationship with Ophelia like? How does he interact physically with his mother? When he acts a short speech for the traveling company of players, is he a good actor or a lousy one? The play poses a zillion questions. Each one needs to be identified, explored, and puzzled out.

But however Hamlet may kiss Ophelia, he only *says* to her what is in the text. However Horatio may dress, he only *says* the lines Shakespeare gave him. The words are the bedrock.

And the words have form.

And that form makes the thoughts behind the words clear and compelling.

"Words, words, words," says Hamlet, and boy, oh boy, did he get that right.

But Claudius adds a disclaimer, and with it, we'll bring our review to a close:

Words without thoughts never to heaven go. (3.3.98)

THINGS FURTHER THOUGHT ON

The Irene Worth Rule

In chapter 4 we discussed the power of *now* and introduced a *Thinking Shakespeare* rule about the importance of stressing that small but extremely important word.

In this chapter, we noted that another small but important word, *all*, arrests the meter of Canterbury's speech and helps drive home his point about the urgency of invading Gallia. This leads to the next . . .

THINKING SHAKESPEARE RULE: Always stress the word *all*.

I've named this rule in memory of Irene Worth, one of the great Shakespearean actresses of the twentieth century. I had the honor of working with her only one time, at a fundraising event for the Public Theater in New York. It was an evening of celebrity actors reading Shakespeare's sonnets. Kevin Kline, Sigourney Weaver, Christopher Walken, Robert Sean Leonard, and others took part in what was a memorable event.

During one rehearsal session, one of the younger actors in the group—I don't recall who—grappled with Sonnet 60, which begins:

Like as the waves make toward the pebbled shore,
So do our minutes hasten to their end;

Each changing place with that which goes before,
In sequent toil all forwards do contend.

Ms. Worth sat nearby, listening. She walked over to the actor and said, in her inimitable voice that could command armies, tame wild beasts, and stop the motion of the stars themselves, "My dear boy. It's simple. *Always* stress the word *all*." Coming from Irene Worth's mouth, the word *all* really was all—the universe, the infinite, the sum total of everything that ever was, is, or shall be. To borrow from Walt Whitman, it contained multitudes.

Ms. Worth meant not just that *all* should sound grand. She meant that the word, like *now*, is always important. Its breadth and size cannot be ignored or given short shrift.

All the world's a stage
And *all* the men and women merely players . . .
As You Like It (2.7.138–139)

How *all* occasions do inform against me . . .
Hamlet (4.4.32)

I know you *all*, and will a while uphold
The unyoked humor of your idleness . . .
Henry IV, Part One (1.2.173–174)

He was a man, take him for *all* in *all*,
I shall not look upon his like again.
Hamlet (1.2.186–187)

> *All* my pretty ones?
> Did you say *all*? O hell-kite! *All*?
> What, *all* my pretty chickens and their dam
> At one fell swoop?
>
> *Macbeth* (4.3.217–220)

It's a good rule. Stress *now*, stress *all*. All the time.

The Joy of Talk

During the post–table work phase of rehearsal, the director will look at each scene in depth. With the actors, she will stage entrances and exits, work on moments and details, and then ask the actors to go through the whole scene, to "run it," so that she can get a look at what everyone has done. Once they finish, the actors will look to the director for "notes," comments that will help hone and refine the work.

As the process continues, most Shakespearean directors will hear themselves give a certain note to their actors again and again. They will all address the way Shakespeare's characters talk—namely, *brilliantly*.

Shakespeare's characters speak with exceptional skill. They are articulate in a way that is somehow beyond the normal. Even the few instances of inarticulacy in Shakespeare are oddly articulate.[33]

---

33 Othello's obsession with the word *handkerchief* is an example of articulate inarticulateness. The word lodges itself in his brain, freezing his capacity to speak. He spits it out again and again in a kind of strange, modernist poem, until, like a computer with a bum hard drive, he locks up and crashes, fainting dead to the floor. As the Folio puts it, he "falls in a trance."

Actors must keep in mind that articulate people *know* they are articulate. They use their facility with language with great dexterity and aplomb. In other words, *they enjoy it*.

A director working on the scene from *Henry V* we analyzed in this chapter will do well to remind the actors that these characters enjoy all this talk. They delight in their ability to voice complex ideas in splendid forms. Think about this enjoyment in the context of the scene. King Henry summons his inner circle to advise him on a momentous national matter. These men, all career politicians and diplomats, talk and debate for a living. If their talk sways the king, it changes the course of the nation's history. That is, the best talker wins. The man who makes the argument that persuades the king gets the gold star that day. Besides, each man enjoys the others' gift of gab. They are friends, colleagues, and debating partners. They know how the others think and use language. It follows that no one is surprised when the Archbishop of Canterbury lays out a long, sensationally accomplished piece of rhetoric—they have heard him do it before, here in the council chamber and certainly in church as well. Whether or not they agree with him, no one can deny that he is awfully good.

It's not hard to imagine Westmoreland and Exeter at the bar later that night, nursing beers and going over the day's debate. "Oh, man," Westmoreland might sigh, "when Canterbury wheeled out that deal about the honeybees, I knew I was sunk."

Relish the language every bit as much as the characters do. Put your character's amazing brain into your own head. Let it hum in your skull, summoning forth language of uncommon vividness and virtuosic accomplishment.

It's what makes Shakespeare Shakespeare. Be confident with it, bask in it, take pleasure from it.

ACT III

David Strathairn as Leontes in *The Winter's Tale*, directed by Barry Edelstein at Classic Stage Company, 2003. Photo © Dixie Sheridan, 2003.

CHAPTER
—Nº—
9

SWEET, VARIED NOTES

THE MUSIC OF THE LANGUAGE, AND ITS RHYTHM, TEMPO, AND PACE

In Shakespeare's violent early tragedy *Titus Andronicus*, the beautiful and innocent Lavinia, daughter of the title character, is brutally raped. Reenacting a famous story from Greek mythology, her attackers cut her tongue out of her mouth so that she won't be able to name them. (Rough justice is dispensed to them later when they are hacked to bits, baked into a pie, and served to their mother for dessert!) Lavinia's uncle Marcus is devastated by the sight of his bloody niece. He remembers the lovely sound of her now-silenced voice:

> O, that delightful engine of her thoughts,
> That blabbed them with such pleasing eloquence,

Is torn from forth that pretty hollow cage
Where, like a sweet melodious bird, it sung
Sweet, varied notes, enchanting every ear.

(3.1.82–86)

These lines draw upon the idea at the heart of *Thinking Shakespeare*: we think, and then we speak. Or, as Marcus puts it, the tongue is the engine that blabs our thoughts with pleasing eloquence. His lovely notion, that words are sweet, varied notes that enchant the ear, is the subject of this chapter.

Shakespearean Language Has a Musical Dimension

Variety is at the core of Shakespeare's technique. We have seen that his writing never stays in the same place for long. Knotty, intricate vocabulary is quickly followed by something direct and unaffected. If a passage is stern and serious, a deflating joke or flash of humor is surely right around the corner. If it's polysyllabic and fast, slow monosyllables aren't far behind, and if it's slow, you can bet it will pick up speed again soon.

This ever-changing, kaleidoscopic effect gives Shakespeare's writing a certain music—"varied notes," as Marcus puts it—of an "infinite variety," as Enobarbus says of Cleopatra. Shakespeare creates rhythms, tempi, and sounds that are his and his alone. Call it the Swan of Avon Swing, the Backbeat of the Bard, the Stratfordian Stomp. Actors need to learn how to jam on it, to bust a move or two when they hear it. The music of Shakespeare—the rhythm, tempo, and pace of his language—adds dimension and nuance to the audience's experience of his plays. The musical aspect of the writing is not to be overlooked. It is our next area of focus.

REHEARSAL TIME

This speech from *Richard II* amply demonstrates the important contributions of rhythm and tempo to the Shakespearean music.

The given circumstances: King Richard II has plunged England's economy into ruin through excessive spending and too much debt. John of Gaunt, uncle to King Richard, is on his deathbed. In the Elizabethan age, folk wisdom had it that dying men are given the gift of clairvoyance. Gaunt welcomes this gift and makes a prophecy about what will happen to his beloved England if his nephew continues his disastrous economic policies.

(Note that for the remaining three acts of *Thinking Shakespeare*, unfamiliar words and ideas in our rehearsal speeches will be glossed with marginal notes signaled by the symbol ° and footnotes, rather than with the more discursive explanations found in Acts I and II. This will allow the emphasis to be placed more squarely on the main point of each chapter, rather than on line-by-line exegesis and supporting observations. You now have all the tools you need to scan the text, piece its argument together, find and use its antitheses, exploit all the changes in the language's height, and phrase it a line at a time. You are ready to look at it from some new perspectives.)

JOHN OF GAUNT	Methinks I am a prophet new-inspired,
	And thus, expiring, do foretell of him.
wastefulness	His rash, fierce blaze of riot° cannot last,
	For violent fires soon burn out themselves.
	Small showers last long, but sudden
	storms are short. 5

early, soon	He tires betimes° that spurs too fast betimes.
	With eager feeding food doth choke the feeder.
	Light vanity, insatiate cormorant,[34]
	Consuming means,[35] soon preys upon itself.
	This royal throne of kings, this sceptered isle, 10
the god of war	This earth of majesty, this seat of Mars,°
	This other Eden, demi-paradise,
	This fortress built by nature for herself
disease	Against infection° and the hand of war,
	This happy breed of men, this little world, 15
	This precious stone set in the silver sea,
capacity	Which serves it in the office° of a wall,
	Or as a moat defensive to a house
ill will	Against the envy° of less happier lands;
	This blessed plot, this earth, this realm, this
	England, 20
	This nurse, this teeming womb of royal kings,
	Feared by their breed[36] and famous by their birth,
	Renowned for their deeds as far from home
	For Christian service and true chivalry
	As is the sepulchre, in stubborn Jewry, 25
	Of the world's ransom, blessed Mary's son;[37]

---

34 insatiate cormorant: literally, hungry vulture; figuratively, glutton

35 means: i.e., the means whereby it lives; its sustenance. The cormorant was thought to eat so ravenously that it sometimes consumed its own talons, in which its food was held.

36 Feared by their breed: i.e., respected by others because of their noble birth and the good qualities that noble birth has given them

37 Renowned . . . blessed Mary's son: famous for their Christian, chivalric exploits (i.e., the Crusades) in the Holy Land, site of the tomb of Christ. To Gaunt, a devout Christian, "Jewry" is "stubborn" for refusing to accept Jesus as savior.

This land of such dear souls, this dear dear land,

Dear for her reputation through the world,

Is now leased out—I die pronouncing it—

capacity / paltry   Like to a tenement° or pelting° farm.   30

England, bound in with the triumphant sea,

Whose rocky shore beats back the envious siege

the god of the sea   Of wat'ry Neptune°, is now bound in with shame,

With inky blots and rotten parchment bonds.[38]

accustomed   That England that was wont° to conquer other   35

Hath made a shameful conquest of itself.

Ah, would the scandal vanish with my life,

How happy then were my ensuing death!

                                            (2.1.31–68)

Sentence Length

That's a mouthful of a speech. As a first step in hearing its particular music, simply ignore the structure of the verse. What would the speech look like as prose?

Methinks I am a prophet new-inspired, and thus, expiring, do foretell of him. His rash, fierce blaze of riot cannot last, for violent fires soon burn out themselves. Small showers last long, but sudden storms are short. He tires betimes that spurs too fast betimes. With eager feeding food doth choke the feeder. Light vanity, insatiate cormorant, consuming means, soon preys upon itself. This royal throne of kings, this sceptered isle, this earth of

---

38 inky blots and rotten parchment bonds: i.e., all the instruments of debt Richard has used to secure his runaway expenditures

majesty, this seat of Mars, this other Eden, demi-paradise, this fortress built by nature for herself against infection and the hand of war, this happy breed of men, this little world, this precious stone set in the silver sea, which serves it in the office of a wall, or as a moat defensive to a house against the envy of less happier lands; this blessed plot, this earth, this realm, this England, this nurse, this teeming womb of royal kings, feared by their breed and famous by their birth, renowned for their deeds as far from home for Christian service and true chivalry as is the sepulchre, in stubborn Jewry, of the world's ransom, blessed Mary's son; this land of such dear souls, this dear dear land, dear for her reputation through the world, is now leased out—I die pronouncing it—like to a tenement or pelting farm. England, bound in with the triumphant sea, whose rocky shore beats back the envious siege of wat'ry Neptune, is now bound in with shame, with inky blots and rotten parchment bonds. That England that was wont to conquer others hath made a shameful conquest of itself. Ah, would the scandal vanish with my life, how happy then were my ensuing death!

Still a humdinger. It's amazing that a dying man can get through all of this!

This monster paragraph, though, helps reveal something obvious, something that iambic pentameter can obscure: this speech is made up of *sentences*, all of different lengths. The first six of them, which occupy lines 1 through 9, are fairly short. Let's recast them with each sentence making up its own paragraph and look at them more closely:

Methinks I am a prophet new-inspired, and thus, expiring, do foretell of him.

His rash, fierce blaze of riot cannot last, for violent fires soon burn out themselves.

Small showers last long, but sudden storms are short.

He tires betimes that spurs too fast betimes.

With eager feeding food doth choke the feeder.

Light vanity, insatiate cormorant, consuming means, soon preys upon itself.

These sentences vary in length. Some are long; some are short. Why do they vary in length? Because *the thoughts they express vary in length.*

Gaunt goes through a five-sentence list of the ways King Richard will exhaust himself. He will burn out like a violent fire, he will end soon like a sudden rainstorm, he will get tired like a horse that goes too fast at the start of the race, he will choke from eating too fast, his own vanity will be his undoing. These are five variations on the same idea: Richard's wild ways will cause his destruction. Why say it five times? Perhaps because the dying Gaunt wants to make sure his listeners take his point now, while he is still alive to make it. Or maybe because he is so disgusted with Richard that no single one of these ideas by itself would sufficiently convey the depth of his feeling.

Whatever choice you and your director make about Gaunt's intention, those five sentences, along with the opening sentence of the speech, create his rhythm. Restore them to their arrangement as verse and this point becomes crystal clear:

Sentence 1—"Methinks . . . him"—*Two lines of verse*
Sentence 2—"His rash . . . themselves"—*Two lines*
Sentence 3—"Small . . . short"—*One line*
Sentence 4—"He tires . . . betimes"—*One line*
Sentence 5—"With . . . feeder"—*One line*
Sentence 6—"Light . . . itself"—*Two lines*

Two verse lines, then two more, then one, one, one, and again, two. Some thoughts are long enough to require a pair of verse lines for their expression; some are short enough to be expressed in only one line. The length of the sentence indicates the length of the thought, and the changing thought and sentence lengths create rhythmic variety in the language.

The next sentence starts on line 10 with "This royal throne of kings." Where does it end? Not until line 30, with "pelting farm." *The sentence is 21 lines long!*

This behemoth is a fairly simple sentence, with a subject—"This England"—and a verb—"is leased out"—just like any other run-of-the mill sentence. "This England is leased out" is the thought; it just takes Gaunt a very long time to say it. We'll talk about why in a moment, but first, let's look at how this sentence's massive length contributes to the overall rhythmic structure of the speech.

Long and Short Phrases

Chapter 7 emphasized phrasing with the verse line, arguing that in Shakespeare, thoughts come in ten-beat bursts, and that the verse lines etch thoughts' beginnings, ends, and contours. Chapter 7 also minimizes the idea that punctuation plays a significant role in shaping a character's thoughts.

But this should not be taken to mean that the punctuation is utterly without value. On the contrary, punctuation does important work in delineating those crucial shifts between fast and slow and long and short that keep the notes in the text sweet and varied. Shakespeare's punctuation can be one of his most effective indicators of rhythm. Here are some exercises that show it at work.

EXERCISE 1: PERIOD MUSICAL CHAIRS

1. Circle the periods in the speech. There are nine of them, as well as one exclamation point. For a more colorful approach, take two markers and highlight each sentence in the speech, alternating colors from one to the next.
2. Set two chairs next to each other and read the speech. Each time you come to a period, change chairs.

Variations

2a. Go into a good-size empty room and start the speech, walking in a straight line as you speak. Each time you reach a period, change directions.
2b. If you're working with a group of actors, sit in a circle. Choose someone to start giving the speech. When that first speaker reaches a full stop, the person to his right starts to speak. At the next full stop, she stops, and the person to her right continues, and so on.

This exercise in each of its variations provides a powerful way to hear the rhythm of Gaunt's thoughts and to get them into your body. The exercise is also a remarkable demonstration of Shakespeare's jazz-like way with rhythm. Short sentences, then longer, then short, short, longer, short. Then veeerrrrryyyy long. Then shortish. Then short, short. Done.

The length of the sentence measures the length of the thought. The changing lengths of the thoughts keep the language varied, dynamic, and interesting.

But a twenty-one-line sentence? How on earth does an actor keep *that* varied, dynamic, and interesting? One way is to widen the net and look not just at full stops but at all punctuation.

EXERCISE 2: ALL PUNCTUATION MUSICAL CHAIRS   This time, look only at Gaunt's bomber of a sentence that starts at "This royal throne" and ends with "pelting farm." Repeat Exercise 1 in all three variations, this time changing seats, direction, or speaker at *every piece of punctuation*, rather than just at the periods.

Here is a visual representation of how it sounds:

This royal throne of kings,

this sceptered isle,

this earth of majesty,

this seat of Mars,

this other Eden,

demi-paradise,

this fortress built by nature for herself against infection and the
    hand of war,

this happy breed of men,

this little world,

this precious stone set in the silver sea,

which serves it in the office of a wall,

or as a moat defensive to a house against the envy of less
    happier lands;

this blessed plot,

this earth,

this realm,

this England,

this nurse,

this teeming womb of royal kings,

feared by their breed and famous by their birth,

renowned for their deeds as far from home for Christian service
    and true chivalry as is the sepulcher,

in stubborn Jewry,

of the world's ransom,

blessed Mary's son;

this land of such dear souls,

this dear dear land,

dear for her reputation through the world,

is now leased out—

I die pronouncing it—

like to a tenement or pelting farm.

The various punctuation in Gaunt's speech reveals the extraordinary variety of rhythms in his thinking. It separates his longest thought (the one that expresses "This England is leased out") into individual sub-thoughts. He articulates a series of single images that together form an overall picture, much as a pointillist painter uses single dots of paint to fill a canvas with a fully detailed composition. Each "dot," each individual image, has its own rhythm. Short, machine-gun spurts ("this earth, this realm, this England") alternate with long, arcing phrases, like the one about the Holy Sepulcher. It is truly a virtuoso performance. The punctuation helps deliver it.

Bringing It Back to the Line

Don't forget that all this sophisticated rhythm lives within a firm framework: the single line of iambic pentameter. In chapter 7 we noted that phrasing with the punctuation has the unfortunate effect of turning verse into prose. Here, we have avoided that pitfall, but instead we have transformed English Renaissance verse into something like a mid-century American modernist free-verse poem. That form worked beautifully for Ezra Pound, but it's not quite what Shakespeare had in mind.

We have to bring the language back into the verse lines that contain it. The good news is that by once again subordinating the punctuation to the dominance of iambic pentameter, we can learn even more about how Gaunt organizes his thoughts.

Each individual line of verse contains a certain number of single, pointillist images. Consider lines 10 through 20.

This royal throne of kings, this sceptered isle,	*two images on one line*
This earth of majesty, this seat of Mars,	*two images on one line*
This other Eden, demi-paradise,	*two images on one line*
This fortress built by nature for herself	
Against infection and the hand of war,	*one image on two lines*
This happy breed of men, this little world,	*two images on one line*
This precious stone set in the silver sea,	*one image on one line*
Which serves it in the office of a wall,	
Or as a moat defensive to a house	
Against the envy of less happier lands;	*one image, with refinements, on three lines*
This blessed plot, this earth, this realm, this England . . .	*four images on one line*

Grab your piece of blank paper and lay it over the text, starting at line 10. Phrasing with the verse line, have a go at Gaunt's long sentence. At each successive line ending, ask the MMM question, *"What else?"* and in that tiny flash of thought, try to discover each next line's worth of images. Work to keep the individual images grouped by number, line by line, and see if you can preserve the dynamic rhythm that you discovered in the Ezra Pound version above. Do that, and you're on your way to thinking rhythmic Shakespeare.

Just Add Acting

And now the question you've been waiting for since this chapter began. *Why is Gaunt using these words now?* Why does it take him twenty-one lines to say, "This England is leased out"?

There are many possible answers to this question. But the one that fuels the speech best is the one that is most obvious: Gaunt loves his country. He is a patriot. It pains him—it literally kills him—to see how the present leader's addiction to debt is harming England.

To say, "England is leased out," would make the point, but it would fail to convey how deeply Gaunt believes this and how much agony it causes him. On the other hand, to say, "This country that I love, that is perfect, that is tough, that is miraculous, that is beautiful, that is Christian, that is famous, that is dear . . . *this* England is leased out," communicates not only the basic idea but also the fiery passion behind that idea. The accumulation of detail is what does the work.

Image by Image

How does an actor make that detail register over the course of such a long sentence? Let's look at just two of Gaunt's lines.

> This earth of majesty, this seat of Mars,
> This other Eden, demi-paradise . . .

"Majesty" and "Mars" make a nice alliterative pair—both start with *m*. "Mars" gets some extra weight thanks to its position at the end of the line. (Listing the final words in the lines will have revealed to you that "paradise" is also emphasized thanks to its placement.) "Mars" has a strong, stalwart sound, which is appropriate for the name of a god of war. "Majesty" has grandeur and size but not the aggression and warfare of "Mars."

The sound of each word helps communicate its meaning.

"This other Eden, demi-paradise" is a bucolic, beautiful line, entirely different from the magnificence and militarism of the line that precedes it. After the harsh *arrrr* of "Mars," "Eden" gives us the sweet sound of a long *e*. "Eden" conjures images of perfection, golden light, beauty. There is no way to say that word in anger or frustration—it wouldn't make sense. The same goes for "demi-paradise," with its happy connotations and three bright, lush syllables. This is a sumptuous, lyrical line.

Make Gaunt's thoughts your thoughts. As you say the constituent images in each of his lines, you must listen to them too. You must allow their sound and their sense to elicit genuine responses in you. *You must feel something about those images.*

The distinct images Gaunt thinks up—tough Mars, idyllic Eden, and all the rest—ring changes in the height of his language. They also create changes in the rhythm, changes in the sound, and changes in the tone.

They are Shakespeare's sweet, varied notes. Play them.

Caesurae Everywhere

Before we leave John of Gaunt to die in peace, we must consider one more aspect of his speech.

In chapter 7, we talked about the caesura, the mid-line pause marked by punctuation. Caesurae create phrasing conundrums that can block a clear push toward the ends of lines.

Technically, every line has a caesura, even when it is not marked by punctuation. Each line of Shakespeare's iambic pentameter is *bifurcated*—split in two—by its caesura, and this bifurcation can be a great help in navigating a big speech like Gaunt's.

Read the speech aloud, with all of the lines split in half at their caesurae.

Methinks I am a prophet	new-inspired,
And thus, expiring,	do foretell of him.
His rash, fierce blaze of riot	cannot last,
For violent fires	soon burn out themselves.
Small showers last long,	but sudden storms are short.
He tires betimes	that spurs too fast betimes.
With eager feeding	food doth choke the feeder.
Light vanity,	insatiate cormorant,
Consuming means,	soon preys upon itself.
This royal throne of kings,	this sceptered isle,
This earth of majesty,	this seat of Mars,
This other Eden,	demi-paradise,
This fortress built by nature	for herself
Against infection	and the hand of war,
This happy breed of men,	this little world,
This precious stone	set in the silver sea,
Which serves it	in the office of a wall,

Or as a moat	defensive to a house
Against the envy	of less happier lands;
This blessed plot, this earth,	
this realm,	this England,
This nurse,	this teeming womb of royal kings,
Feared by their breed	and famous by their birth,
Renowned for their deeds	as far from home
For Christian service	and true chivalry
As is the sepulchre,	in stubborn Jewry,
Of the world's ransom,	blessed Mary's son;
This land of such dear souls,	this dear dear land,
Dear for her reputation	through the world,
Is now leased out—	I die pronouncing it—
Like to a tenement	or pelting farm.
England,	bound in with the triumphant sea,
Whose rocky shore	beats back the envious siege
Of wat'ry Neptune,	is now bound in with shame,
With inky blots	and rotten parchment bonds.
That England	that was wont to conquer others
Hath made a shameful conquest	of itself.
Ah,	would the scandal vanish with my life,
How happy then	were my ensuing death![39]

Try a section of the speech again, this time without breaking at the caesurae. You will find that even though you are not marking

---

[39] Some of these splits are judgment calls, of course. The caesura in line 37 might well fall between "vanish" and "with"; in line 20, you could argue that it comes at any of the commas. There is wiggle room.

it as you speak, the two-part structure of each line has been lodged in your brain. The bifurcated line has become part of the way you *think* through this language.

This almost subconscious awareness of the structure of the lines is very powerful. It adds detail and specificity to each line and gives your phrasing additional nuance, richness, and clarity.

Try to find the caesurae in some of the material we looked at in earlier chapters, or in any Shakespeare speech.

To be or not to be	that is the question . . .
Now is the winter	of our discontent . . .
In sooth,	I know not why I am so sad . . .
Divide your happy England	into four . . .

Each line of verse splits into two. In all of his plays, Shakespeare uses the bifurcated verse line as yet one more way to keep the rhythm of his text varied and compelling and his characters' thinking clear, well-defined, and strong.

The Text at Speed

As we have discovered, although the ten-syllable line rules the roost, Shakespeare writes—and his characters think—in sentences both long and short. Sentences as gargantuan as Gaunt's twenty-line marathon expression of England's glory are exceptions. Mini-sentences of a couple of words ("O! She's warm.") spice up the mix, but they are rare too. Sentences of one to six lines are the norm, and their contribution to the extraordinarily rhythmic symphony that is the Shakespearean music is important enough to merit some discussion.

Sentence length dictates the tempo of Shakespearean speech. We have already discovered that monosyllables often work as brakes that slow down the language. Longer sentences have the opposite effect. They step on the accelerator pedal and zoom the language up to freeway speeds.

HERMIONE AT HIGH SPEED   Here's a speech that makes the point beautifully.

We met Leontes from *The Winter's Tale* in Things Further Thought On at the end of chapter 4. In that scene, we found him unhinged by what he believed to be his wife Hermione's infidelity. He raged on about poisonous spiders and knowledge he wished he didn't have. In truth, Hermione did not cheat on Leontes. He merely imagined it. But that does not stop him from punishing her. He prohibits her from seeing her firstborn child, their young son Mamillius, and publicly accuses her of adultery. He then throws her in jail, where she gives birth to a baby, which, because Leontes is convinced it was fathered by someone else, is seized and exiled to the badlands outside Sicilia.

Midway through the play, Leontes puts Hermione on trial. It is winter, and, cruelly, the trial is held outdoors. On the witness stand, shivering, Hermione answers the charges against her, starting with Leontes's menacing declaration that if she is proven guilty she should "look for no less than death." At long last given the opportunity to speak in her own defense, she responds:

> Sir, spare your threats.
> *bugaboo; nasty thing*   The bug° which you would fright me with, I seek.
> To me can life be no commodity.[40]

....

40 commodity: object of value, i.e., comfort

The crown and comfort of my life, your favor,

count as   I do give° lost, for I do feel it gone   5

But know not how it went. My second joy,

And first fruits of my body,[41] from his presence

I am barred, like one infectious. My third comfort,

Starred most unluckily,[42] is from my breast,

The innocent milk in its most innocent mouth,   10

dragged   Haled° out to murder; myself on every post[43]

i.e., unbounded   Proclaimed a strumpet, with immodest° hatred

belongs   The childbed privilege[44] denied, which 'longs°

To women of all fashion;[45] lastly, hurried

Here, to this place, i'th'open air, before   15

I have got strength of limit.[46] Now, my liege,

Tell me what blessings I have here alive,

That I should fear to die. Therefore proceed.

But yet hear this—mistake me not—for life,

I prize it not a straw; but for mine honor,   20

Which I would free: if I shall be condemned

Upon surmises, all proofs sleeping else[47]

But what your jealousies awake, I tell you

tyranny   'Tis rigor,° and not law. Your honors all,

---

41 **first fruits of my body:** i.e., my firstborn child, Mamillius

42 **Starred most unluckily:** born under an unlucky star (the reference is to astrology)

43 **post:** signpost (news and other important announcements were nailed to community bulletin boards called "posts")

44 **childbed privilege:** i.e., the right to enjoy bed rest after giving birth to a child

45 **all fashion:** every class or social rank

46 **before I have got strength of limit:** i.e., before I have regained my strength after a period of lying-in

47 **all proofs sleeping else:** i.e., all evidence missing except for

appeal to   I do refer me° to the oracle.   25
                               Apollo be my judge.[48]

                                                          (3.2.89–114)

This speech is so juicy, so loaded with the rich detail characteristic of Shakespeare's late period, that we could spend a whole chapter analyzing it. The language changes from high to low in breathtaking ways, the verse lines are fascinating in their irregularity, and the psychology underlying Hermione's argument is revelatory. But this chapter is about rhythm, and right now we are interested in how sentence length indicates tempo. So we will stick to what this speech shows us about that.

Let's start by putting aside the verse lines and rendering the speech in prose, sentence by sentence, like we did with John of Gaunt.

Sir, spare your threats.

The bug which you would fright me with, I seek.

To me can life be no commodity.

The crown and comfort of my life, your favor, I do give lost, for I do feel it gone but know not how it went.

....

48 Apollo be my judge: the Oracle at Delphos was at the temple of the god Apollo. It was believed that wise pronouncements, such as judgments in court cases, could be found there. Earlier, Leontes sent messengers to the Oracle to ask for Apollo's guidance in punishing his wife. The messengers arrive shortly after this speech and read the god's declaration that Hermione is innocent.

My second joy, and first fruits of my body, from his presence I
am barred, like one infectious.

My third comfort, starred most unluckily, is from my breast, the
innocent milk in its most innocent mouth, haled out to murder;
myself on every post proclaimed a strumpet, with immodest
hatred the childbed privilege denied, which 'longs to women
of all fashion; lastly, hurried here, to this place, i'th'open air,
before I have got strength of limit.

Now, my liege, tell me what blessings I have here alive, that I
should fear to die.

Therefore proceed.

But yet hear this—mistake me not—for life, I prize it not a
straw; but for mine honor, which I would free: if I shall be
condemned upon surmises, all proofs sleeping else but what
your jealousies awake, I tell you 'tis rigor, and not law.

Your honors all, I do refer me to the oracle.

Apollo be my judge.

The musicality of this language is hard to miss. Recast in sentences, the speech's rhythmic dimensions become instantly clear.

The speech starts and ends with short sentences. The first
three are completely monosyllabic except for "commodity," a
four-syllable word given an acid prominence because it is surrounded by single syllables. Hermione asks, in paraphrase, "You

want to take away my life? The life I live right now is worthless."
Try to say the lines quickly; it's nearly impossible, because it does
not make sense. The tempo here is slow, defiant, deliberate. It
reflects the strength and certainty of Hermione's thoughts.

Then the language changes. Hermione lists those circumstances that have robbed her life of value—the loss of Leontes'
love, her banishment from her son, the violent exile and likely
murder of her newborn daughter, her public humiliation, her
postpartum exhaustion, and the physical brutality of being tried
outdoors in the cold winter air. Notice that *her sentences get longer
as the list goes on.*

The sentence that begins, "My third comfort" and runs through
"strength of limit" (lines 8 through 16) is the longest of all, clocking
in at seven full verse lines plus two half-lines. It comprises a number
of short clauses separated by commas and semicolons. If we phrase
it according to its punctuation, the sentence looks like this:

> My third comfort,
> starred most unluckily,
> is from my breast,
> the innocent milk in its most innocent mouth,
> haled out to murder;
> myself on every post proclaimed a strumpet,
> with immodest hatred the childbed privilege denied,
> which 'longs to women of all fashion;
> lastly,
> hurried here,
> to this place,
> i'th'open air,
> before I have got strength of limit.

The speech heats up in these lines. The tone grows more militant. Hermione leaves behind the slow monosyllables with which she began, and now her thoughts crash together in a cascade of righteous defiance. As a result, the tempo must pick up. If it does not, if all those short clauses take long chunks of time to say, the sentence turns ponderous, fragmented, and ineffectual. It's simply got to move fast. Hermione's outrage and injured pride drive her on. As her language tumbles out of her, it builds in speed, rushing toward a stunning and climactic moment of protest.

Then, at the end of this long, eight-line list of grievances, her language drops precipitously in height into the stern, spondaic monosyllables of a short, fragmentary sentence: "BUT YET HEAR THIS." *DUM-DUM. DUM-DUM.* Their strength derives from their slowness, and their slowness only registers *if the words preceding them have been spoken quickly.*

Try the speech again, starting off nice and slow and phrasing with the verse line. Listen to what happens to the pace as you move along. It's a remarkable demonstration of how thought has rhythm, and how a great writer treats words and phrases like a composer treats notes and bars. Work with the speech until its varying tempi just flow out of you, with no conscious work required.

....

THINKING SHAKESPEARE RULE: Longer sentences generally mean *speed up*.

....

Variety in Speed Is the Spice of Shakespeare

You can only speed up if you've been going at a slow or normal rate, just as you can only slow down if you've been going at a quick pace.

The speed of Shakespearean speech is relative.

This is an important point. Monosyllables mean slow down. But how slow? Five miles per hour? Ten? Longer sentences generally mean speed up. But how fast? Fifty-five? Ninety? It all depends how fast you've been speaking in the first place.

In a decent professional performance of *Richard II*, Gaunt's "royal throne of kings" speech would take two and a half to three minutes of stage time, depending on how close to death's door the actor decides old Gaunt happens to be. The entire play would run close to three hours. Most modern productions of Shakespeare cut a number of lines, bringing the running times to a more manageable length. (The longest one I ever directed ran two hours and forty-five minutes, including intermission; the shortest, about two hours; the rest hovered around two and a half.) It's hard to generalize, but in most cases a few hundred lines end up on the rehearsal room floor, leaving about 2,500 lines for 150 minutes in the theater. That's about sixteen lines per minute.

You might be thinking, "Oh, no! Now the director's going to whip out a stopwatch and time my performance in lines-per-minute? I quit!!"

No need to worry. No one will point a radar gun at your mouth. Watch Paul Scofield, one of the greatest Shakespearean actors of all time, as King Lear in Peter Brook's film of the play, or as the king of France in Kenneth Branagh's *Henry V*, or as the Ghost in the Mel Gibson / Franco Zeffirelli *Hamlet*. He takes things low and slow, and he is riveting. Ralph Fiennes, on the other hand, played Hamlet in a headlong rush of a production in London's West End and on Broadway. He got through "To be or not to be" in record time, as though the Prince of Denmark had a plane to catch. Yet he too was riveting.

Each actor in each new production has to find his own right pace. To be sure, it's usually faster than he speaks in real life, since Shakespeare's characters think faster than people do in real life. What's best is to establish a baseline speed, then adjust the tempo up and down throughout the performance.

Variety isn't merely the spice of life; it's also the difference between an engaged theater audience and one that wants to swear off Shakespeare forever. Two and a half hours of language delivered at one steady pace is numbing, relentless, and dull, no matter how amazing that language might be.

Vary the rhythm as the thoughts vary. Embrace change, love surprise. Make your Shakespeare sound like jazz. Jam on him. Lay down his smokin' riffs.

Keep the audience on the edge of their seats. The drumbeat of their applause—the only steady rhythm that theater artists desire—will tell you how grateful they are for the treat you gave them.

THINGS FURTHER THOUGHT ON

Words Have Juice

Our discussion of pace in Shakespeare brings up a related and crucial notion.

As we saw when we examined the difference between "this seat of Mars" and "this other Eden," thoughts have different qualities, and words have different weights. Think *majestic, macho, powerful god of war*, and you will speak the word *Mars* in a strong, deep, heavy way. Think *paradisiacal heaven on earth, lush, green and alluring*, and you will speak the word *Eden* in a blithe, inviting, light way. The concepts themselves dictate the way the words are spoken.

But—and this is where acting Shakespeare becomes a sublime pleasure—*all* of Shakespeare's words must be given their due. All of the language must have energy, depth, vigor, and force.

Look at another of Gaunt's wonderful lines:

His rash, fierce blaze of riot cannot last.

(Paraphrase: Richard's reckless, violent flare-up of debauchery can't go on forever.)

I once had the misfortune of hearing an actor blow through this line as though he were commenting on a lousy turkey sandwich he got at the corner deli. "Y'know, too much mayo, tomato's a little mushy, and I prefer rye." It sounded like this: "(*sigh*) . . . his . . . rash fierceblazeofriot . . . cannotlast."

Wrong! This language has weight! It is hugely expressive, thick with disgust and disapproval. "Rash" is sweeping, sudden. "Fierce" is, well, fierce. "Blaze" is on fire. "Riot" is catastrophic, tumultuous, turbulent. These words are powerful and incendiary, muscular and juicy. An actor must deliver them in a way that allows them to be what they are.

Another example: Hermione's "I tell you—*line ending*—*(what??!!)*—'Tis rigor, and not law."

"Rigor," remember, means "tyranny." What an amazing thing to say! The man she's talking to is king, and she is publicly calling him a tyrant, the most offensive, inflammatory name imaginable for any leader. "If you do this, then you're like Hitler!" This ain't kid stuff. Hermione's words have impact, weight, emotion, zing, *cojones*. The actress has to say them that way.

Shakespeare's language has *juice*. Don't be shy of it. Always give it its due.

Lists

Shakespeare loves making lists. They are everywhere in his plays.

Early in her speech, Hermione lists the reasons why her life can no longer be considered a "commodity." "The crown and comfort of my life" is first, "My second joy" follows, "My third comfort" is next, and "lastly" takes up the rear. "Myself on every post" and "the childbed privilege denied" add points five and six to the catalogue of insults.

Gaunt takes twenty-one lines to list all the ways in which England is glorious. Depending on how you count, he enumerates eighteen different ideas, from a royal throne, to a fortress, to a realm, to a womb, to a "dear dear land."

Portia lists the goodies ("house," "servants," "myself") she is ready to turn over to her beloved and victorious husband after having listed all the qualities about herself she wishes she could change, and all those she rather likes.

Hamlet spells out a catalogue of life's "whips and scorns," listing a terrifying vision of the disappointments, small and large, that would lead most of us to commit suicide, were it not for our terror of what we might find after death.

If words express thought, then it follows that a long list of words gives voice to a long and multifaceted thought. The more layers of meaning there are in a certain idea, the more individual items it will take to get that idea into the air.

Like every other kind of language in Shakespeare, a list is a function of a character's need to communicate. When Hermione or Gaunt or Portia or Hamlet don't feel they have made themselves clear with one example of what they mean, they add another, and another, and another, until the idea in question has been completely expressed.

It follows that lists must grow in intensity as they go along. As the speaker works to make himself understood, a pressure builds on the words he uses. Each one counts for more than the last. He asks himself, "Is this the word that's going to wrap up this thought?" When the answer is no, he asks, "Well, then, is this?" No. "All right then, *this*?" Nope. "*THIS?!*"

A excellent illustration of this point can be found in one of Shakespeare's most famous speeches, from *The Merchant of Venice*. It's in prose, not verse (a form we will examine in depth in chapter 14). An excerpt:

He hath disgraced me, and hindered me half a million; laughed at my losses, mocked at my gains, scorned my nation, thwarted my bargains, cooled my friends, heated mine enemies; and what's his reason? I am a Jew. Hath not a Jew eyes? Hath not a Jew hands, organs, dimensions, senses, affections, passions? Fed with the same food, hurt with the same weapons, subject to the same diseases, healed by the same means, warmed and cooled by the same winter and summer, as a Christian is? If you prick us, do we not bleed? If you tickle us, do we not laugh? If you poison us, do we not die? And if you wrong us, shall we not revenge? (3.1.45–56)

At root, the speech is nothing more than a group of lists.

Disgraced . . . hindered . . . laughed . . . mocked . . . scorned . . . thwarted . . . cooled . . . heated

Eyes . . . hands . . . organs . . . dimensions . . . senses . . . affections . . . passions

Fed with food . . . hurt with weapons . . . subject to diseases . . . healed by means . . . warmed / cooled by winter / summer

Pricked / bleed . . . tickle / laugh . . . poison / die . . . wrong / revenge

Shylock has just discovered that Jessica, his beloved daughter and sole family member, has run off to elope with Lorenzo, a gentile. Heartbroken, he wanders the streets of Venice and encounters Salerio and Solanio (whom we met in chapter 6).

Shylock knows that these two are Antonio's friends, and since they seem aware of Jessica's flight, he concludes that Antonio must have been involved in it—yet one more in the long catalogue of injuries the Christian merchant has done him. For their parts, Sal and Sol know that Shylock loaned Antonio 3,000 ducats (for Bassanio to use in wooing Portia) against a peculiar form of collateral: a pound of Antonio's flesh. Sal and Sol unloose a stream of humiliating anti-Semitic bile and ask what use Shylock could ever have for a pound of a man's flesh. "To bait fish withal," he answers. "If it will feed nothing else, it will feed my revenge." Then he launches into his famous speech.

"Hath not a Jew eyes" lays out for two Venetian bigots why a Jew would seek revenge against a Christian. The logic, at least in Shylock's mind, is airtight: 1) Jews and Christians are the same in every way. 2) One of our similarities is the fact that if we suffer a wrong, we are entitled to revenge. 3) This Christian man has wronged me, a Jew. 4) Therefore, since we are the same, I am entitled to be revenged on him.

For Shylock's argument to convince, it must be much more compelling than this bare-bones outline makes it sound. It requires detail, weight, gravity. That's where the lists come in. Shylock *needs* this colossal outpouring of language to express an unusually loaded idea born out of the profound pain in his heart.

Shylock's opening thought is "this Christian has wronged me." But "wronged" doesn't come close to capturing all Antonio has done. So Shylock elaborates. Antonio has "disgraced . . . hindered . . . laughed . . . mocked . . . scorned . . . thwarted . . . cooled . . . heated." If Shylock stopped after any one of these words, the idea wouldn't be complete. "Disgraced . . . hindered . . . laughed" has only a fraction of the power of the entire list. Each new term adds force. And each one has more weight than the last. By the time the list is complete, Shylock has painted a detailed portrait of a monumental history of grievance, one so heinous that only physical retribution can counterbalance it.

Next, Shylock has this thought: "Jews and Christians are alike." But he must provide proof if he is to persuade his listeners. Hence, more lists. Like Christians, Jews have "eyes . . . hands . . . organs . . . dimensions . . . senses . . . affections . . . passions." Jews and Christians are both "fed with food . . . hurt with weapons . . . subject to diseases . . . healed by means . . . warmed / cooled by winter / summer." When pricked, they bleed. When tickled, they laugh. When poisoned, they die. And the clincher, when wronged, they revenge!

You can hear the build in intensity as Shylock continues. Try going through these lists with decreasing energy, trailing off as you near the end of each. It's impossible. It makes no sense. Building in energy is the natural way to communicate the force and import of Shylock's ideas.

....

THINKING SHAKESPEARE RULE: Lists build as they develop.

....

Here's one more list, a personal favorite.

Almost exactly halfway through *Henry V*, King Charles of France finally realizes that England is serious about invading his country. Just when all hope seems lost, he at last gets angry and rouses himself to resist the enemy. He summons all the noblemen of France to join him in the coming fight:

                    Up, princes! And, with spirit of honor edged

hurry   More sharper than your swords, hie° to the field.

                    Charles Delabreth, high constable of France;

                    You Dukes of Orleans, Bourbon, and of Berri,

                    Alencon, Brabant, Bar, and Burgundy;

                    Jaques Chatillon, Rambures, Vaudemont,

                    Beaumont, Grandpre, Roussi, and Fauconberg,

                    Foix, Lestrale, Bouciqualt, and Charolois;

                    High dukes, great princes, barons, lords and
                              knights,

                    For your great seats[49] now quit you of great
                              shames.

block   Bar° Harry England, that sweeps through our
                              land. . .

                                  (3.5.38–48)

    This is one of the most rousing speeches in the play. A sleeping giant awakens, and merely by listing the names of the mighty commanders on his side, he fills his veins with blood, his limbs with muscle and potency, and his countrymen with courage. Only three or four of the men the king names actually appear in the play. Who they are isn't the point; their number is. The increasing intensity of this avalanche of sound makes Charles seem invincible. The piling-on of consonants and vowels bodies forth the prodigious strength of the great nation

---

49 For your great seats: i.e., in the name of your noble titles and positions

over which he reigns.[50] And it's all created by a list that builds as it goes.

Repeats

Near the end of his description of England, Gaunt calls the country "This dear, dear land."

Hamlet wishes, "O, that this too, too solid flesh would melt."

Ophelia laments that the prince, now apparently insane, is "quite, quite down."

Leontes finds his wife's relationship with his best friend "Too hot, too hot."

And Macbeth ruminates on "Tomorrow and tomorrow and tomorrow."

These are lists of sorts, but their components are not new details that add to a growing catalogue. Instead, they are repetitions, restatements of the identical idea.

Why are these repetitions spoken? For the same reason that characters make lists. The idea they are expressing requires so much weight that only by repeating it can they convey its full dimensions.

Like lists, repeats grow in intensity.

"O, that this too, too solid flesh would melt" makes no sense. But, "O, that this too, **TOO** solid flesh would melt," does.

---

50 Directors disagree about how Charles should pronounce the names. Some feel he should say them as a French speaker would: "FWAH, li-STRAHL, boo-see-KOH, and shar-ol-WAH." Others think that Shakespeare intended all the French in the play to be spoken the way it would sound if the words were in English: "FOIKS, LEE-strail, BAW-see-kwalt, and CHAR-o-loyz." Whatever the choice, the effect remains the same. Declaiming an ever-intensifying list of almost nonsense syllables, Charles creates a great army out of thin air. Watch Paul Scofield do this speech in Branagh's movie and you'll get the point. Extraordinary.

Besides, since by now you are accustomed to driving forward toward the ends of lines, it is only natural that you would give the second word in these repeats more oomph than the first.

Try the lines above and see for yourself how repeats call for builds in size.

....

***THINKING SHAKESPEARE* RULE: Repeats require builds.**

....

ACT III

CHAPTER
—№—
10

VERBIAGE

THE POWER OF SHAKESPEARE'S VERBS

One hundred and sixty.

That is the number of words in the juggernaut of a sentence at the center of John of Gaunt's deathbed speech.

Like every sentence, this 160-word mammoth has a subject (the part of the sentence about which something is being said) and a predicate (the part that says something about the subject). We can see them easily in our paraphrase: *England is leased out.* "England" is the subject; "is leased out" is the predicate.

Gaunt takes a lot of space to describe that subject. He doesn't simply say "England," because he is describing not just a country on a map but a philosophy, a people, a beloved way of life. He takes 157 words to paint an elaborate picture of it.

Then, in only three words, he gives his intricate subject a predicate. Gaunt could go on about England for another dozen words, or a thousand: "This royal throne of kings, this earth, this place, this *this*, this *that*, this *the other . . .*" So? What about it? Without "is leased out," we would wonder what on earth this dying old man is trying to say.

The predicate makes his point.[51]

Verbs: The Hardest-Working Words in Show Biz

We could analyze "is leased out" in considerable grammatical detail, getting into the technicalities of *predicate adjectives* and *subject complements* and so on. But we are artists, not grammarians. So rather than discuss a sentence's *predicate*, we'll limit ourselves to the more manageable terrain of Shakespeare's *verbs*.

Subject, verb. Every sentence has them. Verbs are singularly important in dramatic writing. They create dynamism and carry meaning. They are the life force of the language.

Some examples:

To **be** or not to **be**, that **is** the question.

The quality of mercy **is not strained**,
It **droppeth** as the gentle rain from heaven . . .

---

51 I learned how important "is leased out" is to Gaunt's speech from watching Earle Hyman play the role at the Public Theater in 1994. Though best known as Bill's dad on TV's *The Cosby Show*, Hyman is one of the greatest American classical actors. As Gaunt, he sat on a chair center stage and said the famous speech slowly and majestically, building in intensity and pain until "is leased out" boomed from somewhere deep inside him. His *basso profundo* shook the roof of the place. "Izzz leeeeeeeeeased ouuuuuuuut!!" A great moment of theater.

Tomorrow and tomorrow and tomorrow
Creeps in this petty pace from day to day . . .

Why man, he **doth bestride** the narrow world
Like a Colossus, and we petty men
Walk under his huge legs and **peep** about
To **find** ourselves dishonorable graves.

Julius Caesar (1.2.136–139)

But when the blast of war **blows** in our ears,
Then **imitate** the action of the tiger.
Stiffen the sinews, **conjure up** the blood,
Disguise fair nature with **hard-favored** rage.
Then **lend** the eye a terrible aspect,
Let it **pry** through the portage of the head
Like the brass cannon, **let** the brow **o'erwhelm** it
As fearfully as **doth** a **galled** rock
O'erhang and **jutty** his **confounded** base,
Swilled with the wild and wasteful ocean.
Now **set** the teeth and **stretch** the nostril wide,
Hold hard the breath, and **bend** up every spirit
To his full height . . .

Henry V (3.1.5–17)

The verbs are the most expressive words in Shakespeare. Find them, embrace them, and let them rip. They give impetus to what the characters are trying to say.

Verbs provide the energy of Shakespearean thought.

REHEARSAL TIME

This great speech from *Julius Caesar* is an object lesson in the power and sway of Shakespeare's verbs.

Caius Cassius, a Roman nobleman, has grown disenchanted with the great conqueror Julius Caesar. He believes that Caesar is now bent on appointing himself emperor of Rome. Cassius believes that Rome should be a democratic Republic; in addition, he is just plain envious of Caesar's success. So he hatches a plot to assassinate Caesar at the Capitol. He knows that his conspiracy will never succeed without the participation of one of Rome's greatest and most respected political leaders: Marcus Brutus. Cassius finds Brutus alone one afternoon and in a long and detailed argument spells out his vision for Rome's future. Brutus knows immediately where Cassius is heading and warns his friend not to involve him in anything dishonorable, saying, "I love / The name of honor more than I fear death."

Here is Cassius's response:

i.e., honor	I know that virtue° to be in you, Brutus,	
appearance	As well as I do know your outward favor.°	
	Well, honor is the subject of my story.	
	I cannot tell what you and other men	
	Think of this life; but for my single self,	5
	I had as lief not be,[52] as live to be	
	In awe of such a thing as I myself.	
	I was born free as Caesar, so were you.	

---

52 **I had as lief not be:** i.e., I would just as soon be dead

ı

We both have fed as well, and we can both

Endure the winter's cold as well as he.   10

For once upon a raw and gusty day,

churning against The troubled Tiber chafing with° her shores,

Caesar said to me "Dar'st thou, Cassius, now

Leap in with me into this angry flood,

And swim to yonder point?" Upon the word,   15

Accoutred[53] as I was, I plunged in,

And bade him follow. So indeed he did.

The torrent roared, and we did buffet it

With lusty sinews, throwing it aside,

antagonism, rivalry And stemming it[54] with hearts of controversy.°   20

i.e., arrive at But ere we could arrive° the point proposed,

Caesar cried "Help me, Cassius, or I sink!"

Ay, as Aeneas[55] our great ancestor

Did from the flames of Troy upon his shoulder

The old Anchises bear, so from the waves of Tiber 25

Did I the tired Caesar. And this man

Is now become a god, and Cassius is

A wretched creature, and must bend his body[56]

If Caesar carelessly but nod on him.

He had a fever when he was in Spain,   30

take note of And when the fit[57] was on him, I did mark°

---

53 Accoutred: armed and dressed in full military uniform

54 stemming it: holding it back, as a dam holds back water

55 Aeneas: famous Trojan hero who was one of the founders of Rome, Aeneas (uh-NEE-us) carried his father, Anchises (an-KIGH-zeez), out of Troy on his back when the Greeks burned the city.

56 must bend his body: i.e., must bow down

57 the fit: Caesar suffered from epilepsy and had frequent seizures

How he did shake. 'Tis true, this god did shake.

His coward lips did from their color fly;[58]

gaze; glance   And that same eye whose bend° doth awe the world

i.e., its   Did lose his° luster. I did hear him groan,   35

Ay, and that tongue of his that bade[59] the Romans

Mark him and write his speeches in their books,

"Alas!" it cried, "Give me some drink, Titinius,"

As a sick girl. Ye gods, it doth amaze me

weak constitution   A man of such a feeble temper° should   40

So get the start of[60] the majestic world,

i.e., triumph   And bear the palm° alone!

(1.2.92–134)

This exciting speech is worth analyzing from all the viewpoints we have covered so far in *Thinking Shakespeare*. Let's take a moment to do so before turning to the question of verbs.

Argument: The speech's fascinating shape reveals as much about Cassius's peculiar psychology as it does about his political motivations. He starts with an idealistic appeal to honor and liberty, then moves on to a bizarre story about a swimming contest (note the nice, clear, direction-changing "but" smack in the middle) and then turns to schoolyard name-calling ("a sick girl"). He seems to be saying that Caesar shouldn't be emperor not because his imperial power-grab is an affront to Rome's republican principles but because the guy is just too "feeble." The

....

58 **did from their color fly:** i.e., turned pale (literally, fled from their own flag)

59 **bade:** commanded (past tense of "to bid," to give an order)

60 **get the start of:** i.e., gain advantage over

beats of the speech are clear, and each one has its own shape and inner structure.

Scansion: A line such as "ac-COUT-red AS i WAS, i PLUN-ged IN" shows the thrillingly muscular pulse that iambic pentameter can create. There is a dizzy joy in the sheer metrical variety Cassius deploys as he hammers away at Brutus.

Antithesis: It is everywhere in this speech. Lines 23 through 26, including the oppositions of "Aeneas" against "I," "Flames of Troy" against "waves of Tiber," and "old Anchises" against "tired Caesar," show antithesis at its most vivid and rich. When we hear, "this MAN is now become a GOD, and CASSIUS is a WRETCH-ED CREATURE," antithesis is what sparks the shocking realization that pure envy, and not political idealism, is the petty motivation driving Cassius to murder.

Height of language: Here too the speech is a dazzler. The language starts out simply enough. Cassius takes a rational and lucid approach at first, cunningly but calmly speaking of the ideals he knows will appeal to Brutus: virtue, honor, and freedom. Later, he shifts into the soaring language of mythology, reeling off the legendary names of Aeneas and Anchises, the Roman equivalents of Washington, Jefferson, and Franklin. Then the gears change again, and the language downshifts into bluntness, taunts, and mocking. In the final lines, the language leaps back up to the heights of philosophical majesty. Occasional monosyllables, as in lines 31, 32, 34, and 39, give our ears (and Cassius's tongue) some relief and leave the torrential Tiber behind.

Phrasing with the verse line: Almost every line ending in the speech works with spectacular efficiency to hone Cassius's thoughts. Take a stab at lines 6, 25, 26, 27, 38, and 39 through 41, using the Paper Trick and MMM, and you'll see a crystal-clear demonstration of Shakespeare's wizardry with verse structure and enjambment. Speak the final word in each line, and you'll feel in your own voice just how consistently Shakespeare eases the juiciest ideas toward the ends of lines.

Exercise: Making a List

Now back to the verbs, which are, after all, their own kind of heightened speech. The action they express provides a jolt, giving Cassius's thoughts electricity and immediacy.

The central passage of the speech most merits attention. Cassius's language surges during his extravagant story of diving into the Tiber. Its energy leaps up, until this Roman politico sounds like a great play-by-play announcer calling the most epic gold medal swim meet in Olympic history.

What gives this beat of the speech its marvelous intensity? The verbs.

Break out those colored highlighters once again. Just as we have learned to attack a speech by focusing in isolation on its antitheses, line endings, or sentence lengths, so now we will see how to unlock a character's thinking by zeroing in exclusively on his verbs.

Work through lines 11 to 26, noting every verb Cassius uses.

> troubled
> chafing
> said
> dar'st
> leap
> swim
> accoutred

plunged

bade

did

roared

did

buffet

throwing

stemming

arrive

proposed

cried

help

sink

did

bear

did

tired

Read this list aloud, and you may as well be reading the full speech. The verbs are its backbone.

When you encounter a passage of Shakespeare for the first time, start by pulling out its verbs. They will tell you what the speech is really about.

A Nondoctrinaire Approach to Grammar

You might object that "troubled," as it is used in this speech, is not technically a verb. You're correct. It is an adjective that describes "Tiber." But for the purposes of *Thinking Shakespeare*, it's a verb too.

Verbs can mutate into all kinds of shapes in the English language. They can turn into nouns and adjectives, and, with the addition or subtraction of a few letters, they can tell when in time a certain action took place or is taking place or has not yet taken place. As you're working on a speech, don't worry about what part of speech a certain verb has morphed into or about the difference between intransitive, infinitive, and gerundial verbs. Instead focus on the idea that *every form of verb is useful.*

Verbs' Verve

Each verb in the list from Cassius's speech, regardless of its tense or form, has vitality.

Caesar, whom Cassius quotes, uses commanding, authoritative, present-tense verbs: "leap," "swim," "help," and "sink." Cassius himself uses a more nuanced variety of forms, all of them superbly expressive: "buffet," "stemming," "throwing," "troubled," "did," and "bear." These verbs have *juice.* They communicate great vigor and activity.

Be bold and let the verbs be as expressive as they can be.

Say the verbs with all the energy they demand. Let them work their way from your brain to your mouth with all their force intact.

The torrent roared . . .

You can practically hear the raging Tiber in those words. The noisy river must be there when you say them.

. . . throwing it aside, / And stemming it . . .

The ferocious effort of this swim is embedded in each word. You need juice when you say "throwing" and "stemming."

. . . the tired Caesar . . .

Cassius is already planting in Brutus's mind the notion that Caesar's physical limitations undercut his political potency. He might describe the drowning Caesar as wet, cold, breathless, shrieking, or flailing. But "tired" is the verb he chooses. When you speak that word, you must let Cassius's disdain for Caesar's weakness drip through the two lugubrious syllables. Note that the vowel sound long *i* echoes many times in this section of the speech ("Ay," "Tiber," "I," "tired").

Later in the speech Cassius uses some spectacularly charged verbs.

mark

shake (said twice)

fly

awe

lose

hear

groan

bade

mark

write

cried

give

amaze

get

bear

How thrilling these verbs are! They have an almost physical presence. "Shake," "awe," "lose," and "groan" soar right off the page, swooping around Cassius, Brutus, and the audience. Their vowel sounds are full and spacious yet shaped by sharp and percussive consonants. The sounds of these verbs communicate meaning just as vividly as do the thoughts they represent.

AN AMAZING WORD   *Amaze* is a particularly juicy verb, with a big long vowel singing out in the middle and a scissor-like *z* at the end chopping it off. Even its most colorful synonyms—*astonish, dumbfound*—don't quite match the unique energy of *amaze*. Nor do they express all the overtones the verb carried with it in Shakespeare's day.

The word *amaze* comes from the same root as *maze*. Mazes were hugely popular in Elizabethan England, and wealthy landowners often built shrubbery mazes on their estates. (The well-known one still standing at Hampton Court, south of London, dates from just before Shakespeare was born.) Getting lost in a maze is at first confusing, and then scary. It can bring on panic, and then an immobilizing terror characterized by a physical state of arrested movement and an emotional state of perplexity and despair. That paralysis is what Shakespeare meant by *amazement*. The word is one of his favorites. Time and again Shakespeare (and his contemporaries) jams a character into an irresolvable dilemma. Frozen in his tracks and completely overwhelmed, the character will declare himself "amazed."

That's what Cassius does here. *Why is he using this word now?* Because he can't believe that a wimp like Julius Caesar is only inches away from becoming the most powerful man on earth. The man can't swim. He had epileptic seizures in Spain. He cried to Titinius for a drink. He's not even a man; as far as Cassius is concerned, he's just a sickly little girl. Yet somehow, Rome, the greatest nation in history, is about to crown him emperor. It astonishes Cassius. It flabbergasts him. It stuns, staggers, and stupefies him. In a word, it *amazes* him.

One verb communicates so much. Give it full permission to do so.

There's juice in all these verbs. Squeeze it out.

Verbs Take You Places

Open your *Complete Works* to any page and you'll see countless examples of Shakespeare's verbs doing their amazing work.

More than any other words in the text, verbs have a mysterious way of making you feel emotion. Something about the fact that verbs describe physical action—that they carry tangible, material force—makes them especially and powerfully effective. If you commit to them, saying them with all the strength and pressure they demand, you will instantly click into exactly what your character is thinking and feeling. It's a peculiar kind of magic.

Think the verbs, and your mind becomes the character's. Thinking verbs is *Thinking Shakespeare*.

MORE REHEARSAL TIME

Here are two speeches I like from early in Shakespeare's career, and one of my favorites from his late period. Each one depends on its verbs to make its argument vivid and to keep its energy from flagging.

First, Helena from *A Midsummer Night's Dream*. This speech comes near the climax of the play's series of confusions and mistakes. The mischievous fairy Puck has placed a magic love potion in Lysander's eyes, making the young man fall in love with Helena and reject his own girlfriend, Hermia. When Puck realizes the trouble he has caused, he decides to fix the situation by putting the love potion in Demetrius's eyes, so that he falls in love with Helena too. Both men tell her how much they adore her, but the embarrassed and self-conscious Helena is convinced that they are mocking her. She also believes, wrongly, that Hermia is in cahoots with the boys to humiliate her. Helena wonders how her best friend in the world could betray her and cause her so much pain.

Read the speech one line at a time and listen to the verbs do their work.

conspiracy	Lo, she **is** one of this confederacy.°
come together	Now I **perceive** they **have conjoined**° all three
lying entertainment /	To **fashion** this false sport° in spite of me.°—
i.e., to spite me	Injurious Hermia, most ungrateful maid,
	Have you **conspired, have** you with these **contrived** 5
	To **bait** me with this foul derision?
confidences	**Is** all the counsel° that we two **have shared**—
	The sisters' vows, the hours that we **have spent**
reprimanded	When we **have chid**° the hasty-**footed** time
	For **parting** us—O, **is** all quite **forgot**? 10
	All schooldays' friendship, childhood innocence?
	We, Hermia, like two artificial gods,[61]

---

61 artificial gods: gods of artifice, or art (in this case, embroidery)

Have with our needles **created** both one flower,

Both on one sampler, **sitting** on one cushion,

Both **warbling** of one song, both in one key,   15

As if our hands, our sides, voices, and minds,

Had been incorporate.[62] So we **grew** together,

Like to a double cherry: **seeming parted**,

But yet an union in partition,

Two lovely berries **molded** on one stem.   20

So, with two **seeming** bodies but one heart,

Two of the first[63]—like coats in heraldry,

Due but to one and **crowned** with one crest.

rip   And **will** you **rend**° our ancient love asunder,

To **join** with men in **scorning** your poor friend?   25

It **is** not friendly, 'tis not maidenly.

Our sex as well as I may **chide** you for it,

Though I alone **do feel** the injury.

(3.2.193–220)

Remarkably, the sense of the speech emerges immediately, even from a cold reading, when the verbs are allowed to lead the way. The verbs carry Helena all the way through her thought process. First they communicate her love for her friend (we *have shared* counsel, we *have spent* hours, we *have chid* time for *parting* us, we *grew* together, we *had been incorporate*, we are *crowned* with one crest). Then they etch Hermia's betrayal (*rend* our ancient

---

62 incorporate: i.e., of one body

63 of the first: this phrase refers to heraldry. In a coat of arms, the *first* is the image in the upper-left quadrant, which is often duplicated elsewhere. Helena means that even though she and Hermia are two separate people, they share one common identity.

love, *join* with men, *scorning* [her] poor friend). Finally, they portray Helena's anger and heartbreak (I may *chide* you, I alone *do feel* the injury). Practice this speech a few times, allowing the verbs to pull you through the full spectrum of Helena's feeling.

A second speech comes from *Henry VI, Part One.*

The English army has laid siege to the French town of Orleans, where the French king's son, known as the Dauphin, has his headquarters. Certain that there's no way he can turn back the English forces, the Dauphin is about to surrender. But just then, word reaches him of a young shepherdess, Joan la Pucelle (a.k.a. Joan of Arc), who claims to have been sent by heaven to help the French. She arrives, tells the Dauphin who she is, explains how God blessed her with supernatural powers, and welcomes the Dauphin to challenge her to a fight to prove that she is genuine.

Once more, work through the speech line by line, letting the verbs carry the argument forward.

	Dauphin, I **am** by birth a shepherd's daughter,
	My wit **untrained** in any kind of art.
	Heaven and our Lady gracious[64] **hath** it **pleased**
low social standing	To **shine** on my contemptible estate.°
	Lo, whilst I **waited** on my tender lambs, 5
	And to sun's **parching** heat **displayed** my cheeks,
	God's mother **deigned** to **appear** to me
	And in a vision full of majesty
	Willed me to **leave** my base vocation
	And **free** my country from calamity. 10

....

64 our Lady gracious: i.e., the Virgin Mary

Her aid she **promised** and **assured** success.

In complete glory she **revealed** herself;

swarthy; dark complected And, whereas I **was** black and swart° before,

shone With those clear rays which she **infused**° on me

That beauty **am** I **blessed** with which you **see**. 15

Ask me what question thou canst possible,

And I **will answer unpremeditated**.

My courage **try** by combat, if thou **darest**,

And thou **shalt find** that I **exceed** my sex.

be certain of **Resolve** on° this: thou **shalt** be fortunate,   20

If thou **receive** me for thy warlike mate.⁶⁵

(1.3.51–71)

The verbs describing Joan's vision of the Virgin Mary express brilliantly the drama of her religious rapture. Joan *waited* on her innocent sheep, her face *displayed* to the *parching* sun, when Mary *deigned* to *appear*, then *willed* her to *leave* her flock and *free* the country, *promised* and *assured* of success. Give those words their full weight, and Joan—and you—will be full of feeling. (Joan is not the only one who is enraptured. The Dauphin is stunned by her speech, and he lets loose a great verb when she's done: "Thou *hast astonished* me with thy high terms.")

Fifteen years or so after writing *Henry VI, Part One*, deep in his late period, Shakespeare wrote *Cymbeline*. In the following speech, the play's comic villain, a dangerous prince named Cloten (rhymes with "rotten"), declares his "love" and "hate" (antithesis!) for Imogen, his stepsister. She is a beautiful princess,

---

65 mate: partner, with the overtone of "lover"

which is why he loves her, but she is in love with another man,
Posthumus, which is why he hates her.

because	I **love** and **hate** her. For° she**'s** fair and royal,
features	And that she **hath** all courtly parts° more exquisite
	Than lady, ladies, woman—from every one
	The best she **hath**, and she, of all **compounded**,[66]
	Outsells[67] them all—I **love** her therefore; but 5
	Disdaining me and **throwing** favors on
insults, discredits	The low Posthumus, **slanders**° so her judgment
otherwise	That what's else° rare is **choked**; and in that point
	I **will conclude** to **hate** her, nay, indeed,
	To **be revenged** upon her. 10

(3.5.70–79)

As the speech progresses, Cloten's verbs turn angry, violent,
nasty. He's a brute of a guy, and his language reflects that. (Before
the play is over, he will have his head chopped off by a savage
in the wilderness.) *Disdaining, throwing, slanders, choked, hate, revenged*—by letting those verbs really rip in all their menace and
thuggery, you will connect with the ferociousness of Cloten's
feelings.

Energizing his verbs—saying his words—*thinking his thoughts*—
will lead to feeling his emotions and living his experiences.

Let the verbs do their stuff!

....

66 **of all compounded:** i.e., composed of all of them

67 **Outsells:** i.e., exceeds in value

....

THINGS FURTHER THOUGHT ON

....

NSP?

One of the most oft-repeated pieties of acting Shakespeare is what I call the NSP Rule: Never Stress Pronouns.

Theater folk may disagree about everything from playing to the punctuation to splitting abutted consonants. But when it comes to handling pronouns, there's near-universal agreement. *Never stress 'em.*

Thinking Shakespeareans should not aspire to be contrarian. But the NSP Rule is ripe for a serious challenge.

Consider the Cassius speech we analyzed in this chapter. It has over fifty pronouns in its forty-two lines. Beat out the meter of the speech, and you'll find that sixteen of these fall in positions of stress according to iambic pentameter. Allowing for the usual syncopation of the language and the frequent departures from the meter as they seek the natural scansion of the lines, most actors will find about a half dozen pronouns here that simply *must be stressed* for the speech to make sense. Those are:

you	line 4
I	line 7
I,, you	line 8
he	line 10
I	line 26

Try these lines aloud.

I cannot tell what you and other men
Think of this life; but for my single self   5
I had as lief not be, as live to be
In awe of such a thing as I myself.
I was born free as Caesar, so were you.
We both have fed as well, and we can both
Endure the winter's cold as well as he.   10
    . . .
Ay, as Aeneas our great ancestor   23
Did from the flames of Troy upon his shoulder
The old Anchises bear, so from the waves of Tiber   25
Did I the tired Caesar . . .

NSP? Not in these cases. Except for "I" at the beginning of line 8, all of these pronouns fall in places of iambic stress. That "I" gets stress because it is one half of an antithesis with "you" at the end of line 8; both words need emphasis (and the line therefore starts with a trochee). "You" has to be stressed as well—it's the word that's antithetical to "I," and the thought is not clear if both aren't heard. "He" gets stress in line 10 because it is the antithesis of "we" in line 9 (and some actors might well argue that the first "we" in that line should be stressed too), and Cassius's entire point depends on the comparison between himself and Brutus on one hand ("we"), and Caesar on the other ("he"). All these, then, are pronouns that simply must be stressed.

The other forty-odd pronouns in the speech do not get stress. In general, pronouns are the low men on the Shakespearean parts-of-speech totem pole. Verbs do the heavy lifting and get lots of stress, nouns are all-important, adjectives can communicate color and vividness, but pronouns are usually best left alone. That's why so many people are inclined to stick to the NSP Rule.

But *never* stressing pronouns is extreme. There are always exceptions. Certain other features of the lines may force stress to fall on a pronoun—features such as antithesis, meter, or the demands of clarity of thought. Most pronouns live out their Shakespearean lives in quiet anonymity. But plenty of their kin demand to be underlined for the thinking to come clear.

With that in mind, let's ditch the NSP Rule in favor of another: GASPBCSOCRYDS. Generally Avoid Stressing Pronouns, But Check to See if Other Considerations Require You to Do So.

Names on Billboards

Shakespeare is very interested in his characters' names. He frequently seems amused and a little amazed that one word represents an entire human being, in all his or her complexity. In *Henry VI, Part One*, merely the name of a great English general causes a French city to fall in battle. A delighted English soldier tells us:

> The cry of "Talbot" serves me for a sword,
> For I have loaded me with many spoils,
> Using no other weapon but his name.
>
> (2.1.81–83)

In *Henry IV, Part Two*, we hear how reinforcements abandoned Hotspur, another incredibly gifted English military man, at a crucial moment in battle, with the result that "Nothing but the sound of Hotspur's name / Did seem defensible" (2.3.37–38) (i.e., Hotspur's name was the only thing capable of providing defense).

In *Hamlet*, the prince takes a fateful voyage to England during which he foils Claudius's attempt to have him killed by turning the tables on his would-be assassins, Rosencrantz and Guildenstern, killing them instead. (Poor Rosencrantz and Guildenstern are "hoist with their own petard," in the prince's familiar phrase.) When Hamlet arrives back in his native Denmark, he emerges from the shadows to proclaim, "This is I, Hamlet the Dane!" (5.1.241) His own name has power now. By calling himself "the Dane"—i.e., the Danish monarch—he takes on the full authority of kingship. (And he stresses the pronoun "I" while he's doing it.)

And in *Romeo and Juliet*, Juliet famously mulls the power of names, wondering,

why	O Romeo, Romeo, wherefore° art thou Romeo?
	Deny thy father and refuse thy name,
	Or if thou wilt not, be but sworn my love,
	And I'll no longer be a Capulet . . .
	'Tis but thy name that is my enemy.
	Thou art thyself, though not a Montague.
	What's Montague? It is nor hand, nor foot,
	Nor arm, nor face, nor any other part
	Belonging to a man. O, be some other name!
	What's in a name? That which we call a rose
	By any other word would smell as sweet.
	So Romeo would, were he not Romeo called,
owns	Retain that dear perfection which he owes°
	Without that title. Romeo, doff [68] thy name,

_____

68 doff: remove (as if it were a hat)

And for that name—which is no part of thee—
Take all myself.

(2.1.74–91)

Names have magic in Shakespeare. Respect them. Whenever you say a name—especially if you are the first to speak another character's name in the play—give it special prominence, highlighting the peculiar power that simple word has to represent an entire human being.

There is an acting term that describes giving a word particular prominence: *billboarding*. It was taught to me by Mark Linn-Baker, the great comic actor who was a brilliant Touchstone in my production of *As You Like It*. In Act III of the play, Touchstone decides to take his relationship with Audrey, the "country wench" he has fallen for, to the next level. "I will marry thee," he tells her, "and to that end I have been with Sir Oliver Martext, the vicar of the next village, who hath promised to meet me in this place of the forest, and to couple us." These lines mark the first time the audience hears the vicar's name, and I asked Mark to underline "Martext," which is a pun that captures how inept the guy is. Here's how our conversation went.

MARK	Oh, you want me to billboard it.
BARRY	What?
MARK	Billboard it. Y'know, say it as though it were up on a billboard in Times Square.
BARRY	Um . . .
MARK	COCA-COLA! KODAK! PANASONIC!
BARRY	That's called "billboarding"?
MARK	Yup.

BARRY   Hm. (*pause*) Well, then. As I was saying, I think
             you should billboard Sir Oliver Martext.

MARK   No problem.—I will marry thee; and to that
             end I have been with SIR OLIVER MARTEXT,
             the vicar of the next village, who hath promised
             to meet me in this place of the forest, and to
             couple us.

....

THINKING SHAKESPEARE RULE: Billboard all names (those of
both people and places), especially if you are the first person
in the play to say that name.

....

CHAPTER
—№—
11

BUT HOW DO YOU REALLY FEEL?

IRONY, WIT, HUMOR, AND EMOTION

One of my favorite passages in Shakespeare is a still and quiet moment just prior to the violent climax of *Othello*.

It's late at night in Cyprus, on the military garrison Othello has come from Venice to defend against a Turkish invasion. Desdemona, Othello's wife, at a loss to understand why her husband has so angrily accused her of betraying him, waits apprehensively in their room for him to come to bed. Emilia, Desdemona's friend and chambermaid, is helping her mistress get changed into her night clothes. The two women make small talk, avoiding the real issues weighing on their minds. Desdemona remembers Lodovico, the Venetian diplomat who came to visit Cyprus earlier in the day. "This Lodovico is a proper man," she says (4.3.33). Emilia agrees:

"A very handsome man." But Desdemona didn't quite mean that he was good looking. She corrects her companion: "He speaks well."

When I directed *Othello*, this line always grabbed me. It still does whenever I see a production of the play. I find it very touching. This innocent young woman, who seems to sense that her already anxious situation will only get worse, still manages a moment of kindness, paying a sweet compliment to a man she little knows.

The nature of that compliment is revealing. In one of his great speeches earlier in the play, Othello says he used to spend hours at Desdemona's house, telling stories of the many dramatic episodes in his life. Through relating these tales—by "speaking well"—Othello made Desdemona fall madly in love with him. Lodovico's good speaking apparently had the same effect on another young woman, as Emilia notes: "I know a lady in Venice would have walked barefoot to Palestine for a touch of his nether lip." (4.3.33–37)

In Shakespeare, men who speak well get the girl. Good looks don't hurt. Wealth is attractive too, and power adds appeal. Warmth, generosity, charisma—all are helpful.

But *speaking well* is the kicker.

Talking the Talk

Shakespeare's characters speak well.

Moreover, time and again, characters in Shakespeare actually *talk about* how well they speak. They note pithy turns of phrase. They quote one another. They call attention to their own eloquence (as Salerio does with "as it were," and "in a word" in the excerpt from *Merchant* we studied in chapter 6) and to the eloquence of others.

How can we describe that aspect of Shakespearean speech Desdemona calls "speaking well"? What is it about the "special providence in the fall of a sparrow" that makes us say of the man who utters that phrase, "Gosh, he sure speaks well"? What makes us swoon for Rosalind or wish we had a friend like Falstaff or volunteer to follow King Henry V into battle? Can we give their quality of speech a label?

The Elizabethans had one. Wit.

Wit, Whither Wilt?

These days, the word *wit* is associated almost exclusively with humor. A witty person is quick with a joke or an amusing bit of light banter. But 400 years ago, the word *wit* had broader implications. It referred not just to comedic chops, but also to general intellectual acuity. A person's wit was her intelligence, insight, power of observation, and ability to size up a situation in an instant. [69]

Most important for Shakespearean actors, wit meant not just perception but also *the ability to express one's thoughts about what one perceived* in a diverting, incisive, and memorable manner.

Wit is that very particular quality of mind that boggles us when we hear a Shakespearean character speak. "He speaks well"? That's right. Because he has wit.

---

[69] People in Shakespeare's time believed that everyone had five types of wit, not just one. (In *King Lear*, Edgar, disguised as the mad Poor Tom, tells the king, "Bless thy five wits!") This belief reached all the way back to Aristotle. The five wits are common sense, imagination, fantasy (i.e., artistic invention or creativity), judgment, and memory. (In *Much Ado about Nothing*, Beatrice remembers a time when she got in a verbal battle with Benedick, and "four of his five wits came halting off"—i.e., were crippled. For 400 years, scholars have been trying to guess which one survived uninjured.)

We have seen plenty of examples of wit in earlier chapters of *Thinking Shakespeare*. When Cassius says, "I had as lief not be as live to be / In awe of such a thing as I myself," he is being witty, not only by punning on the similar-sounding words "lief" and "live," but by calling himself (and, by clever implication, Caesar) a "thing." When the Archbishop of Canterbury describes how the bees "with merry march" bring their loot home to the hive, and how the sad-eyed justice has a "surly hum," he is being witty, anthropomorphizing bees and ascribing to one of their chief citizens a distinctly bee-like sound. When Portia says that she is unpracticed and unschooled, but not too dull and not too old, and that the full sum of herself is the sum of something, she is being incredibly witty. She manages to remain charmingly self-deprecating even as she executes some showy verbal gymnastics. When Exeter says that England has "pretty traps to catch the petty thieves," he is being witty. When Westmoreland compares England to an eagle and Scotland to a weasel, he is being witty. When Richard Gloucester talks about his deformity with an arch euphemism about being "unfinished," he is being witty, just as he is with his outrageous claim that his profound ugliness causes dogs to yelp when he walks past them.

This list could go on and on. Eventually it would encompass nearly every single line in the plays.

Wit abounds in Shakespeare. The word itself occurs several hundred times in his canon. Linguistic cleverness and ear-catching inventiveness are quite simply *everywhere*.

Wit and Heart

Michael Langham, that great Shakespearean director whom we met in Things Further Thought On after chapter 7, coined a phrase that wittily captures wit's importance in Shakespeare's plays. He said (with an expert use of antithesis), "You act Chekhov with your heart. But you act Shakespeare with your wit."

I hear copies of *Thinking Shakespeare* dropping to the floor from the hands of acting students everywhere.

Isn't emotion the center of the actor's work? Didn't Stanislavski and Strasberg and Meisner and every acting teacher of the past 100 years dedicate their lives to helping actors create real emotion on stage?

Certainly. Feeling is an indispensable component of an actor's job. Langham's dictum means not that there is no heart in Shakespeare, or no wit in Chekhov. But it does mean that in Shakespeare, *wit comes first*. In classical material, feeling must be balanced with the understanding that *what the character says* is as important as what he feels. In classical acting, the way in which a character expresses his thoughts points to the nature, texture, and emotions of the thoughts themselves.

Before we spin off into the stratosphere of theory, though, let's turn to Shakespeare for a concrete illustration of exactly what this means.

REHEARSAL TIME

Here is one of the most famous speeches in the canon—one of the Shakespeare Top Ten—preceded by the less famous lines that cue it in. It's from *As You Like It*, one of the wittiest of the plays, and one overtly concerned with witticism and how wonderful and easy it is to fall in love with someone who is truly witty. This speech is a great laboratory for exploring the challenges and rewards of Shakespearean wit.

Duke Senior and his men, who live in the Forest of Arden in heartbreaking exile from the royal court, have just been accosted by Orlando, a young man desperate for food for himself and his friend, an old man who, he says, is starving nearly to death. On the verge of tears, Orlando practically begs the duke, who grants help and sends him to fetch his friend so they can both be nursed back to health. As soon as Orlando goes, the duke speaks to Jaques, a lord in the duke's company, who has observed the entire exchange.

DUKE SENIOR   Thou seest we are not all alone unhappy:
               This wide and universal theater
               Presents more woeful pageants[70] than the scene
               Wherein we play in.

JAQUES[71]   All the world's a stage,
               And all the men and women merely players: 5
               They have their exits and their entrances;
               And one man in his time plays many parts,
               His acts being seven ages. At first the infant,
crying   Mewling° and puking in the nurse's arms.
               And then the whining school-boy, with his satchel,   10
               And shining morning face, creeping like snail
               Unwillingly to school. And then the lover,
               Sighing like furnace,[72] with a woeful ballad

---

70 **woeful pageants:** sad spectacles

71 **Jaques:** the French pronunciation "zhahk" is not used. Instead, the name is pronounced as though it were English: JAY-queez.

72 **Sighing like furnace:** i.e., sighing very heavily; sighing as much as a furnace giving off hot air

Made to his mistress's eyebrow. Then a soldier,

Full of strange oaths, and bearded like the pard,[73] 15

Jealous in honor,[74] sudden and quick in quarrel,

Seeking the bubble[75] reputation

Even in the cannon's mouth. And then the justice,

In fair round belly with good capon[76] lined,

With eyes severe, and beard of formal cut, 20

sayings Full of wise saws° and modern[77] instances;

And so he plays his part. The sixth age shifts

Into the lean and slippered pantaloon,[78]

With spectacles on nose and pouch on side,

stockings; socks His youthful hose° well saved, a world too wide 25

lower leg; calf For his shrunk shank;° and his big manly voice,

Turning again toward childish treble, pipes

i.e., its And whistles in his° sound. Last scene of all,

That ends this strange eventful history,

utter; total Is second childishness and mere° oblivion, 30

without (French) Sans° teeth, sans eyes, sans taste, sans everything.

(2.7.135–165)

....

73 **pard:** leopard, whose whiskers the soldier's beard resembles

74 **Jealous in honor:** i.e., extremely particular, even angrily so, where questions of honor are concerned

75 **bubble:** an image of something temporary and ultimately insubstantial

76 **capon:** a kind of chicken, raised to be very fatty—an expensive delicacy. The implication is that the judge has grown fat from eating rich meals, presumably given to him as bribes to influence his decisions.

77 **modern:** new—and, by implication, not so wise

78 **pantaloon:** i.e., a silly old man; specifically, a stock character from the Italian *commedia dell'arte* tradition

Our first impression of Jaques? He speaks well. His remarkable speech is built upon a dazzling flight of wit: human life is like theater, he says, and all human beings are like actors playing parts that unfold in seven acts. (Flashback to chapter 4: that seven-part list is the organizing principle that structures Jaques's argument.) Jaques's powers of observation are phenomenal. We recognize ourselves or people we know in every one of his Seven Ages. And his gift of language allows him to paint pictures of these types with penetrating, even ferocious, precision. Each age is rendered with economy, yet each is replete with dense detail:

1. The infant screams and vomits in its nanny's arms.
2. The schoolboy with the freshly washed face walks ever so slowly to school, a place he hates.
3. The lover sighs like a windbag and writes elaborate poems about silly things, such as his girlfriend's eyebrow: "Ohhhh, my love! Thine eyebrows are magical rainbows in the sky of my heart!"
4. The solider curses a lot, has a bizarre animal-like beard, cares only about honor, gets angry quickly and picks lots of fights, and worries so much about his reputation (as fleeting as that is) that he is willing to risk being fired upon in order to burnish it.
5. The justice is fat and stern and spouts endless streams of canned wisdom and newfangled nonsense.
6. The skinny old man, with thick eyeglasses, an odd handbag, and a thin, reedy voice, saves the clothes he wore in his youth and tries them on now and then, even though they look ridiculous hanging on his shriveled form.

7. The senile invalid is blind, toothless, and completely out of it.

In the lines that precede Jaques's speech, the duke makes the same basic argument that Jaques does: the world is like a theater. But the duke's language is generic and bland, devoid of color and specificity. No wonder we remember Jaques's speech rather than the duke's. Jaques is the witty one. His imagery—the schoolboy inching his way to school, the lover writing earnest and absurd poetry, the tough solider so concerned with his reputation that he puts himself in harm's way just to enhance it—sketches funny and truthful vignettes. His turns of phrase are incredibly winning, and Jaques himself, beguiling. Like Emilia's lady friend, we would walk barefoot to Palestine just for a touch of him.

You act Shakespeare with your wit. You can't play Jaques without it.

WHERE'S THE FEELING?   But what about your heart? As amusing as he is, Jaques also has a dark view of life. None of his Seven Ages has much room for happiness; each features some form of ridiculousness, misery, or embarrassment. Is Jaques simply a cold cynic, a misanthrope who sees other people as self-deluded, vain, and destined only for decay? Why is he talking like this? *Why is he using these words now?*

Read the rest of the play and you will discover a character deeply invested in humanity. Jaques likes nothing more than observing people, analyzing their idiosyncrasies, and talking with them and about them. He sees the world as sick with the disease of foolishness, and he regards himself as a kind of physician whose life's work is to cure the ills of humanity by lashing out at them with his considerable wit. "Give me leave / To speak my mind," he urges the duke a few lines earlier, "and I will through and through / Cleanse the foul body of th'infected world / If they will patiently receive my medicine." It pains Jaques that people are so silly and that life is ultimately so futile. His love of humanity is what fuels his harsh diagnosis of its problems. He thrives on the very spectrum of human existence that he dismisses so savagely in his most famous speech. His excess of wit expresses his excess of emotional attachment.

Work through the speech again, one line at a time, and listen in particular to how its height drops drastically at the end. Those amazing monosyllables—*sans. teeth. sans. eyes. sans. taste.*—slow Jaques to the snail's pace of the reluctant schoolboy. They toll like a funeral bell, ringing out in somber tones all the pain Jaques feels. It tears him apart that every man's destiny is infirmity, and that the sum total of life is oblivion.

The simultaneous presence of humor and darkness is what makes this speech such an interesting conundrum. The wit on the surface interacts with the pain underneath, masking it, covering it, deflecting it, and giving it purpose. And the dark vision at the speech's heart sharpens the wit into a lacerating verbal weapon. Jaques's wit exists not in the absence of his heart but because his heart beats so strongly. The wit and the pain are intertwined, wrapped around each other in a double helix of Shakespearean poetry.

That's what Michael Langham's advice leaves unsaid. Shakespeare contains both wit and heart, as does Chekhov. *But they exist in relationship to each other.*

Joe's Irish Coffee

The great producer Joseph Papp, founder of New York's renowned Public Theater and its equally famous and widely imitated

Shakespeare in the Park, is one of the heroes of American Shakespeare. I had the privilege to work for him in the last few years of his life. Now and then he would stop everything in his busy day and simply recite Shakespeare. He wasn't a bad actor, and he had dozens of speeches in his head, letter perfect. But he didn't simply quote lines. He also talked about how Shakespeare worked, and how to do the plays.

One night before a performance of *The Taming of the Shrew* in Central Park (Morgan Freeman played Petruchio and Tracey Ullman played Kate; I was fresh out of school and was lucky to be the assistant director), Mr. Papp told me that the key to the play, and to all of Shakespeare's comedies, was that they were like Irish coffee.

I knew that drink was a mix of strong java and hot whiskey topped with sweet cream, but what did Irish coffee have to do with this play? It took me a few years to understand what Mr. Papp meant: underneath the frothy cream of Shakespeare's comedies lie dark, murky depths.

Irish coffee is the perfect metaphor for the relationship between wit and emotion in the plays. Where there's cream on top, there's got to be coffee underneath. The spectacular and seemingly effortless brightness of Shakespeare's wit almost always rests atop a turbulent, roiling emotional undercurrent. In fact, in general, the more dazzling the wit, the more intense the subterranean passions.

....

THINKING SHAKESPEARE RULE: Always look for the depths of feeling underneath the witty language of Shakespearean speech.

....

Cassius's Bitter Brew

When Cassius describes Caesar's "fever when he was in Spain," he says, "His coward lips did from their color fly." On one level, the line is simply descriptive: Caesar's lips turned pale as he fell ill. But these are not regular lips; they are cowardly lips. They didn't merely grow ashen; they flew from color to paleness. The image suggests an army in retreat: soldiers are said to "fly from their colors" when they turn and run away from their own flags. In one phrase, Cassius manages to say "he turned pale," "he's a coward," and "he's always retreating from difficult battles." It's a breathtakingly witty line.

And it's a layer of cream on top of the bitterest coffee. Cassius hates Caesar deeply and passionately. He cannot believe that such a misfit would presume that he could rule all of Rome. Cassius's furious hatred sparks something deep in the language center of his brain and drives his words to a level of high and lacerating wit.

The key for the actor is to let the line be witty. Avoid allowing the hatred underneath to overwhelm the wit, so that we get 100% coffee and 0% cream. Feel all that hatred, but express it in the form of a funny and cutting remark.

Where the Coffee Meets the Cream

Had Shakespeare met Joseph Papp (and I like to think he has, in the outdoor theater of the afterlife), I believe he would have enjoyed that Irish coffee metaphor. Shakespeare is fascinated by the links between emotion and wit. Indeed, you might say that his writing method involves placing his characters right on the boundary of the cream and the coffee. That line shifts a lot. But Shakespeare lives astride it.

The contrast between the surface luster of the language and the submerged emotion burbling beneath it generates a particular charge of energy that is the life force of Shakespearean characterization. We feel that energy in Cassius, for example, as he whets the blade of his fury into a knife of wit.

We also feel it in Hamlet, when he leaps with Laertes into Ophelia's grave and competes with him in a contest of incontinent grief. Laertes has called out to be buried with his sister under a huge mountain of earth, but Hamlet does him one better:

> Be buried quick with her and so will I.
> And if thou prate of mountains, let them throw
> Millions of acres on us, till our ground,
> Singeing his pate against the burning zone,
> Make Ossa like a wart.

(5.1.264–268)

Hamlet is saying, in paraphrase, "Go ahead, be buried alive with her. I will be too. And if you want to rant about mountains, then let them throw millions of acres of earth on top of us, until this plot of land grows so tall that it burns its head on the sun; until it makes Mt. Everest look like a pimple." [79] That final image is surprising, funny, and strange. It is also witty, which is astonishing in the circumstances. Hamlet feels overwhelming grief at the death of his beloved Ophelia and titanic rage at her brother's

---

[79] Ossa is the tallest mountain mentioned in Greek mythology. In one story, a group of giants decide to get to the top of Mt. Olympus, where the gods live. To achieve their goal, they lift Pelion, another mountain, atop Ossa. But they fail. Not even this stack of earthly mountains reaches as high as what Laertes calls "the skyish head of blue Olympus."

ostentatious mourning. When the pain reaches a crescendo, it comes out of him in some weird, edgy joke, in language that drips with bilious yet nimble wit.

"Make Ossa like a wart." In this single line of *Hamlet*, Shakespeare manages to contain within one character's bosom a great vastness: the yawning distance between the intensity of Hamlet's sorrow and the magnificence of his imagination. It is our privilege as an audience to spend time with a person who can hold so much in his heart, and who can find such striking words to express it. That is why we come to see the play again and again and again. The space between the profundity of his agony and the radiance of his speech is what makes Hamlet, Hamlet.

That shadowy border zone where coffee meets cream is what Shakespeare is all about.

Isn't That Ironic?

Literature has a word for the distance between what we feel and what we say: *irony*.

You are on your way home from a vacation. Your plane is delayed. When it leaves, you are seated next to a wailing baby for five hours. There is terrible turbulence. The movie is one you hate. The airline forgets that you ordered a vegetarian meal. Then they lose your luggage. Finally, you get home. A friend asks, "How was the flight?" You answer, deadpan, "It was the most enjoyable journey I've ever taken."

You say one thing even though you mean another. There is a gap between the words you use and the feeling you have. That is irony.

Shakespeare deploys it in all of his plays, sometimes savagely, sometimes hilariously, but always to tremendous effect.

MORE REHEARSAL TIME

Another of Shakespeare's Top Ten speeches is also one of the greatest illustrations of his use of irony. It comes from *Richard II*, a play we encountered in chapter 9 while analyzing John of Gaunt and his phenomenal sense of rhythm.

Remember that Gaunt is scathingly angry about how King Richard has plunged England into economic insolvency by borrowing too much money. Richard incurred this massive debt to finance, among other things, a huge increase in military spending, primarily so that he can invade Ireland to suppress an anti-British uprising there. While Richard is away leading his army into battle, Gaunt's son, Henry Bolingbroke (BAH-ling-brook), stokes the national hatred of the king into a full-fledged rebellion that most of the ruling elites in the country eventually join. When Richard returns home, a series of messengers inform him of all the great men who have gone over to Bolingbroke's side. It becomes clear that Bolingbroke is unstoppable. He will certainly usurp the throne, seize the crown, and put Richard to death. Richard absorbs the devastating news while two of his last remaining supporters—the Duke of Aumerle, son of the still-loyal Duke of York, and the Bishop of Carlisle—stand with him. The young Aumerle holds out hope that his father will come to the rescue. "Comfort, my liege," he says twice to the king. Then, desperate, he asks, "Where is the duke my father with his power?" Here is King Richard's famous answer.

No matter where. Of comfort no man speak.
Let's talk of graves, of worms and epitaphs,

Make dust our paper, and with rainy eyes[80]

Write sorrow on the bosom of the earth.

Let's choose executors and talk of wills—   5

And yet not so, for what can we bequeath

Save our deposed[81] bodies to the ground?

Our lands, our lives and all are Bolingbroke's;

And nothing can we call our own but death,

And that small model[82] of the barren earth   10

Which serves as paste[83] and cover to our bones.

For God's sake, let us sit upon the ground

And tell sad stories of the death of kings—

How some have been deposed, some slain in war,

Some haunted by the ghosts they have deposed,   15

Some poisoned by their wives, some sleeping killed,

All murdered. For within the hollow crown

encircles   That rounds° the mortal temples of a king

jester   Keeps Death his court; and there the antic° sits,

Scoffing his state[84] and grinning at his pomp,   20

Allowing him a breath, a little scene,

To monarchize,[85] be feared, and kill with looks,[86]

---

80 rainy eyes: i.e., eyes wet with tears

81 deposed: Note that the word scans with three syllables here—de-POS-ed—but with only two syllables at the end of line 15. (One reason is because in this line the word is a past participle [a verb used as an adjective], whereas in 15 it's part of the normal past tense verb phrase that makes up the predicate of the subject "they.")

82 model: parcel; small piece; i.e., Richard's grave

83 paste: a thick mixture of clay and water used in pottery, or perhaps a pastry shell that surrounds a filling. Richard imagines the earth enveloping him in his grave.

84 Scoffing his state: i.e., mocking his formal bearing

85 monarchize: i.e., act like a monarch

86 kill with looks: i.e., sentence people to death with nothing more than a glance

Infusing him with self and vain conceit,[87]
As if this flesh which walls about our life
Were brass impregnable; and humored thus,[88] 25
Comes at the last, and with a little pin
Bores through his castle wall; and farewell, king.
Cover your heads,[89] and mock not flesh and blood
With solemn reverence. Throw away respect,
Tradition, form, and ceremonious duty, 30
For you have but mistook me all this while.
I live with bread, like you; feel want,
Taste grief, need friends. Subjected thus,[90]
How can you say to me I am a king?

(3.2.140–173)

This great speech is so rich that it merits a whole chapter of
Thinking Shakespeare. Here, though, our focus is on irony—the
difference between how Richard feels and what he says.

How he feels is obvious: sad. He wants to sit and tell melancholy stories, talk about graves, make out his will, and write
his epitaph on the ground by weeping bitter tears into the dust.
Look closely at the end of the speech: lines 32 through 34. These
amazing monosyllables sound a dirge of woe from a man who is
grief-stricken, lonely, and afraid.

....

87 **Infusing . . . conceit:** i.e., filling him with ego and vanity

88 **humored thus:** i.e., and Death having enjoyed himself in this way

89 **Cover your heads:** put your hats back on (said to Aumerle and Carlisle, who have
removed theirs as a sign of respect to the king, their superior)

90 **Subjected thus:** exposed to these things in this way; also a pun meaning, roughly,
"transformed by all this into a mere subject, as opposed to a king."

But look at lines 17 through 27. Here is a paraphrase:

> Inside the circular crown that surrounds the all-too-human skull
> of a king, Death presides over a royal court of his own. And that
> clown sits there, making fun of the king's dignified behavior and
> laughing at what a big shot the king thinks he is. Death grants him
> a few short breaths, a brief performance, in which he can act regal,
> intimidate people, and have them killed with a mere glance. Death
> fills the king with thoughts of vanity and self-importance, as if his
> flesh-and-blood body were actually made of brass—impenetrable
> and invulnerable. Then, having amused himself in this way, Death
> makes his appearance at last, and with nothing more powerful than
> a tiny pin, drills through the skull, and, "*Ciao*, King-o!"

Sad? Not quite. Savage? Yes. Bitter? You bet. *Ironic*? A text-book case!

Richard articulates a vision of life that is absurd and darkly comic. Imagine: a king, the mightiest man alive, who can murder simply by batting an eye, is no more than a plaything for Death, who is not some sickle-wielding specter, but is instead a jester, a fool, a farceur. The distance between the reality of things as Richard knows them and the black humor of the way he presents them here is the essence of irony. When we expect sadness, we get bitter comedy. That is vintage Shakespeare.

Richard is doing with this ironic image precisely what Jaques does in the "Seven Ages of Man" speech: using his wit to push down his dread and terror. Irony is a defense mechanism used to ward off overwhelming grief.

Try the speech again, working not on the sadness of Richard in defeat but the caustic and bitter humor of his view of kingship.

Let wit cut through the grief just like a bright beacon through a foggy night.

What you'll discover is this: just as there is coffee underneath the cream, there is cream atop the coffee. That is, just as darkness runs underneath Shakespeare's comedies, humor shines out of his tragedies. Not that every tragedy is a comedy, of course. *King Lear* is hardly a barrel of laughs. Yet even Lear cracks a string of horrifying jokes when he first spots his old friend Gloucester stumbling around blind. Time and again in that play, and in *Julius Caesar* and *Othello* and *Hamlet* and even *Macbeth*, wit and irony surprise us and keep us on our toes. In the same way that Shakespeare's rhythm always changes to stave off monotony, his tone shifts constantly for the same purpose. And, remarkably, the injection of levity actually deepens the tragedy. It provides relief. It gives us something against which to measure our pain.

....

THINKING SHAKESPEARE RULE: Always look for the humor in Shakespeare's darkest moments.

....

Many Witticisms, Great Emotion

These lines about the antic Death sitting atop the king's head are not the only witty ones in the speech. Near its start, Richard's list of funereal items he wants to discuss—graves, worms, epitaphs, dust, sorrow, executors, wills—generates a tone of over-the-top exaggeration. It sounds like an extravagant, childish temper tantrum: "I don't wanna talk about comfort! I wanna talk about death and dying and burials and eulogies and coffins and mortuaries and undertakers!" The excessiveness is itself a kind of irony. Richard's ceaseless invention expresses his determination to make light of his desperate circumstances even as it demonstrates his fixation on them. Once again, his wit serves simultaneously to give voice to his pain and also to distance himself from it.

The same is true of lines 14 through 17, which contain Richard's list of how kings die. He says they are always murdered: overthrown, killed in battle, whacked by their wives, done in while sleeping, or haunted to death by the ghosts of the kings they knocked off to get the crown for themselves. According to Richard, no king has ever died of a heart attack, old age, prostate cancer, or a fall from a horse. Richard admits no possibility for royal death other than the fate about to befall him—extreme violence. This is another great stretch of ironic wit. The outlandish one-sidedness of the images generates a comic tone that even veers perilously close to camp.

Thinking Shakespearean actors know not to fall into the trap of playing sadness just because the situation is sad. When the language is funny, *let it be*, especially when the given circumstances seem most unbearable.

When you read Richard's speech with wit and irony in mind, the sad stories Richard wants to tell turn out to be not that sad after all. Or, more precisely, they turn out to be unbearably sad, but their dolefulness is leavened by a mind racing to intercept the pain before it reaches the heart. Only at the end of the speech does the true horror of the situation drop in.

The last seven lines of the speech contain as stunning a change of height in language as any in the canon. The high wit of Richard's irony crashes down into unadorned straight talk. In paraphrase, he tells Carlisle and Aumerle:

Put your hats back on. And don't mock a normal guy like me
by being worshipful and dignified in my presence. Stop being
respectful. Ignore custom, proper behavior, and elaborate
expressions of obedience. Because all this time, you've been
making a mistake. I eat bread, as you do. I feel pain. I know
what grief is. I need friends. I've been transformed into a
regular citizen by all this. So how can you call me "King"?

Those thudding monosyllables in lines 32 and 33 release the
searing agony in Richard's guts. The words come out slowly, with
effort and deep anguish. The shame burns in the king's face, and
the bishop and the duke suffer as they watch him.

I'll never forget seeing Richard Thomas, who achieved television immortality as John-boy Walton, play this role in Michael
Kahn's wonderful production at the Shakespeare Theater in
Washington, D.C., many years ago. He worked his way through
the speech with bitter glee, describing antic Death with an
acrid archness. Then everything changed. When he got to "need
friends," it was as if a hole opened in his chest and his lifeblood
poured out. He let loose a strangulated howl, a plaintive wail of
loneliness. Those two syllables seemed to take minutes to finish.
Nnnneeeeeeeeddddddd frieeeeeeeeeeeennnnndddsssss!! The hair on
the back of my neck still stands up when I think about it.

Actor and director looked at the speech and asked, *Why
is Richard saying these things now?* They recognized all the sour
wit and keen irony coursing through the first two-thirds of the
speech, and they understood the heartbreak underneath this glittering surface. They then observed the change in the language at
the speech's end and used it to express all the emotion that had
been tamped down by the earlier lines.

They used their own wits to help Shakespeare's wit work its magic.

Look for the wit in Shakespeare. Cherish it when you find it, and give it wing. It will lift Shakespeare's heaviness and deepen his lightness.

Act Shakespeare with your wit.

....

THINGS FURTHER THOUGHT ON

....

Out of One, Many

Thinking Shakespeare has made much of monosyllables. Mono-syllabic lines slow the text down and spread the iambic stress evenly across each word. They indicate central thoughts and deep emotions.

And sometimes, they come with interesting variations. Both speeches in this chapter contain one of Shakespeare's favorites—a monosyllabic line with a polysyllabic word at the end:

Sans teeth, sans eyes, sans taste, sans everything.
Our lands, our lives and all are Bolingbroke's

This pattern appears countless times in the plays. Why? What does it do?

We already know that important words often move toward the ends of lines. "Everything" and "Bolingbroke's" get special attention for that reason alone. But they also stand out because they each have three syllables, in contrast to the single-syllable words that come before them. They are more elaborate and more complicated than "sans," "teeth," "our," "lands," and "lives," so they really roar out on the heels of these slow, heavy words.

These three-syllable words also sing because of the thoughts they express. "Everything" encompasses all that we lose when we hit old age: not just our senses and our teeth but the sum total of what makes us human. We end our days sans *ev-ery-thing*. This giant word lets Jaques give voice to a hugely bleak idea.

Similarly, the word "Bolingbroke" encompasses for Richard all of the world's troubles. As far as he is concerned, *everything* awful in life, all that is frightening, hateful, violent, torturous, and loathsome, can be expressed in his rival's long, strange, and choppy name. Saying "Bolingbroke" is hard for Richard, emotionally and physically. He's like a child saying to his mother, "I—do—not—want—to—eat—this—BROCCOLI!" The word's many syllables choke him, embitter him, shake him, disgust him.[91]

Polysyllabic words at the end of monosyllabic lines always have power.

New Words and Latin Words

Some statistics about Shakespeare's use of words:

- There are 884,647 total words in the *Complete Works*.
- Shakespeare's vocabulary consists of over 17,000 words—more than four times the size of the average English speaker's.
- He uses over 7,000 unique words one time only.
- The *Oxford English Dictionary* credits him as the first to use over 3,000 words in the English language.

This last point is of special interest to actors. Shakespeare added over 3,000 words to our language!

Since actors regard Shakespeare's language as living thought rather than prewritten speech, it follows that when Shakespeare makes up a word, as far as actors are concerned, it is *the character*

---

[91] Note two more *Thinking Shakespeare* ideas in this line: Richard *billboards* a name, and he uses the Irene Worth Rule, stressing "all."

now talking who is making up that word. He has an idea he wants to express, and if no existing word will do, he will simply create one.

The word for making up a word is *neologize*, and a newly created word is called a *neologism*—from the Greek *neo* (new) and *logos* (word).

Shakespeare created many neologisms in the German style—by jamming more than one little word into one bigger compound word. "Moonbeam" and "leapfrog," believe it or not, are Shakespearean neologisms of this type.

Shakespeare also made new words by turning nouns into verbs. A famous example: Cleopatra worries, presciently, that her reputation as a great lover will be lampooned by actors in theaters around the world for generations to come. In Shakespeare's day, women were not allowed to act in public playhouses, so female characters like Cleopatra were portrayed by young boys in women's clothing. (Never mind that Cleopatra is in ancient Egypt, where there was no theater at all!) She laments,

> I shall see
> Some squeaking Cleopatra boy my greatness
> I'th'posture of a whore . . .
>
> (5.2.220–222)

Shakespeare—and, for the actor's purposes, Cleopatra—turns the noun *boy* into a verb meaning "to portray onstage by a boy playing a woman."

We saw another noun-as-verb in this chapter. Richard II turns the noun *monarch* into the verb *monarchize*, meaning, "to act like a royal ruler." Richard finds the new word himself (although, of course, Shakespeare puts it in his mouth). Here, the neologism is formed by the addition of the Latin suffix -*ize* to the noun. (Our modern English is full of such transformations: *computerize, jeopardize, prioritize,* even *Midasize.*)

Shakespeare loves to drag Latin into the English language. We've already noted that he studied the ancient language in school. He was obviously an A student, since his plays are full of Latinate words—forms derived directly from the Latin. These are not always neologisms (though many are, such as *obscene,* a word that is very familiar to us but was first used in English by Shakespeare), but Latin words and Latinate forms in Shakespeare almost always do something special. Luckily, the characters who use them tend to translate them so that the people to whom they're speaking (and the audiences who are listening) know what they mean.

For example, in *As You Like It,* Orlando complains that his overwhelming love for Rosalind makes him unable to speak:

> Can I not say, "I thank you?" My better parts
> Are all thrown down, and that which here stands up
> Is but a quintain, a mere lifeless block.

> (1.2.215–217)

A quintain is a wooden post used as a target in jousting.[92] In other words, it is just what Orlando goes on to explain it is: a lifeless block. (In rehearsal for this scene, some wag inevitably shouts, *Huh?!* after "quintain," so that Orlando is forced to define

---

[92] The word comes from the Latin *quintus,* or "fifth," which refers in this case to the section of a Roman military encampment where battle practice was held.

the word for the room, sheepishly, or peevishly, or exasperatedly. Not a bad rehearsal technique!)

Look for neologisms and Latinate forms, and know they have value for the actor.

Irony Beyond the Lines

Irony not only charts the difference between what is said and what is felt, but it also describes the difference between what is expected and what actually occurs. Shakespeare uses this kind of irony to spectacular effect.

Here is just one example.

Polysyllabic Henry Bolingbroke usurps the crown and has Richard II killed, just as Richard feared he would. But when he takes the throne under the name King Henry IV, Bolingbroke hardly enjoys it. He is wracked by guilt over murdering his way to power. Haunted by the ghost he has deposed, Henry longs to atone for his sin, and he finds a way to do so when he hears a prophecy that he will die in Jerusalem. He interprets this to mean that he should lead a crusade to the Holy Land and die, if necessary, in the glorious act of spreading Christianity far and wide. But a series of events delay the launch of his crusade, and the passing years and gnawing guilt eventually ruin his health. One day, he collapses in a small room in his castle. Aware that he is about to die, he wonders about the room where he fainted:

```
KING HENRY   Doth any name particular belong
             Unto the lodging where I first did swoon?
WARWICK      'Tis called Jerusalem, my noble lord.
KING HENRY   Laud be to God! Even there my life must end.
             It hath been prophesied to me many years
```

I should not die but in Jerusalem,
Which vainly I supposed the Holy Land;
But bear me to that chamber; there I'll lie;
In that Jerusalem shall Harry die.

(4.3.360–368)

All his life, Henry thought *Jerusalem* meant the great city holy to three world religions. But it turns out to mean some tiny room in a cold English castle. What came to pass is a long way from what was expected. Henry's dream of a redemptive death in a noble cause is mocked by the reality of an eternal sleep in an ignominious spare bedroom.

That's irony. Look for it in the way Shakespeare builds his plots and structures his stories.

THOUGHT, TEXT, AND STAGE BUSINESS

In an ironic and strangely amusing scene late in *Troilus and Cressida*, the valiant Trojan warrior Hector meets his rival Achilles the night before they are due to fight to the death on the field of battle. Like a boxer at a press conference before a title bout, Achilles boasts of the damage he's going to do and wonders aloud which parts of Hector's body he should pierce with his sword: "whether there, or there, or there?" Hector comes right back at him, predicting that he won't merely wound specific parts of Achilles. He tells his foe, "I'll kill thee everywhere, yea, o'er and o'er." Hector and Achilles are like two little boys taunting each other in the schoolyard. All that's missing is the iambic pentameter version of "Nyah nyah-nyah NYAAAAH nyah!"

Then Hector does something unexpected. Noting that a noble warrior is supposed to be above such arrogant and silly behavior, he apologizes for boasting so extravagantly: "You wisest Grecians, pardon me this brag." However, just so everyone understands that he means business, he adds this thought: "I'll endeavor deeds to match these words." (4.7.138–143)

Deeds to match words. This is the next area of inquiry in *Thinking Shakespeare.*

Lots of Stage Business

An actor in a Shakespeare play spends a great deal of stage time standing and talking, or sitting and talking, or crouching and talking, or perched in some other position and talking. In most cases, a good rule of thumb is "don't just do something, stand there." *What you say* is all-important, and it's best to minimize any physical movements that might distract from the words.

Still, every now and then, a Shakespearean actor has to quit talking and start doing. The requisite task might be simply walking on or off stage. It might be sitting in a chair or rising from one. Some characters are required to giggle on cue, others to tiptoe, others to faint, and still others to dance. Violence is common; swinging a broadsword or whipping a rapier comes up every few plays.

During the course of his play, for instance, Hamlet has to stab Polonius, leap into Ophelia's grave, swipe some musical instruments out of Rosencrantz and Guildenstern's hands, catch Yorick's skull in midair and hold it at arm's length, nick Laertes with a sword, run Claudius through (having earlier brandished a dagger above his head), and then pour some poisoned wine down his throat. On top of all this, in most productions he also has to manhandle both Ophelia and Gertrude, gallivant about the castle like a lunatic, and finally swoon into Horatio's arms in a decorous Danish version of Michelangelo's *Pietà*. In one inventive production I saw, Hamlet even tagged Elsinore's walls with some Shakespearean graffiti. That's an awful lot of activity for a guy who goes on and on about how common it is to "lose the name of action."

Given how much talking Hamlet does in the play, when, exactly, does he have the opportunity to do all this? And given the general rule that too much activity makes it hard to hear the text—an especially relevant rule in the case of words as complicated as Hamlet's—are there ways to slip all this action in so that the words keep going, uninterrupted and unobstructed?

The Almighty Line Ending

Most theater artists know this old saw: "In contemporary plays, you walk and talk at the same time, but in classical plays, you talk first, then you walk." There are a million exceptions to this truism, but, typically, they only serve to reinforce the rule's power. Shakespeare has his own version of this law, and it centers on—*surprise!*—his line endings.

Chapter 7 showed the power of line endings to shape breath, phrasing, and, ultimately, thought. Line endings make one additional, indispensable contribution. They shape *stage business*.

Nine times out of ten, when you have to do something onstage, the line ending provides the best place to do it. Need to walk from point A to point B? Do it in a line ending. Need to open a book and jot something down? Try it at a line ending. Toss a coin to a servant? Look at the line ending. Slap someone's mug? Line ending.

The springboard to thought at the end of every line is also an endlessly useful springboard to physical action.

REHEARSAL TIME

One of Shakespeare's busiest and most charming speeches comes from *The Two Gentlemen of Verona*, which may be his first play.

Proteus has written a love letter to his girlfriend Julia and given it to Julia's maid, Lucetta, to deliver. Lucetta playfully refuses to hand over the letter. She knows how much Julia loves the guy and decides to tease her a little. But Julia is too proud to reveal her feelings in front of her maid, and when she finally gets her hands on the letter, she tears it into a million pieces to prove to Lucetta how little it means to her. The instant Lucetta leaves, Julia reverses herself and pours forth regret for destroying Proteus's tender missive.

Here's what she then says and does. Cover the lines with your trusty piece of paper, and give the speech a whirl.

	O hateful hands, to tear such loving words;	
	Injurious wasps, to feed on such sweet honey	
	And kill the bees that yield it with your stings.	
separate	I'll kiss each several° paper for amends.	
	Look, here is writ "Kind Julia"—Unkind Julia,	5
as if	As° in revenge of thy ingratitude	
	I throw thy name against the bruising stones,	
	Trampling contemptuously on thy disdain.	
	And here is writ "Love-wounded Proteus."	
	Poor wounded name, my bosom as a bed	10
thoroughly, completely	Shall lodge thee till thy wound be throughly° healed;	

healing, medicinal	And thus I search [93] it with a sovereign° kiss.
	But twice or thrice was "Proteus" written down.
	Be calm, good wind, blow not a word away
	Till I have found each letter in the letter 15
	Except mine own name. That, some whirlwind bear
overhanging	Unto a ragged, fearful, hanging° rock
	And throw it thence into the raging sea.
look, behold	Lo,° here in one line is his name twice writ:
	"Poor forlorn Proteus," "passionate Proteus," 20
	"To the sweet Julia"—that I'll tear away.
since	And yet I will not, sith° so prettily
	He couples it to his complaining [94] names.
	Thus will I fold them, one upon another.
	Now kiss, embrace, contend, [95] do what you will. 25

(1.3.106–130)

The actress playing Julia is required to do an awful lot in this speech. First, she scolds her own hands. Then she picks up some pieces of the letter and reads them. Next she throws one piece to the ground and tramples on it. She picks up another, reads it, and tucks it into her bosom after kissing it. She calms the wind. Then she picks up another piece of the letter, this one with Proteus's name on it twice. Seeing that one is adjacent to her own name, she begins to tear that off, stops, and folds the two names onto each other.

---

93 **search:** examine, probe; possibly also seal

94 **complaining:** expressing pain (Proteus is *poor* and *forlorn* when he's not around Julia)

95 **contend:** engage in physical struggle; tussle

That's quite an agenda. It takes almost as long to list all of Julia's actions as it does to perform the speech.

Given how much talking there is in these twenty-five lines of text, *when should Julia actually do all of that stuff?*

The Private and the Public: Julia's Choice

To answer that question, we need to ask another one: *To whom is Julia speaking?*

Julia is delivering a *soliloquy*, a speech made when a character is alone onstage, or thinks she is alone. All soliloquies present what we might call "Julia's Choice": either she is talking *to herself*, or she is speaking *directly to the audience.*

We have already worked on some soliloquies that call for Julia's Choice to be made. Richard of Gloucester is alone on stage at the beginning of *Richard III.* The context of that speech suggests that he is speaking directly to the audience. He provides information about current events in the kingdom, he shares confidences about his own lack of fitness for these times, and he lays out his master plan for stirring up trouble. He wants the audience on his side as allies and cheerleaders in his quest for the crown. Therefore, he turns to us and spills his guts, hoping to win our approval. It's possible that he is talking to himself, but the speech feels too outwardly aimed, too energetic, to be the ruminations of a man mulling something over in private.

King Henry VI, on the other hand, is surely working something out for himself when he speaks in soliloquy. His Molehill Speech has an inwardly focused energy. It is quiet, pensive, contemplative, and resigned. These qualities suggest that Henry has withdrawn into his own thoughts, just as he has been removed from the seat of power by his domineering queen. It's hard to imagine Henry announcing to the audience his desire to grieve his life away, or his fantasy of spending his life as a shepherd. No, his manner is different from Richard of Gloucester's. Henry is simply cogitating, contemplating his situation, talking to himself.

Even when Julia's Choice goes that way, and the soliloquy is inwardly directed, the text must still have vibrancy—the audience has to hear it, after all. But the actor has to find a way to be audible without violating the interiority of the experience. It's a tricky balance, and its success relies on the conventions of the theater. We in the audience know that Henry is speaking much louder than someone in real life does when pondering things to himself. And we accept that his loud speech is a theatrical device, a way for us to hear his innermost thoughts out loud.[96]

Some soliloquies can work in either direction. In the majority of *Hamlet* productions I've seen, "To be or not to be" has been played as a private meditation, although I have seen a few handle it publicly, as a debate club proposition to be solved with the audience's help. I've seen some Henrys shift between private and public as the Molehill speech progressed. "Here on this molehill will I sit me down" works fine as a piece of public information; the "I wish I were a shepherd" beats reveal Henry at his most vulnerable and seem to call for privacy.

Most Julias I've seen have played the letter speech big, broad, and straight to the crowd (*out front* or *to the balcony*, in theater

---

96 The cinema solves the problem differently, and, perhaps, more elegantly, through the use of voiceover. In that technique, we hear a character's private thoughts even though we do not see him speak. Laurence Olivier takes this approach to the soliloquies in his film version of *Hamlet*; so does Ethan Hawke. Kenneth Branagh, in his *Hamlet* movie, speaks the soliloquies out loud, as though he were on stage. It works less well. Interestingly, audience-directed soliloquies often clunk in the movies. The camera seems uncomfortable with the more heightened theatrical device of direct address.

lingo). Its comic tone and full-blooded, hormonally charged energy seem to demand that. But the prevalence of this choice needn't rule out its opposite. No matter how public this soliloquy may be, some of its lines may well work better as the quiet, lovelorn broodings of a sweet teenaged girl. It is perfectly legitimate to explore both sides of Julia's Choice. As we have seen, Shakespeare's language never stays one way for very long.

Whichever choice you make, know that talking to the audience and talking to herself are not the only options available to Julia. Analyze the speech with the question, "To whom is she speaking?" in mind, and it becomes apparent that in fact Julia is addressing various objects, people, and ideas. We can list them:

Lines	Addressee
1 through 3	her hands
4 and first part of 5	herself or the audience
second part of 5 through 8	the word *Julia* on the scrap of the letter
9	herself or the audience
10 and 11	the phrase "poor wounded Proteus" on the next scrap of the letter
12 and 13	herself or the audience
14 through 18	the "good wind"
19 through 24	herself or the audience
25	the scrap of the letter with Proteus's complaining names folded on each other

As you approach this speech, the first step (first, that is, after looking at the scansion, antitheses, changes in the height of the language, line endings, verbs, and so on) is to be very specific about to whom or to what you're speaking. The addressee of a speech changes often, and in surprising ways. By keeping track of those changes and exploiting them, you will keep your thinking fresh and particular.

Try Julia's speech again, concentrating only on speaking to the person, place, or thing she is addressing. Right away, the speech will begin to make sense, and Julia's argument will start to emerge. Miraculously, the speech will become easier to do, and you will find yourself holding Julia's thoughts in your mind naturally and effortlessly.

. . . .

THINKING SHAKESPEARE RULE: Always note to whom or to what your character is speaking and speak specifically to that person or thing as you work through the speech.

. . . .

Doing It an Action at a Time

Now let's get back to all the things Julia has to do in the speech.

1.   *She scolds her own hands.*

> O hateful hands, to tear such loving words;
> Injurious wasps, to feed on such sweet honey
> And kill the bees that yield it with your stings.

She speaks the first line directly to her hands, stressing the antithesis between "hateful hands" and "loving words." An MMM at the first line ending asks, "What else?", and Julia comes up with an image for her hands, comparing them to injury-causing wasps. Why that image now? Perhaps her hands are tightened and claw-like, fluttering through the air like aggressive wasps buzzing around a nest. Or maybe her fingernails remind her of angry stingers. Whatever answer you choose, find a real, concrete inspiration for Julia's metaphor, one that makes the image of wasps inevitable. (And don't miss the great verbs "feed" and "kill.")

2.   *She tells us of her plan to kiss the papers and make up for the hurt she caused them.*

> I'll kiss each several paper for amends.

The idea comes in the ending after line 3.

3.   *She scans the scraps on the ground and picks up one of them, then tells us what's written on it.*

Julia must look around and spot a piece of paper to kiss before she gets to line 5, when she says what she has found. This means that *in the line ending between lines 4 and 5*, she has to spend a moment glancing at the torn bits of paper on the ground. That action happens between lines, while she's not talking. It can take a little time or a lot of time, depending on the effect actor and director want to achieve. Is Julia in a comic frenzy, speed-reading the words on the scraps of paper? Or is she in a romantic mood, slowly reviewing all the scraps as she searches for words to kiss?

When Julia finds a scrap that interests her, she stands up again and continues speaking.

> Look, here is writ "Kind Julia"—Unkind Julia

At the caesura, the dash midway through the line, she changes her mind about kissing the paper, as the antithesis between "Kind" and "Unkind" makes clear. She decides to take revenge against her unkind self, and an MMM at the next line ending helps her decide how to do it:

> As in revenge of thy ingratitude   (*what?*)

4.   *She throws the name "Julia" against the stones.*

> I throw thy name against the bruising stones,

This action leads to another.

5.   *She tramples on it.*

> Trampling contemptuously on thy disdain.

The great verbs "throw" and "trample" force the actress to make some decisions. When does she throw the piece of paper down, and when does she trample it?

She could throw it on the word "throw." Simple enough. She could then trample it on the word "trampling." That's a little trickier, because her trampling feet make noise, maybe so much that the audience can't hear what she's saying. (The Lord of the Dance doesn't talk much, for good reason.)

She could also throw and trample *before* she says the words:

> As in revenge of thy ingratitude   (*throw the paper*)
> I throw thy name against the bruising stones
> (*trample it*)
> Trampling contemptuously on thy disdain . . .

Or, she could say what she's going to do *first*, and then do it:

> As in revenge of thy ingratitude
> I throw thy name against the bruising stones   (*throw*
> *the paper*)
> Trampling contemptuously on thy disdain . . .
> (*trample it*)

Try both approaches. What's the difference between them?

- If you do first and talk second, the action has an impulsive quality, and Julia seems impetuous and peevish. The audience sees Julia's actions, then waits for her to find words that describe what she did. Those words come as a surprise. They reveal a slightly bratty girl who is petulant but controlled in her anger. It's a great choice.

- If you *talk* first and *do* second, you put the audience in the position of waiting to see *how* Julia will throw and trample. Does she throw in an unathletic, uncoordinated manner, or with the precision of a major league pitching ace? Is her contemptuous trampling a hard, nasty stomp, or a long, sneering, ball-of-the-foot twist? You have the chance to be especially inventive as you execute Julia's actions, and your audience has a moment to relish the surprise of what Julia does. Also a wonderful choice.

Both approaches work. Both create a distinct relationship between the action and the words that describe it. This relationship can be ironic, straightforward, comic, or absurd. I once saw an actress spend thirty hilarious seconds trampling with increasing contempt, until she was leaping up and down on the piece of paper in gymnastic contortions worthy of a classic routine from *I Love Lucy.*

Note that whether you and your director choose talking followed by doing, or doing followed by talking, *both approaches make the action happen in the line endings!*

The line endings give you the opportunity to do what the character needs to do, without interrupting what the character needs to say. They phrase the action every bit as much as they phrase the language.

Next:

6. *She picks up another piece of the letter and reads it.*

Again, Julia scans the ground; again, she does so in the line ending; again, she spots an interesting scrap of paper:

> And here is writ "Love-wounded Proteus."
> Poor wounded name, my bosom as a bed
> Shall lodge thee till thy wound be throughly healed;

Proteus's name is "wounded," so Julia decides to heal it by giving it bed rest on her bosom. This, in turn, gives her another idea.

7. *She kisses the piece of paper and then tucks it into her décolletage.*

> And thus I search it with a sovereign kiss.

She decides to kiss the wounded name as part of the treatment. ("Sovereign" here means medicinal, curative.) When does the course of medication begin? When does Julia kiss the paper?

We learned about *index words* in Things Further Thought On at the end of chapter 5. "Thus" is one. It indicates, or points to, the action described: in this instance, kissing. Julia can kiss the paper as she says the words. Try it:

> And thus I search it (*smooch!*) with a sovereign kiss.

That's fine, but it's a bit sloppy, and it puts a break in the middle of a line of verse where we may not want one. So try it at the end of the line:

> And thus I search it with a sovereign kiss. (*mmmmwwah!*)

Better. After kissing the paper, she tucks it into the bed that is her bosom, which means that the tuck also happens in this same line ending.

Julia's next thought is that Proteus's name was written two or three times in the letter:

But twice or thrice was "Proteus" written down.

Why does this thought come now? The answer refers back to the previous action: because putting Proteus's name down her shirt *feels good*! Why not take two or three opportunities to do it again?

The action itself leads to a new thought.

We have seen line endings link thought to thought. Now we see that they make it possible for *action* to trigger thought. The action at the end of line 12—tucking the scrap of paper into her bosom after kissing it—becomes a kind of Mamet Moment, asking *What?* and keeping the flow of ideas moving forward.

Now, to find more scraps to tuck, Julia must solve a new problem.

8. *She calms the wind and calls for a tornado to carry off to the sea any pieces of paper with her name on them.*

> Be calm, good wind, blow not a word away
> Till I have found each letter in the letter
> Except mine own name. That, some whirlwind bear
> Unto a ragged, fearful, hanging rock
> And throw it thence into the raging sea.

Speaking to the wind, Julia encounters more MMMs, which prompt her to specify where the tornado should carry the papers, and what it should do with them.

Next, in the line ending after "sea," she looks around at the papers for the third time and discovers another interesting scrap.

9. *She picks up a paper with Proteus's name on it twice and tells us about it.*

> Lo, here in one line is his name twice writ:
> "Poor forlorn Proteus," "passionate Proteus,"
> "To the sweet Julia"—

10. *She sees that one "Proteus" is linked to her own name and begins to tear that off, but stops before doing so.*

Where does she change her mind about tearing away her own name? You got it: *in the line ending!* And there's even a nice "yet" to signal the 180-degree turn.

> that I'll tear away.   (*goes to tear, stops*)
> And **yet** I will not, sith so prettily
> He couples it to his complaining names.

11. *She folds the two names onto each other.*

> Thus will I fold them, one upon another.
> Now kiss, embrace, contend, do what you will.

This is the most fun piece of business in the whole speech. "Thus," a useful index word, appears again, this time referring to the action of folding the paper, which happens in the line ending after "another."

Question: which way does Julia fold them? We know that they are folded "one upon another," but which name is on top, and which is underneath? Maybe she tries it one way, thinks better of it, and then flips them over.

When, in the final action of the speech, she talks to the two names, she tells them first to "kiss," then to "embrace," then to "contend," or engage in a physical struggle, and finally to "do what you will," whose meaning ought to be clear enough to any actress who can imagine the mentality of a love-struck teen-age girl. I like to think that at the end of this line, Julia actually manipulates the paper into doing what she describes, perhaps by rubbing the two folded names back and forth on each other, to the accompaniment of gales of knowing laughter from the audience.

Putting It All Together

Here's the speech again, with all the action described. Try it one more time, noting how smoothly all the business flows right out of the language, without breaking it up or interrupting it.

[to her hands] O hateful hands, to tear such loving words;
Injurious wasps, to feed on such sweet honey
And kill the bees that yield it with your stings. [has an idea]
[to audience] I'll kiss each several paper for amends.   [scans
                                                    pieces of paper]
Look, here is writ "Kind Julia"—[to the paper] Unkind Julia,
As in revenge of thy ingratitude
I throw thy name against the bruising stones,   [throws paper
                                                    down]
Trampling contemptuously on thy disdain.   [stomps on
                                                    paper, scans
                                                    ground again]
[to audience] And here is writ "Love-wounded Proteus."
[to paper] Poor wounded name, my bosom as a bed
Shall lodge thee till thy wound be throughly healed;

And thus I search it with a sovereign kiss.   [*kisses paper,
                                                     tucks it into her
                                                     neckline,
                                                     remembers
                                                     something*]

[*to audience*] But twice or thrice was "Proteus" written down.
[*to the air*] Be calm, good wind, blow not a word away
Till I have found each letter in the letter
Except mine own name. That, some whirlwind bear
Unto a ragged, fearful, hanging rock
And throw it thence into the raging sea.   [*spots a piece
                                                  of paper*]

[*to audience*] Lo, here in one line is his name twice writ:
"Poor forlorn Proteus," "passionate Proteus,"
"To the sweet Julia"—that I'll tear away.   [*goes to tear it;
                                                   stops*]

And yet I will not, sith so prettily
He couples it to his complaining names.
Thus will I fold them, one upon another.   [*folds the
                                                  paper, perhaps
                                                  tries different
                                                  combinations of
                                                  which name is
                                                  on top and
                                                  which on
                                                  bottom*]

[*to the paper*] Now kiss, embrace, contend, do what you will.

What a beguiling piece of theater!

Julia's language here is not particularly dense, but it's not modern English either, and simply making it clear is its own challenging task. Add to the actress's burden all the stage business and physical activity required, and this charming little speech becomes a real bear. That's why it's so helpful to let the structure of the verse organize it all. Just as the line endings help make complex ideas comprehensible, so they arrange physical action into manageable segments. Just as the actress playing Julia uses line endings as springboards to thought and opportunities for breath, so should she use them as tools to sculpt the shape of her stage business.

During rehearsal it will become clear that this simple approach allows for the creation of all sorts of wonderful effects. The language can plant expectations in the audience that the physical actions then either fulfill or deny. Stage business can become an elaborate routine, only to be undercut by a descriptive piece of language in ironic opposition to what just happened.

The placement of physical action relative to the text is one of a Shakespearean actor's most powerful tools. Few techniques in the theater are more effective than savvy juxtapositions of words and business.

Just be sure to do your business at the ends of the lines.

THINGS FURTHER THOUGHT ON

No Directions

This chapter of *Thinking Shakespeare* wouldn't have been necessary had Shakespeare written out the actions he wanted his characters to perform. Alas, the early printed texts of his plays have practically no stage directions at all. The few that do appear are extremely brief.

Most scenes start with the word *Enter*, followed by a list of the characters who come on to speak, and end with a simple *Exit*, or the plural Latin form, *Exeunt*. Once in a while there will be a concise description of some crucial action, as in *They stab Caesar*, and, a few lines later, *Dies*. Shakespeare occasionally describes sounds, especially during battle scenes, which are liberally sprinkled with *Flourish*, *Alarum*, *Trumpets sound*, or *Drum within*. Even highly unusual bits of stage business get short shrift, as with the most famous Shakespearean stage direction of all, *Exit, pursued by a Bear*, from *The Winter's Tale*.

The Tempest, printed only in the First Folio, which appeared seven years after Shakespeare's death, is an exception. It has many evocative stage directions. They include, *Enter Mariners, wet* and *Thunder and lightning. Enter Ariel like a Harpy, claps his wings on the table, and with a quaint device the banquet vanishes.* Because these are so much longer and more descriptive than Shakespeare's usual directions, many scholars believe they were not written by Shakespeare but were added during the publication process by someone who had seen or been in the original production of the play.

Our modern editions of Shakespeare, printed over 400 years later, contain similar added stage directions. The *Oxford Shakespeare*'s *Two Gentlemen of Verona*, for example, includes this direction a few lines into Julia's letter speech: *She picks up some of the pieces of paper.* Earlier, it says, *She tears the letter and drops the pieces.* Neither direction was written by Shakespeare; the text of the play printed in the First Folio says nothing about what Julia does during the speech. As the editors make clear in their introduction, the *Oxford* directions are intended to help readers—not necessarily actors—understand the gist of what is happening during the speech. Actors should regard the stage directions in most modern editions of Shakespeare with skepticism. Unless they are clearly marked as deriving from the original published texts, they are probably additions made by the editors. Think the character's thoughts, look at the line endings, and decide what you need to do. Look to the editors for guidance, and trust your director for the rest.

Shakespeare: Rated R

Every time I teach Julia's speech, I am greeted with titters and laughter when I discuss the business implied by its last line: "Now kiss, embrace, contend, do what you will." I remind my students that Julia is a healthy teenager in love. I ask them to think about the progressions from "kiss" to "embrace," "embrace" to "contend," and "contend" to "do what you will." Then I tell them that "what you will," usually the Elizabethan equivalent of *whatever*, could in some contexts be a euphemism for sex.

Sex? In *Shakespeare*?! (*Titters and laughter.*) REALLY??!!

Really. Shakespeare deals with every aspect of being human—birth, death, laughter, sadness, ambition, fear, hunger, loneliness, loss. Why would he leave out sex, an impulse as basic as eating and sleeping? Like every other great author in world history, Shakespeare knows that not even the most compelling story is complete without a little good old-fashioned physical passion.

Richard Gloucester's line about how soldiers have stopped making war so that they can "caper nimbly in a lady's chamber / To the lascivious pleasing of a lute" sounds naughty, and it is. "Lascivious" literally means "lecherous, sexually exciting." Later in the speech, "sportive tricks" sound naughty, and they are. When Richard says that he is "not shaped" for them, that his body is "deformed" and "cheated of feature," it's not only the dirty-minded who grasp exactly which part of his anatomy he is referring to. It sounds naughty, and it is.

Romeo and Juliet is about teenagers in love. They flirt, they kiss, they spend the night together. Their relationship is sexy, hot. *As You Like It* ends with four pairs of lovers cavorting together in the woods—Touchstone calls them "country copulatives." They are sexy, alive in their bodies, lustful and loving. Falstaff in *Henry IV, Part One* and *Part Two* and *The Merry Wives of Windsor* is a randy old fellow who loves food, booze, and girls. His favorite woman is a prostitute whose habits in bed are reflected in her name: Doll Tearsheet. *Antony and Cleopatra* tells the story of a middle-aged couple enjoying a passionate physical love affair. The Roman soldier Philo spells out the play's sexual subject matter in its very first speech: he says his great general Antony's "captain's heart" has "become the bellows and the fan / To cool a gypsy's lust." This list could go on and on and on and on.

Sex is everywhere in the plays. It's part of life, and it's a huge part of Shakespeare. Titter and laugh at it, but don't be afraid to embrace it.

....

THINKING SHAKESPEARE RULE: When something in Shakespeare sounds naughty, it is.

....

(That's one of my favorite *Thinking Shakespeare* Rules.)

ACT IV

Jeffrey Wright as Mark Antony in *Julius Caesar,* directed by Barry Edelstein
at the New York Shakespeare Festival / Public Theater's "Shakespeare in the
Park," 2000. Photo © Michal Daniel, 2000.

WHAT THE OTHER GUY IS THINKING

THINKING THE TEXT IN SCENES

It wasn't until a few hundred years after his death that one Will Shake-speare, actor and playwright, born in Stratford-upon-Avon, 1564, became William Shakespeare, the Greatest Writer of All Time.

Surprises abound in the history of his reputation's evolution over the centuries. During some periods since his death in 1616, Shakespeare's works fell out of favor. Some plays were ignored altogether, while others were performed only in versions so heavily abridged and rewritten that the playwright himself would hardly have recognized them. In other periods, every single word of every play was venerated, and Shakespeare was worshipped as though he were a god. The great—and greatly envious—George Bernard Shaw found this amusing. He coined a name for the pseudo-religion whose deity was the Bard of Stratford-upon-Avon: "Bardolatry."

As Shaw observed, Shakespeare was not nearly as revered in his own lifetime as he was in Britain's Romantic era. The Bard was famous while he lived, to be sure, but he wasn't idolized. He was regarded as a talented writer among a group of luminaries, including Ben Jonson, Christopher Marlowe, and Thomas Middleton. As if they somehow knew that their colleague would one day be far more celebrated than they, these writers were happy to pick on Shakespeare. Jonson notoriously called a speech in *Julius Caesar* "ridiculous." He also sniped that Shakespeare's work needed pruning. "The players have often mentioned it as an honor to Shakespeare that in his writing he never blotted out a line," Jonson wrote. "My answer hath been, 'Would he had blotted a thousand!'"

Robert Greene, a playwright who was popular around the time Shakespeare was getting started, called the younger man "an upstart crow" who "supposes he is able to bombast out a blank verse" with the best of them. Greene accused the newcomer from Stratford of believing himself to be "the only Shake-scene in a country."

The Special Qualities of Shakespearean Scenes

I suspect Shakespeare would have enjoyed Greene's wisecrack. "Shake-scene" is the kind of wonderfully odd, specific turn of phrase he loved. What's more, the insult acknowledges that there is something unique about the way Shakespeare writes drama. He doesn't just write scenes. Any hack can do that. No, Shakespeare writes "Shake-scenes"—special exchanges, stylized conversations among original, eccentric, and inimitable characters.

"Shake-scenes" are *sui generis*, the only example of their kind. They are different from everything else in Western drama, in the same way that "Beckett-scenes" or "Molière-scenes" or "Shaw-scenes" are entirely unique. They have particular rhythms, complex forms, a strange and arresting musicality, and, most of all, powerful structural devices that hold them together and make them sparkle onstage.

The Same Rules Apply in Scenes as in Speeches

Almost every piece of material we have examined thus far in *Thinking Shakespeare* has involved one actor speaking at length. Soliloquies (long speeches delivered to oneself or to the audience that reveal one's inner thoughts) and monologues (extended speeches that comprise one side of a conversation between two or more people) have been our bread and butter. These have revealed the basic building blocks of the Shakespearean technique, but in the context of *only one speaker.*

Now it's time to look at what happens when someone else participates. Does the meter determine which words the other guy stresses? Can the two sides of an antithesis come from two different characters? Will an MMM sculpt the thoughts of the next person to speak? Does the height of the language change not only line by line within a speech but also speech by speech within a longer dialogue?

Once we've asked, "Why am *I* using *this* word now?" should we also ask, "Why is *the other guy* using *that* word now?"

The answer to all of these questions is yes, which leads to a . . .

. . . .

THINKING SHAKESPEARE RULE: Shakespearean characters think and speak according to the same principles whether they are talking by themselves or with others.

. . . .

Acting a scene in Shakespeare is essentially the same project as acting a monologue in Shakespeare. The techniques used by a thinking Shakespearean always apply, whether he is onstage by himself or whether he is one member of a huge group.

In the context of Shake-scenes, however, there are some variations on the *Thinking Shakespeare* approach:

- Scansion indicates which words to stress *as well as when the other character should come in.*
- The line endings cue not just your own thoughts *but also the thoughts of the next person to speak.*
- Changes in the height of the language signal not only the changes in one character's thoughts *but also the changes in the tone of the scene and the relationships among the characters in conversation.*

REHEARSAL TIME

Keep all the *Thinking Shakespeare* fundamentals close at hand, grab a scene partner, and let's look at these special Shake-scene considerations, plus one or two more.

Shared Verse Lines

In chapter 3, we learned how to scan single lines of verse. In chapter 6, we looked at a scene from *The Merchant of Venice* in which a single verse line was broken in two and shared between two speakers. A reminder:

SOLANIO	And every object that might make me fear
	Misfortune to my ventures, out of doubt
	Would make me sad.
SALERIO	My wind cooling my broth
	Would blow me to an ague when I thought . . .

"Would make me sad. My wind cooling my broth" is one line of iambic pentameter.

Would make | me sad | My wind | cooling | my broth

Why does Shakespeare choose to split the line between Solanio and Salerio?

This is Shakespeare's way of telling the actor playing Salerio *to come in with his line immediately on cue.*

Salerio should have his breath ready and jump right in on Solanio's "sad," with no pause, no air, and no space. In rehearsal, the director would call this *picking up the cue.* The meter requires the line to be spoken as if by one voice, not two. The line is a *pick-up.*

Most of the time, but not all, the text's editor will signal shared verse lines by indenting the second half of the line to the right, as it is printed above. Although modern Shakespeare editions are pretty reliable, it's always a good idea to beat out the meter yourself to make sure that what seems to be a pick-up really is one.

You'll find some that are pretty hairy, as in this passage from the Scottish Play. Macbeth has just murdered King Duncan in the upstairs guest bedroom of his castle. Terrified, his hands drenched in blood, he reports to his wife.

MACBETH	I have done the deed. Didst thou not hear a noise?
LADY MACBETH	I heard the owl scream and the crickets cry. Did not you speak?
MACBETH	When?
LADY MACBETH	Now.
MACBETH	As I descended?
LADY MACBETH	Ay.
MACBETH	Hark! Who lies i'the second chamber?
LADY MACBETH	Donalbain.

(2.2.14–18)

Here's a concrete way to see how iambic pentameter controls the pace and intensity of this scene. Try this *Macbeth* snippet without treating the shared verse lines as pick-ups. That is, insert pauses after each of Mr. and Mrs. Macbeth's lines.

LADY MACBETH	I heard the owl scream and the crickets cry. Did not you speak? **(pause)**
MACBETH	When? **(pause)**
LADY MACBETH	Now. **(pause)**
MACBETH	As I descended? **(pause)**
LADY MACBETH	Ay. **(pause)**
MACBETH	Hark! Who lies i'the second chamber?

Pretty ponderous, and not very exciting.

Now try it again, making sure to follow the verse structure and keep those chunks of iambic pentameter together.

That central shared line—did NOT you SPEAK when NOW as I de-SCEND-ed—generates all the speed, excitement, and energy the scene requires. Both characters are reeling from the violence and exhilaration the murder of Duncan has unleashed. The tight pick-ups, the rapid back-and-forth, and the machine gun pace of the text communicate their palpitating and breathless states. Similarly, Macbeth's "Hark!" taken as a sharp and precise pick-up, is startling, even frightening. It shows the audience how jumpy the couple is, and it points the actors toward the rush of adrenaline coursing through their characters' bodies and the jagged fragments piercing their minds.

It takes a lot of rehearsal, but by honoring those shared lines and pick-ups, two actors can make this scene crackle.

....

THINKING SHAKESPEARE RULE: Shared verse lines are pick-ups.

....

MORE REHEARSAL TIME

Here is another short scene from *Merchant*, this one from near the end of that great play.

In Venice, Shylock is pressing hard for his pound of flesh, agonizing Antonio and Bassanio (the former's life is in danger; the latter is racked with guilt over it). Shylock's daughter, Jessica, has eloped with her boyfriend, Lorenzo. They have arrived at Portia's house in Belmont. Portia has gone to Venice, where she hopes to help Bassanio with the Shylock situation. She has left Lorenzo and Jessica to mind the house. The newlyweds seemed terrific together at first, despite the differences between them (she is Jewish; he is not), but now things change.

It's a beautiful, moonlit night. There is a soft, balmy breeze. Jessica steps outside and Lorenzo follows. Grab a scene partner and two blank pieces of paper and have a go.

LORENZO   The moon shines bright. In such a night as this,
            When the sweet wind did gently kiss the trees,
            And they did make no noise, in such a night
            Troilus methinks mounted the Trojan walls
            And sighed his soul toward the Grecian tents,   5
            Where Cressid lay that night.[97]

JESSICA   In such a night
            Did Thisbe fearfully o'ertrip the dew,
            And saw the lion's shadow ere himself,
            And ran dismayed away.[98]

LORENZO   In such a night
            Stood Dido with a willow in her hand   10
            Upon the wild sea banks, and waft her love
            To come again to Carthage.[99]

....

97 Troilus . . . Cressid: The story of Troilus and Cressida is told in Shakespeare's play named after the characters. Briefly: during the Greek siege of Troy, Troilus and Cressida, young Trojans, fall in love. The Trojan elders separate them by sending Cressida to the Greek camp in a prisoner exchange. Cressida promises to remain faithful to Troilus but instead falls for the Greek Diomedes, breaking Troilus's heart.

98 Thisbe . . . away: On her way to meet her lover, Pyramus, Thisbe encounters a lion and runs away. In her hurry, she drops a piece of her clothing. Pyramus finds it and assumes the lion has killed Thisbe. Devastated, he commits suicide, and Thisbe later does the same. Shakespeare presents a burlesque version of the story, performed by the "rude mechanicals," in *A Midsummer Night's Dream*.

99 Dido . . . Carthage: the Trojan warrior Aeneas abandons Dido, Queen of Carthage, breaking her heart. Shakespeare references the story in many plays. The willow tree is the traditional symbol of unrequited love. *Waft* = waved.

JESSICA	In such a night
	Medea gathered the enchanted herbs
	That did renew old Aeson.[100]
LORENZO	In such a night

escape; also, rob Did Jessica steal° from the wealthy Jew   15
spendthrift And with an unthrift° love did run from Venice
As far as Belmont.

JESSICA   In such a night
Did young Lorenzo swear he loved her well,
Stealing her soul with many vows of faith,
And ne'er a true one.

LORENZO   In such a night   20
Did pretty Jessica (like a little shrew)
Slander her love, and he forgave it her.

JESSICA   I would out-night you, did nobody come:

footsteps But hark, I hear the footing° of a man.

(5.1.1–24)

This tone of this lovely scene is very complex—romantic and lush on one hand (the moon, the breeze, all those mythological lovers) but dark and painful on the other (those love stories all end badly).

Let's briefly track the argument. Lorenzo opens with beautiful language about the moon and the trees and then reaches out to Jessica with the image of forlorn Troilus pining for his distant

---

100 Medea . . . Aeson: Though best known for the savage murder of her own children, Medea appears in other myths as a famous healer and magician. She helps Jason and the Argonauts find the Golden Fleece, and she cures Jason's sick old father Aeson with herbal remedies. The story of Jason and the Fleece is mentioned many times in *Merchant*, and Portia is associated more than once with Medea.

love. Jessica responds with the story of a frightened woman running from a lion. Lorenzo continues with the story of a woman hoping her beloved will soon return to her arms. Jessica counters with the story of a woman famous for restoring a sick father figure to health. Lorenzo, who knows his mythology, interprets this as a reference to Jessica's own father, Shylock, made sick by her abandonment of him. Dropping mythology, Lorenzo bluntly reminds Jessica that it was because of her love for him that she chose to leave home in the first place. Jessica rejects this argument, calling Lorenzo a liar who never loved her. Lorenzo takes the hit but doesn't take the bait, choosing to forgive Jessica rather than respond in kind. The footsteps of an approaching man prevent Jessica from saying any more.

The characters' arguments take the form of a game, a witty tit-for-tat of digs both subtle and blatant, a web of mythological references to nighttime heartbreak combined with frank talk about their own delicate situation.

Pick-ups and Line Endings Work in Tandem

Each mythological reference in the scene is preceded by the phrase "in such a night," used twice in Lorenzo's first speech and starting the subsequent ones. "In such a night" is a half-line pick-up that completes the previous speaker's unfinished iambic pentameter. Each repetition of the phrase also creates an enjambed line ending after itself, with an MMM just begging to know what comes next:

> Where Cressid lay that night. / In such a night   *(what?)*
> Did Thisbe fearfully o'ertrip the dew . . .

And ran dismayed away. / In such a night   *(what?)*
Stood Dido with a willow in her hand . . .

To come again to Carthage. / In such a night   *(what?)*
Medea gathered the enchanted herbs . . .

That did renew old Aeson. / In such a night   *(what?)*
Did Jessica steal from the wealthy Jew . . .

As far as Belmont. / In such a night   *(what?)*
Did young Lorenzo swear he loved her well . . .

And ne'er a true one. / In such a night   *(what?)*
Did pretty Jessica, like a little shrew . . .

This is Shakespeare directing the scene from beyond the grave. The verse structure is his way of saying to each of the two actors, "Each 'in such a night' is a pick-up, and thou must speak it as tightly on cue as thou possibly canst. But then thou must use the line ending to *find* the image that cometh next."

As the scene moves forward, each speech tops the one before it, or puts a spin on it, or swats it away. The split second in which the characters think, *What will I say about what kind of night this is?* comes *after* each "in such a night," not before it. Jessica and Lorenzo are forced to listen carefully to the ideas being pitched by the other person and then respond with new ideas that advance their own agendas.

Again, for proof that Shakespeare intends the scene to unfold like this, all you need to do is try it the other way. Run the scene with long pauses before each "in such a night," and you'll find that it just sits there, dead as Pyramus on the cold ground.

Observe and follow the verse structure, though, and suddenly you have a piece of theater, a real scene. A fascinating, unusual, involving, and moving scene. A Shake-scene.

Height Changes in Shake-Scenes

Let's look at the way the height of the language changes as the scene moves forward and what that tells us about what is happening between the characters.

It's clear that Lorenzo and Jessica's relationship is on the skids. Under the combined stresses of Antonio's peril, Bassanio's apprehension, Portia's absence, and even Jessica's regret at the pain her elopement caused her father, their affair has soured. It's also clear that Lorenzo wants to reverse this hurtful change more than Jessica does.[101] His language is elevated: romantic, lush, and seductive. He introduces mythology, heightening the tone further. Jessica responds in kind, but her eventual reference to Aeson prompts Lorenzo to abandon mythology and describe the here and now in direct language. Jessica then drops into stark monosyllables: "and ne'er a true one." In response, Lorenzo keeps his language simple and unadorned as he attempts to communicate as plainly as he can. Jessica stays at that level too; her blunt "I hear

---

[101] Most directors infer from his opening speech that something bad happened between them just before the start of this scene. Many believe that Lorenzo cites Troilus because to him Jessica is a Cressida figure who has rejected her true love and gone somewhere far away. Some directors raise the stakes by surmising, as I did in my 1995 production at the Public Theater, that this rejection must be sexual in nature—that Lorenzo and Jessica were in bed together when something made her bail out. Hence, you will often see renditions of this scene in which the characters are dressed in pajamas, wrapped in bed sheets or blankets, or naked. Remember, if something in Shakespeare seems naughty, it is.

the footing of a man" is 180 degrees different from the earlier poetic talk of Medea, Thisbe, Dido, Aeneas, Troilus, and Cressida.

These changes in height direct the scene.

When Lorenzo and Jessica reject sophisticated wordplay, their straightforward plain talk connects them and allows them to address the real problem. That is, when the fanciness drops away, the gloves come off. In nine out of ten productions, directors reflect this shift of tone in the staging of the scene, placing Lorenzo and Jessica physically far away from each other during the mythology section and close to each other in the plainspoken part.

This physical proximity gives Jessica a wonderful moment before her last speech. She has been on her toes throughout the scene, jumping on Lorenzo's every line with quick pick-ups that throw his overtures right back at him. But now, inches away from him, she slows down. She has enough time after the line ending "and he forgave it her" to hear the footsteps of a man arriving in the distance and to decide that she is done playing the "in such a night" game. She looks into Lorenzo's eyes and says, perhaps with bitter triumph, "I would outnight you . . . " What she means is, "I'm smarter than you, and quicker than you, and still very upset with you, but I'm going to stop this conversation rather than continue to engage you." An actress can discover this complex moment simply by looking at how the height of the language changes as the scene moves ahead.

This brief but rich exchange is a textbook case of Shake-scene technique. As in a long speech spoken by one character,

- Verse structure dictates rhythm.
- Line endings create opportunities for thought.
- Changes in the height of the language mark shifts in tone and intention.

But in addition to happening within the speeches of each participant in the scene, all of these dynamics unfold between speakers as well.

EVEN MORE REHEARSAL TIME

If we've asked the central *Thinking Shakespeare* question once, we've asked it 100 times: *Why am I using this word now?*

The previous chapters have proposed all kinds of answers to this question, and now, in the context of the Shake-scene, we encounter one more:

I'm using these words now because the other character used those words then.

Just as the end of each line of iambic pentameter creates a springboard for thought as one character speaks, so each line ending spurs a new thought in the person who talks next. The last character's line ending gives the next character a compelling reason to say what he says. And just as each actor thinks a full line and then asks *"What?"* before thinking up what comes next, so each actor must "think" his scene partner's lines by listening to her very attentively. In this way, your scene partner's line endings help you find the right thing to say. Her line endings create MMMs *for you.*

Here's a nifty little exercise that shows just how this works.

An Exercise: Listening to the Last Word

We've spent quite a bit of time on Shakespeare's *Richard II*, with John of Gaunt in chapter 9 and with King Richard himself in chapter 11. Now we're going to check in with three of Richard's closest associates, Bushy, Bagot, and Green.

Although they sound like a law firm in some Dickens novel, Bushy, Bagot, and Green are actually King Richard's closest friends and most intimate advisors. In the early part of the play, they are almost always with him, counseling him, supporting him, amusing him. They are medieval yes-men, reflexively reinforcing their boss's beliefs and indulging his whims.

When Bolingbroke's rebellion takes hold, the three realize that if King Richard goes down, they are sure to go down with him. They are reluctant to desert Richard in his time of need, but they know they've got to do something if they are to avoid being jailed or even killed. This short scene finds them together, wondering what to do. Should they join Richard in Ireland? Should they stay in England and fight? Should they hide until the trouble passes?

Our exercise starts with a pass through the scene to get familiar with what's being argued. Take it one line at a time, paying particular attention to how the line endings within each individual speech make Mamet Moments that spring the thinking forward into the next line.

BUSHY	The wind sits fair for news to go for Ireland,
raise an army	But none returns.[102] For us to levy power°
	Proportionable to the enemy
	Is all unpossible.

---

102 The wind . . . returns: i.e., the direction of the wind makes it possible for ships to sail from England with dispatches to Ireland (where Richard is), but no news is arriving back.

	GREEN	Besides, our nearness to the King in love	5
i.e. implies		Is near° the hate of those love not the King.	
	BAGOT	And that is the wavering commons;[103] for their love	
		Lies in their purses, and whoso empties them	
		By so much fills their hearts with deadly hate.	
	BUSHY	Wherein the King stands generally condemned.	10
	BAGOT	If judgement lie in them, then so do we,[104]	
		Because we ever have been near the King.	
	GREEN	Well, I will for refuge straight to Bristol Castle.	
		The Earl of Wiltshire is already there.	
service	BUSHY	Thither will I with you; for little office°	15
		Will the hateful commons perform for us,	
wild dogs		Except like curs° to tear us all to pieces.	
		Will you go along with us?	
	BAGOT	No, I will to Ireland to his majesty.	
		Farewell: If heart's presages[105] be not vain	20
		We three here part that ne'er shall meet again.	
	BUSHY	That's as York thrives to beat back Bolingbroke.[106]	
	GREEN	Alas, poor Duke, the task he undertakes	
		Is numb'ring sands and drinking oceans dry.	
		Where one on his side fights, thousands will fly.	25
	BAGOT	Farewell at once, for once, for all and ever.	

---

103 wavering commons: the common people (whose loyalty to any leader depends on how his policies affect their fortunes—"It's the economy, stupid" was as apt a slogan in the days of King Richard II as it is today.)

104 If judgement . . . we: i.e. if justice is in their hands, then we are too

105 heart's presages: omens; ill feelings in the heart that predict bad things to come (Stress is on the first syllable—PRESS-i-jiz—creating a syncopation in the rhythm of the line.)

106 That's as York . . . Bolingbroke: i.e., That depends on whether the Duke of York (still loyal to Richard) can manage to defeat Bolingbroke.

BUSHY   Well, we may meet again.

BAGOT   I fear me never.

                                                    (2.2.123–149)

Before we get to the exercise, a few quick observations:

The passage has one shared verse line (split between Bushy and Bagot on line 27), which is a pick-up for Bagot. This makes sense. Throughout the scene, Bagot has been the one saying that the three friends will never meet again, that they will be left at the mercy of the angry commoners, and that this goodbye is "for all and ever." He's not about to agree with Bushy's sentimental and unrealistically optimistic hope that they may survive this ordeal. He's also in a hurry to get to Ireland before the wind, which now "sits fair" for that journey, changes direction. And he's got to complete the final rhymed couplet that ends the scene, rather stunningly, on "never" in answer to his own "ever." For all of these reasons, it's logical that he would jump on this cue and start talking immediately.

The scene has two half-lines, like the ones we saw in Things Further Thought On at the end of chapter 6. Those create pauses and shape the emotions onstage. In line 4, the odd word "unpossible" hangs in the air like a guillotine blade about to descend on the three men. "Unpossible" is an inspired word, a much weirder and more striking term than the familiar *impossible* we would expect from anyone other than William Shakespeare. The absolute finality of the word rattles Green so badly that he needs a moment before he can go on. How long a moment? That's up to the actor playing Green and his director to decide. The second pause, in line 18, after "Will you go along with us?" gives Bagot a moment to think before he makes a decision that will separate him from his friends forever. Again, the half-line hangs while Bagot thinks, perhaps looks sadly at his friends, and then pronounces the awful monosyllable "no" that seals his fate.

In these instances—lines 4, 18, 27, and 28—the verse structure determines the rhythm, tempo, and even emotional content of the scene.

The individual speeches contain some terrific Mamet Moments. Bushy comes up with the odd phrase "Is all unpossible" by searching for an answer to the Mamet *"What?"* after line 3, which asks how hard it will be to raise a force powerful enough to defeat Bolingbroke. Line 8's Mamet Moment gives Bagot a great chance to use antithesis to explain how fickle the commoners are when it comes to their leaders and their money ("empties their purses" versus "fills their hearts"). And on line 23, Green's line ending sets up the best poetry in the scene. The Duke of York has undertaken a hopeless task. Mamet asks, *"What is it?"* Green thinks, and then says it is like counting every grain of sand and drinking the ocean dry. That is a memorable image for a job so overwhelming in size that it is literally undoable. (Try it on your boss the next time he gives you some preposterous assignment. "You want me to copy and file all the company correspondence since 1962?! That's numbering sands and drinking oceans dry!")

Now, to the repetition exercise. It is deceptively simple. *Each actor repeats the last word of the previous character's speech before beginning his next line.*

It sounds like this:

BUSHY   The wind sits fair for news to go for Ireland,
          But none returns. For us to levy power

Proportionable to the enemy
Is all unpossible.

GREEN **unpossible** . . . Besides, our nearness to the King
            in love
Is near the hate of those love not the King.

BAGOT **King** . . . And that is the wavering commons; for
            their love
Lies in their purses, and whoso empties them
By so much fills their hearts with deadly hate.

BUSHY **hate** . . . Wherein the King stands generally
            condemned.

BAGOT **condemned** . . . If judgement lie in them, then so
            do we,
Because we ever have been near the King.

GREEN **King** . . . Well, I will for refuge straight to Bristol
            Castle.
The Earl of Wiltshire is already there.

BUSHY **there** . . . Thither will I with you; for little office
Will the hateful commons perform for us,
Except like curs to tear us all to pieces.
Will you go along with us?

BAGOT **us** . . . No, I will to Ireland to his majesty.
Farewell: If heart's presages be not vain
We three here part that ne'er shall meet again.

BUSHY **again** . . . That's as York thrives to beat back
            Bolingbroke.

GREEN **Bolingbroke** . . . Alas, poor Duke, the task he
            undertakes
Is numb'ring sands and drinking oceans dry.
Where one on his side fights, thousands will fly.

BAGOT	**fly** . . . Farewell at once, for once, for all and ever.
BUSHY	**ever** . . . Well, we may meet again.
BAGOT	**again** . . . I fear me never.

I always find hearing this scene in this way so provocative that I can't believe Shakespeare wasn't actually doing it himself as he wrote!

This powerful exercise reveals that each character's thoughts arise *specifically from the thoughts of the other characters.*

Consider line 11: "**Condemned** . . . then so are we." In the word "condemned," Bagot feels the commoners' deadly verdict land on his and his friends' shoulders.

Or line 19: "**Us?** . . . No." Bagot hears Bushy's hopeful use of the pronoun that would keep the group of three together and then makes his decision to depart alone.

Or line 23: "**beat back Bolingbroke** . . . an impossible task." Green, too, hears Bushy's optimism, finds it hollow and misguided, and rejects it.

The exercise also reinforces an idea we first encountered in chapter 7. *The important words gravitate toward the ends of lines.* In that chapter we saw how listing the words at the end of lines reveals the basic argument of a speech. Here, listing the words at the end of lines reveals the basic argument of a *scene*:

Ireland

power

enemy

unpossible

love

King

love

them

hate

condemned

we

King

Castle

there

office

us

pieces

us

majesty

vain

again

Bolingbroke

undertakes

dry

fly

ever

never

The whole scene unfolds in those twenty-seven words. Each one is crucial, not only because of its placement at the end of a line but also because it is so important *to the thinking of the person who speaks next*. Each character hears the idea articulated by the previous speaker and responds accordingly. The characters *listen* to one another, and then speak.

By requiring the actors to repeat the last word they hear before it's their turn to speak, this exercise forces them to listen, hear, think, choose their words, and respond. Listening is central to the actor's art, as this exercise proves. It's a great one to try in rehearsal.

Sometimes it yields astonishing results, as it does when applied to this brief exchange from *Othello*.

Iago, Othello's ensign, seems loyal but is secretly plotting to destroy the general. In this exchange, he plants in Othello's mind the idea that his devoted wife, Desdemona, is having an affair with another officer, Michael Cassio. I've included in the scene the repeated words the actors would say while working through the exercise. They are in **boldface**. Read the passage and the repeated words aloud, as you did in the *Richard II* scene. (To hear the unadorned Shake-scene, simply skip the repeats. And note that the scene is written in both verse and prose, so some of the speeches that here appear to be half-lines are in fact full lines of prose. We'll explore this subject more fully in the next chapter.)

IAGO	Did Michael Cassio, when you wooed my lady,
	Know of your love?
OTHELLO	**love** . . . He did, from first to last. Why dost thou ask?
IAGO	**ask** . . . But for a satisfaction of my thought;
	No further harm.
OTHELLO	**harm** . . . Why of thy thought, Iago?
IAGO	**Iago** . . . I did not think he had been acquainted
	with her.
OTHELLO	**her** . . . O, yes; and went between us very oft.
IAGO	**oft** . . . Indeed!
OTHELLO	**Indeed** . . . Indeed! Ay, indeed. Discern'st thou
	aught in that?
	Is he not honest?
IAGO	**honest** . . . Honest, my lord!

OTHELLO	**my lord** . . . Honest! Ay, honest.
IAGO	**honest** . . . My lord, for aught I know.
OTHELLO	**know** . . . What dost thou think?
IAGO	**think** . . . Think, my lord!
OTHELLO	**my lord** . . . Think, my lord!
	By heaven, he echoes me . . . [107]

(3.3.96–110)

The Shake-scene unfolds a thought at a time, just as the Shake-speech does. The repeated word exercise is a great way to hear how it works.

Shake-Scene Volleyball

The Shakespearean technique of antithesis produces powerful results when used in multicharacter scenes. In the Bushy, Bagot, and Green excerpt, each man finishes antitheses started by someone else. In lines 10 and 11, for example, Bushy introduces the idea that "the King" stands condemned, and Bagot answers with an antithesis: so do "we" (i.e., we too are condemned). "The King" versus "we." Antithesis. In lines 18 and 19, Bagot's "I" is antithetical to Bushy's "you," and his "his majesty" opposes

....

[107] Not only does this exercise make each actor focus intensely on the words the other uses, but it also allows the actors (and us) to hear what the great early-twentieth-century critic G. Wilson Knight famously described as "the Othello music." The sound of this play is unique in the Bard's canon. This passage has a modern ring that seems to echo the voices of Samuel Beckett and Harold Pinter, writers who weren't born until nearly 350 years after Shakespeare's death. It's one of the wonders of Shakespeare that his plays always seems to contain ideas that didn't exist in his lifetime and that he couldn't have predicted: the theories of Marx and Freud, the dramaturgy of Brecht, the nihilistic rhythms of Beckett. All the wisdom, insights, discoveries, and yes, follies, of generations yet to come find themselves represented in the Bard's pages.

Bushy's "us." "Will you go with us" versus "I will [go] to his majesty." Two antitheses.

Antitheses are more complicated when more than one speaker is involved. When an individual character uses antithesis within his own lines ("Now is the winter of our discontent / Made glorious summer by this son of York"), he is alone responsible for stressing both sides of the antithesis as he delivers the lines. He must *think* "winter" versus "summer," or "to be" versus "not to be." But when antithesis unfolds across the lines of two speakers, both together share the responsibility for making the thought clear. Bushy has to stress "the King," and Bagot has to lift "we." If either neglects to do so, the antithesis doesn't work, the lines don't make sense, and the Shake-scene falls flat.

Here are a few lines from *Hamlet* that demonstrate this point.

Having confirmed at his specially arranged performance of *The Mousetrap* that Claudius is guilty of murdering Old Hamlet, the prince hastens to his mother Gertrude's bedroom (a.k.a. her "closet") to confront her with the facts and ask why she has stayed loyal to her husband's killer. Here are the first few lines of their confrontation.

> GERTRUDE Hamlet, thou hast thy father much offended.
> HAMLET   Mother, you have my father much offended.
> GERTRUDE Come, come, you answer with an idle tongue.
> HAMLET   Go, go, you question with a wicked tongue.
>
> (3.4.8–12)

The antitheses in this exchange are easy to hear. In the first two lines: "Hamlet" versus "Mother"; "thou" versus "you"; "thy father" versus "my father." In the second two lines: "come, come" versus "go, go"; "answer" versus "question"; "idle" versus "wicked."

The actress playing Gertrude and the actor playing Hamlet must do two jobs to make these antitheses work: 1) They have to know that these antitheses are in their lines (they've read *Thinking Shakespeare*, as have their director and dramaturg, so that's no problem), and 2) they have to stress the antithetical terms as they say them, by thinking them clearly, just as they would antitheses within their own speeches.

But that second task is not so straightforward in the context of a scene. After all, each actor is only able to think and speak *his own* side of the antithesis. Neither can control how the other person says his line. Still, both players are on the same team, and together they must make the Shake-scene work, using these antitheses to keep the confrontation between the characters energetic and vehement.

One way they can make the scene work is to think of each shared antithesis as a volleyball.

In the game of volleyball, points are scored when one teammate lofts the ball off his fingertips and into the perfect spot for his teammate to spike it over the net and hammer it to the ground. As you work on a scene, think of the antithesis as a ball that one character lofts into the air for another character to spike.

Gertrude sets up the ball with *Hamlet / thou / thy father*. Hamlet spikes it home with *Mother / you / my father*. Gertrude lofts another one: *Come, come / answer / idle*, and Hamlet jams it back with *Go, go / question / wicked*. The actors must match each other in intensity. If Gertrude doesn't put enough lift on, say, "answer" and "idle," Hamlet can go as wild as he wants with "question" and "wicked," but the exchange won't work. The spike won't happen;

the point won't be scored. Conversely, Gertrude can lob "answer" and "idle" into the sweetest spot ever heard on a Shakespearean stage, but if Hamlet doesn't ram them home with "question" and "wicked," again, the exchange lays an egg.

Both actors are on the same team. Call it Team Antithesis. If they work together, they will make the sense of the thoughts clear. They will make Shake-scene Volleyball a thrilling spectator sport. And they will show that Robert Greene was right: William really is "the only Shake-scene in a country."

THINGS FURTHER THOUGHT ON

Crazy Word Number One: Stichomythia

Stichomythia. stick-uh-MITH-ya. It sounds like something that has to be treated with antibiotics.

Actually, it's a form of dramatic writing invented by the ancient Greeks. *Stichomythia* is the technical name for dialogue in which two characters speak to each other in alternating, and often rhymed, single lines of verse.

Shakespeare uses stichomythia a lot, particularly in his early plays. One of the rare examples from his middle period is the short snippet of *Hamlet* we looked at in this chapter. In it, Gertrude and Hamlet deliver single, complete verse lines that bounce back and forth in rapid stichomythic succession.

Here are two other brief examples from the earlier work *The Comedy of Errors.* Adriana, wife of Antipholus of Ephesus, isn't happy with married life. She resents having to stay home all day while her husband is out doing his business and, Adriana suspects, cheating on her. Her younger sister Luciana, meanwhile, pines for marriage and tries to convince Adriana that a woman's place is in the home and that men should be in charge. "A man is master of his liberty," she says. "Time is their master, and, when they see time / They'll go or come. If so, be patient, sister." Adriana's response begins the stichomythic exchange:

ADRIANA   Why should their liberty than ours be more?

LUCIANA   Because their business still lies out o' door.

ADRIANA	Look, when I serve him so, he takes it ill.
LUCIANA	O, know he is the bridle of your will.
ADRIANA	There's none but asses will be bridled so.
LUCIANA	Why, headstrong liberty is lashed with woe.

(2.1.10–15)

Later in the scene, the sisters continue their debate:

ADRIANA	This servitude makes you to keep unwed.
LUCIANA	Not this, but troubles of the marriage-bed.
ADRIANA	But, were you wedded, you would bear some sway.
LUCIANA	Ere I learn love, I'll practice to obey.
ADRIANA	How if your husband start some other where?
LUCIANA	Till he come home again, I would forbear.
ADRIANA	Patience unmoved! No marvel though she pause;
	They can be meek that have no other cause.

(2.1.26–33)

Both snippets are fast and furious. Both depend on the quick wits of the speakers. Both are great fun for the audience to hear. If the antitheses in the stichomythic dialogue between Hamlet and Gertrude call volleyball to mind, these exchanges beg comparison to another sport: tennis.

Adriana and Luciana are the Venus and Serena Williams of Shakespeare. In this scene they hold a fierce rally, bouncing text back and forth. Each woman challenges the other to take her best shot, and each fires back with precision and variety.

Grab a scene partner and try these exchanges, one line at a time, slowly at first, then faster and faster. Keep the idea of mutual challenge in the front of your mind. Think tennis.

You'll find that the language takes on a fast, dazzling rhythm, and a competitive texture. That is the characteristic feel of stichomythia. It's a very exciting subcategory of Shake-scene stagecraft.

Crazy Word Number Two: Tutoyer

Tutoyer. too-twa-YAY. It sounds like something a French cheerleading squad might shout when their team scores a goal.

In French, as in many European languages, there are two forms of the second-person pronoun *you*. Generally, the formal form, *vous*, is used to address an elder or a superior, and the informal, *tu*, is used to address a younger person or an inferior. An employee uses *vous* to his boss; a student uses *vous* for her teacher; a grandchild uses *vous* for his grandparents. On the other hand, the bank president addresses the newly hired teller using *tu*; the teacher speaks to his student with *tu*; the grandma coos at her granddaughter with *tu*; and close friends call each other *tu*. In French, *tutoyer* means *to address someone using the informal pronoun* tu. (Its opposite, *vouvoyer*, means *to address someone using the formal pronoun* vous.) By extension, *tutoyer* is used to describe the rules governing the use of formal and informal second-person pronouns in all languages.[108]

"That's fascinating," you're thinking. "What's it got to do with Shakespeare?"

During Shakespeare's time, and really until the nineteenth century, common English usage included two forms of the second-person pronoun. While to our modern ears *thou* sounds

---

[108] Grammarians use a more technical term: a *T-V distinction*. Although this sounds like an alternate name for the Emmy Awards, it borrows the first letters of *tu* and *vous* to describe the process of switching between the formal and informal.

poetic, excessively formal, and biblical, in fact it was the informal pronoun, and *you* (and sometimes *ye*) was the formal pronoun. *You* was used by subjects addressing royalty, by children addressing parents, and by servants addressing masters. *Thou* was used in the opposite direction. *You* was also used as the plural of both the formal and informal case. (A teacher would say to one student, "thou hast failed the test," but to the whole class, "you have failed the test.") [109]

As exemplified by the Ten Commandments, the informal case has its own set of verb forms: *Thou shalt*, not *thou shall*; *thou dost*, not *thou does* or *thou do*; *wilt thou*, not *will thou*. When these verb declensions disappeared from English, the language got much simpler to use.

Thou canst see more Shakespearean tutoyer at work in the brief bit of *Hamlet* in this chapter.

GERTRUDE   Hamlet, thou hast thy father much offended.
HAMLET   Mother, you have my father much offended.

Gertrude, Hamlet's mother and the Queen of Denmark, uses the familiar "thou" to address her son; he uses the formal "you" to answer back.

Tutoyer gets really interesting when someone decides to break the rules. If a subordinate uses *thou* to a superior, he is being wildly insulting (as happened during the trial for treason of Sir Walter Raleigh in Shakespeare's day, when a lowly prosecutor shouted at

....

109 There are some places where both forms are still in use, such as Yorkshire and other parts of northern England, in so-called Quaker plain speech, and among the Amish communities in the Pennsylvania Dutch country. "Wilt thou help me at the barn raising, Jann?"

the nobleman, "I thou thee, thou traitor!"). If a superior uses *you* to an inferior, he is injecting a level of formality that reminds the subject of the status distance between them. (This is similar to when your mother gets angry at something you've done and uses your full name and a formal tone to put you in your place: "Mr. Barry Genis Edelstein! What have you done now?" Big trouble ahead.)

In chapter 11 we heard King Richard II tell his subjects Carlisle and Aumerle, "you have but mistook me all this while," and "I live with bread, like you." The use of "you" in those phrases is very interesting. It might be the plural of the familiar "thou," used by the king to address two inferiors. But it might also be the formal pronoun in the singular. If the latter interpretation is correct, then the king, "subjected"—transformed into a subject—by the humiliations to which he has been exposed, now sees himself as inferior to his betters the bishop and the young duke, and so he accords them the status of the formal pronoun.

Tutoyer can also help illuminate hidden shifts in the dynamics of a Shake-scene.

The Merchant of Venice provides an interesting example. At around line 26, the clown Launcelot Gobbo, Shylock's servingman, is visited by his father, Old Gobbo, who is "sand-blind" and can't see a thing. Old Gobbo literally bumps into Launcelot, and, not knowing it's his son, asks him for directions to Shylock's house. "Master young man, I pray you, which is the way to Master Jew's?" He reflexively uses *you* in case the unknown man is his social superior. (Better to show too much deference than not enough.) Later in the scene, Old Gobbo realizes that the stranger he is addressing is actually his son and immediately switches to *thou*. "I'll be sworn thou art my own flesh and blood." The switch in pronoun marks a shift in power between the two characters.

While Old Gobbo uses "you," he is deferential, well-mannered, and formal. When he switches to "thou," he assumes an air of familiarity, casualness, and fatherly superiority.

In the theater, these two tiny words, *you* and *thou*, fly by in fractions of a second. But Shakespeare's actors—not to mention his audience—would have heard them loud and clear. Today, actors have to be on the lookout to notice the subtle information *thou* and *you* convey. Even if the audience does not catch the difference between the two words, they will notice the power shifts that the words bring about. "Why am I using *you* and not *thou?*" is as good a question as any in the *Thinking Shakespeare* universe.

Why Iambic Pentameter?

The shared verse lines in the Shake-scenes in this chapter show once again how deliberate Shakespeare is with verse structure and how much care he takes in fashioning where his lines start, end, break off, and continue. The number of different effects he can achieve with ten syllables of alternating stress, the sheer variety of music he can make with that simple rhythm, is truly staggering. Of course, he is no slouch with all sorts of other meters too, and he is pretty good with prose, which has no meter at all (as we're about to discover in the next chapter). So, of all the forms he could have chosen as his mainstay, why is the vast majority of his work composed in iambic pentameter?

Scholars advance different theories. Some say Shakespeare relies on iambic pentameter because his predecessor, Christopher Marlowe, wrote in this meter, establishing a convention for London's newly emerging professional play-writing industry. That may well be, though it must be pointed out that Shakespeare's iambs swerve away from their regular pulse much more frequently than Marlowe's do. "Is this the face that launched a thousand ships?" and thousands of other Marlowe lines stick to iambic pentameter with metronomic precision. Shakespeare is much looser, as we have seen, syncopating and varying the rhythm at every opportunity.

Another theory holds that English poets tried to imitate the rhythm of Italian, since Italian literature, specifically the Italian sonnet, was a direct inspiration to most poets writing in English at Shakespeare's time. Anyone who speaks that beautiful language will tell you that its inherent rhythm is heavily iambic.

More mystically inclined scholars will suggest that Shakespeare wrote in iambs because that is the rhythm of the human heart: *bi-BUM bi-BUM bi-BUM bi-BUM*.

I think the explanation is simpler. Like Italian, the English language naturally comes out in iambic pentameter. Listen to yourself speak sometime and you'll hear how often your words are unconsciously phrased ten beats at a time.

Good morning, sweetie. Would you like some coffee?
My mom and dad are coming out to visit.
I love my iPod. Couldn't live without it.

All iambic pentameter. Each and every line.
Or consider these famous American phrases:

Four score and seven years ago our fathers
Brought forth on this continent a new nation
Conceived in liberty and dedicated
To the proposition that all men
Are created equal . . .

That's iambic pentameter too. (Historians remind us that Lincoln loved Shakespeare and often read speeches aloud to White House visitors, sometimes dissolving in tears before he could finish. The cadences obviously worked their way beneath his skin.)

Listen to the language around you and you'll hear blank verse all the time. It's how English likes to sound.

ACT IV

CHAPTER
—№—
14

**MORE PROSAIC
CONCERNS**

THINKING SHAKESPEARE'S PROSE

We have thought a lot of Shakespeare in the preceding thirteen chapters of *Thinking Shakespeare*.

From the lyrical to the blunt, from the quick to the slow, from the earnest to the ironic, from the wacky to the despairing, we've explored the panoply of modes and styles that make up this grand body of work.

And we have skipped something huge.

Despite their variety, the texts we have considered share one important feature: they are all verse. But a vast tract of Shakespeare—perhaps as much as a third—isn't written in verse at all. It's written in *prose*.

The Prose Postulate

Prose just flows.

Whereas verse consists of a regular pattern of stressed and unstressed syllables grouped in a given number per line, prose is unregulated by syllable count and undisciplined by line length. There is no scansion, no "feet," no fancy Greek labels to describe the rhythm. Essentially, prose is plain old speech.

That's not to say that prose is just commonplace language. Shakespeare's prose is as artfully composed and meticulously crafted as is his verse. It can communicate elevated thought as well as simple sentiment, swooping from one to another and back again in a flash. Indeed, some Shakespearean prose is as rich and complex as his most celebrated verse. Here's one example:

> What a piece of work is a man! How noble in reason, how infinite in faculty, in form and moving how express and admirable, in action how like an angel, in apprehension how like a god—the beauty of the world, the paragon of animals! And yet to me what is this quintessence of dust?
>
> (2.2.286–290)

Hamlet's famous speech may be prose, but it most certainly isn't prosaic.

In fact, Shakespeare's prose is quite similar to his verse. It contains antithesis, changing height of language, great verbs, monosyllables, wit, irony—the works. The only thing it lacks is the thing that makes verse, verse: meter.

One way to think of this is as a kind of mathematical equation: call it the *Thinking Shakespeare* Prose Postulate. It looks like this:

$$P_s = V_s - M$$

where . . .

P_s = Shakespeare's Prose

V_s = Shakespeare's Verse

M = Meter

Shakespeare's prose is his verse minus the meter.

Why the Pros Write Prose

Those masterpieces of Shakespeare's middle period, *Henry IV, Part One* and *Part Two* (called by the English critic Kenneth Tynan "the twin summits of Shakespeare's achievement"), are split pretty evenly between verse and prose. Their verse is spoken largely by the aristocrats of the king's royal court, and their prose is spoken mainly by the unruly denizens of Falstaff's hangout, the tavern at Eastcheap.

This linguistic class distinction has given rise to a view of Shakespeare's use of verse and prose that has become convention-al wisdom: Shakespeare's upper-class characters speak verse and his lower-class characters speak prose.

Like most pieces of conventional wisdom, this one is an oversimplification.

Hamlet often speaks in prose, and he is royalty: the prince of Denmark. Falstaff, who speaks *only* in prose, is a knight: Sir John Falstaff. Mistress Quickly, Poins, Bardolph, and Nim are as far from bluebloods as it's possible to be, and they speak prose. But their cohort and social equal, Pistol, fires off some of the wildest verse in the canon. Prince Hal shuttles back and forth between the two kinds of speech, using prose when he is with Falstaff and verse when he is with his father, the king. Portia and Shylock switch between verse and prose. So does Rosalind. And Iago. And Beatrice. And Benedick. And many more.

There is no general rule that accounts for all of Shakespeare's switches between verse and prose. The only categorical statement it's possible to make is that he swings from one to the other *when he wants to make a rhythmic or tonal change.* Prose and verse sound different. The plainest verse isn't the same as prose, and the most vaunted prose doesn't create the same aural texture as verse does. The ability to shift back and forth between them is yet another weapon in Shakespeare's arsenal of techniques that keep the language vibrant, fresh, and alive.

He deploys this weapon in nearly every play, including all of his greatest works. Only four of Shakespeare's plays have no prose at all: *Richard II, King John*, and *Henry VI, Part One* and *Part Three*. Only one—*The Merry Wives of Windsor*—has almost no verse. Prose is a crucial thread in the Shakespearean fabric, woven with his many varieties of verse into a beautiful and lush tapestry.

Thinking Shakespeare has stressed the Bard's kaleidoscopic variety and rapid shifts between the high and the low, the fast and the slow, the complex and the simple. Now there is one more shift to be aware of: from verse to prose, and back. Each time this shift occurs, the same fundamental question must be asked: *Why?*

Why does Hamlet switch to prose when his old college chums Rosencrantz and Guildenstern arrive? Why does he speak verse with Horatio in some scenes and prose with him in others? Why does *The Winter's Tale*'s Polixenes speak verse when visiting Leontes in Sicilia, prose at home with his advisers, and verse again when spying in disguise on his wayward son?

As always, beneath all these questions lurks the most basic question of all. *Why am I using this word—deployed <u>in this form</u>—now?*

The answer will arise from the exciting ebb and flow of the rehearsal room's creative atmosphere.

The Improved Prose Postulate

Shakespeare's prose is Shakespeare's verse without the meter.

This means that all the fundamentals of *Thinking Shakespeare* apply *except for the ones that depend on the presence of meter*—the principles in chapters 3 (Scansion) and 7 (Phrasing with the Verse Line). No meter means no scansion. No verse line means no phrasing with the verse line.

But if you don't phrase with the verse line, then how do you phrase? If there's no MMM, where do you find the next thought? What do you do if you can't do the Paper Trick? And when do you breathe?

Oh my goodness! How do you do this stuff?!

Many Shakespearean actors argue that Shakespeare's prose is actually harder to perform than his verse. With the latter, you know that if you can count to ten and breathe, the language itself will go a long way toward taking care of you. Without that ten-beat framework, however, the whole process can feel unwieldy and out of control.

Not to worry. Shakespeare is too thoughtful and generous an artist, and just too talented a writer, to leave his actors hanging when he feels like writing in prose. In place of the missing meter, he adds all sorts of other goodies to shape the characters' thoughts and help the actors along as they work to make those thoughts clear.

An improved version of the Prose Postulate tells us how he does it:

$$P_s = (V_s - M) + S_{os}$$

where . . .

P_s = Shakespeare's Prose

V_s = Shakespeare's Verse

M = Meter

and

S_{os} = Shakespearean

Organizing Structures

Shakespeare's prose is full of S.O.S.'s (Shakespearean Organizing Structures). It features devices, patterns, groupings, and arrangements that give the prose a governing logic and help it phrase thought as efficiently as verse does.

REHEARSAL TIME

The adamantine and altogether glorious verse in *Henry V* exemplifies Shakespeare's mid-period brilliance. So does the play's supple and dynamic prose. In this example, the Boy who worked for Falstaff as his page (servant or attendant) before Falstaff's death now finds himself working the supply lines of King Henry's expeditionary force in France. The rest of Falstaff's gang—the drunken Bardolph, with his alcohol-ravaged, red, and carbuncled face; the mousy and pusillanimous Nim; and the loudmouthed and lying Pistol—are also there. The siege of Harfleur is underway, and Henry has roused his troops to fight with his famous rallying cry of, "Once more unto the breach, dear friends, once more!" But the Falstaff Three will have none of it, instead doing everything they can to avoid actual combat. The Welsh martinet,

Captain Fluellen, finds them lingering at the rear and literally beats them toward the front lines and the fight. The Boy, who is no more than fifteen years old, watches it all. Once the other characters have exited, he turns to the audience.

As young as I am, I have observed these three

swashbucklers swashers.° I am boy to them all three, but all they three, though they should serve me, could not be

clowns man[110] to me, for indeed three such antics° do not

cowardly amount to a man. For Bardolph, he is white-livered° and red-faced—by the means whereof a'[111] faces it out,[112] but fights not. For Pistol, he hath a killing tongue and a quiet sword—by the means whereof a' breaks words, and keeps whole weapons. For Nim, he hath heard that men of few words are the best men, and therefore he scorns to say his prayers, lest a' should be thought a coward. But his few bad words are matched with as few good deeds—for a' never broke any man's head but his own, and that was against a post, when he was drunk. They will steal anything, and call it "purchase."[113] Bardolph stole a lute-case, bore

---

110 man: 1) adult male or grownup; 2) serving man or underling

111 a': i.e., he. Throughout this play, Shakespeare uses spelling to capture the regional dialects of the various Britishers in Henry's army. (Fluellen, for example, says "plud"— "blood" with a thick Welsh accent.) The contraction *a'* renders the working-class London sound that today would be a Cockney's *e'*—"'e's awryte, mite!" for "he's all right, mate!" In 1598, *a'* would have sounded like *uh*, but a modern actor should feel free to substitute *e'* or plain old *he*. Make the thought clear and make the argument understandable to the audience, even if it means taking a very slight liberty with the text.

112 faces it out: i.e., acts like a big shot; puts on a brave face

113 purchase: booty taken from the enemy in conquest

it twelve leagues,[114] and sold it for three halfpence.

stealing Nim and Bardolph are sworn brothers in filching,° and in Calais[115] they stole a fire shovel. I knew by that piece of service the men would carry coals.[116] They would have me as familiar with men's pockets as their gloves or their handkerchiefs—which makes much against[117] my manhood, if I should take from another's pocket to put into mine, for it is plain pocketing up of wrongs.[118] I must leave them, and seek some better service. Their villainy goes against my weak stomach, and therefore I must cast it up.[119]

(3.2.26–49)

Elements Shared with Verse

First, a brief paraphrase to clarify the argument.

Even though I'm young, I know all about these three knuckleheads. They're cowards and fools who talk a big game

....

114 twelve leagues: over thirty miles—a long way to carry something as large and bulky as a lute case when all they're going to get for it is three half-pennies

115 Calais: the French port city where ships crossing the English Channel arrive even today

116 carry coals: a complicated pun. Since they stole a fire shovel—an andiron used for tending the embers in a fireplace or stove— Nim and Bardolph would literally "carry coals" with it. But the phrase is also slang for "do a dirty job," or "get the short end of the stick." The point is that their thievery isn't very smart and seems always to be their undoing.

117 makes much against: goes against; does offense to

118 pocketing up of wrongs: 1) weakly tolerating insults; 2) pocketing stolen merchandise

119 cast it up: be rid of it (literally, vomit it up)

but do nothing. They steal worthless junk and get zilch for it.
They want me to pick pockets for them, but I'm not about to do
it. I've got to ditch them and find somebody else to work for.
They make me sick.

Or, even shorter:

I know these guys. They're jerks. I've got to leave them.

Second, antitheses. The speech has plenty.

- I am boy to them / they could not be man to me
- three antics / a man
  (some productions rewrite "a" to "one" to make the
  antithesis even sharper)
- white-livered / red-faced
- faces it out / fights not
- killing tongue / quiet sword
- breaks words / keeps whole weapons
- few bad words / few good deeds
- take from another's pocket / put into mine
- their villainy / my weak stomach

Third, the changing height of the language. The Boy's speech
is generally simple, but wonderfully juicy words stand out here
and there, giving the speech texture and humor. "Swashers"
is one. Another is "purchase," the superbly ironic euphemism
Pistol, Bardolph, and Nim use to dignify their thievery. ("Oh,
my word, no, I didn't *steal* that, I *purchased* it.") But what really
gives this text moments of height is the Boy's amazing talent for

making jokes and puns. The speech has the tenor of a stand-up comedy routine, with punch lines so sharp that you can almost hear the rim shot on the drums. ("And that was against a post when he was drunk!"—*ba-dum bum!*) To be sure, some of these jokes—the one about lugging the lute case twelve leagues and selling it for chump change, the one about carrying coals—are not as funny to modern ears as they may have been to Shakespeare's audience. But their rhythm and tempo, the music of the piece, still communicate a loose-limbed and fun tone.[120] And that music changes throughout, just as it does in a long verse speech. The Boy uses polysyllabic words and bursts of monosyllables. "I must leave them," the central point of the speech, rings out thanks to its four sharp single-syllable words. Similarly, "I must cast it up" ends the speech with a decisive flourish. The verbs in each statement are powerful: "must leave," "must cast," illustrating that, as in the verse, verbs do special and vivid work.

Argument, antithesis, height of language. All good, all the same as in verse.

---

120 These jokes, and other similarly time-worn bits of Shakespearean comic banter, are often slightly rewritten by modern theater artists in the interests of clarity and "making it work." When I directed this play, the Boy said, "In Calais, they stole an outhouse bucket. I knew by that piece of service the men would end up in the dumps." In one memorable production, I heard him say, "Bardolph stole a piano, bore it twelve miles, and sold it for three cents." Perhaps neither rewrite is destined for immortality. But both at least keep the sense intact and give the Boy a fair shot at getting a laugh. Prose is much more amenable to such changes than verse; after all, in prose, no strict meter limits the choice of words available as replacements. In addition, these stand-up-comedy-style monologues depend for their success on a feeling of spontaneity. Shakespeare himself complained that his clowns frequently departed from the written text. Though certainly not an endorsement of rewriting, the complaint is testimony to the fact that it was standard practice in the Elizabethan theater. Now, as then, the practical requirements of stagecraft trump the fastidiousness of even the most eloquent playwright.

Enter the Prose Postulate

Fourth on our list of analytical techniques would be phrasing with the verse line, but we can't do that here, since there is no verse line in this prose speech.

So the Prose Postulate kicks in, and those Shakespearean Organizing Structures do their work.

S.O.S. ONE: THE SENTENCE   The Boy's speech consists of thirteen sentences:

1. As young as I am, I have observed these three swashers.

2. I am boy to them all three, but all they three, though they should serve me, could not be man to me, for indeed three such antics do not amount to a man.

3. For Bardolph, he is white-livered and red-faced—by the means whereof a' faces it out, but fights not.

4. For Pistol, he hath a killing tongue and a quiet sword—by the means whereof a' breaks words, and keeps whole weapons.

5. For Nim, he hath heard that men of few words are the best men, and therefore he scorns to say his prayers, lest a' should be thought a coward.

6. But his few bad words are matched with as few good deeds—for a' never broke any man's head but his own, and that was against a post, when he was drunk.

7. They will steal anything, and call it "purchase."

8. Bardolph stole a lute-case, bore it twelve leagues, and sold it for three halfpence.

9. Nim and Bardolph are sworn brothers in filching, and in Calais they stole a fire shovel.

10. I knew by that piece of service the men would carry coals.

11. They would have me as familiar with men's pockets as their gloves or their handkerchiefs—which makes much against my manhood, if I should take from another's pocket to put into mine, for it is plain pocketing up of wrongs.

12. I must leave them, and seek some better service.

13. Their villainy goes against my weak stomach, and therefore I must cast it up.

Listed this way, the sentences reveal the extraordinary rhythmic structure of the speech. Sentences 2 through 6 are almost identical in length. They are bracketed by the short, staccato bursts of sentences 1 and 7. Sentence 11 goes on for a long while, in counterpoint to the brief sentences 10 and 12.

Still have that blank piece of paper that's come in handy for phrasing the verse one line at a time? Grab it and lay it over all but the first sentence of this speech. Move along sentence by sentence, saying them one at a time.

It's a miracle! Our trusty Paper Trick makes the speech instantly clear, just as it does with verse.

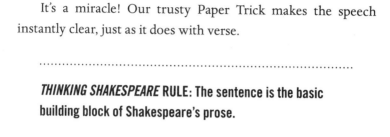

THINKING SHAKESPEARE RULE: The sentence is the basic building block of Shakespeare's prose.

When you're working on prose, recast a block paragraph into a list of the sentences that compose it. Read them one at a time, careful not to glance at the next until you've finished the one you're working on. You will find the speech remarkably clear.

S.O.S. TWO: PARALLELISM The verse line has the meter to keep it together. What is the equivalent in the sentence? What keeps sentences 2 through 6 in the Boy's speech from sounding repetitive and flat? How do you keep the thinking fresh?

Look carefully at the composition of the three sentences about the cowardice of the "antics"—sentences 3, 4, and 5. Each begins with "For" and a name. After the name, the first two sentences unfold identically, following this pattern:

For (NAME), he has (BAD FEATURE 1) and (BAD FEATURE 2), by the means whereof, a' (DOES SILLY THING) but not (GOOD THING).

We can put this pattern in the form of a chart that lays out the sentences schematically:

	Sentence 1	Sentence 2
Name	Bardolph	Pistol
Bad feature 1	white-livered	killing tongue
Bad feature 2	red-faced	quiet sword
Silly thing	faces it out	breaks words
Good thing	fights not	keeps whole weapons

Read vertically down the columns labeled *Sentence 1* and *Sentence 2*. You'll hear the basic thought behind each sentence. As the table reveals, the two sentences have a special relationship to each other: they are *parallel*.

Parallel structure is one of the key S.O.S's that hold Shakespeare's prose together.

The X-ray Method

If making a table seems a little too scientific for an acting exercise (when Iago calls Cassio a "mathematician," he does not mean it as a compliment), there is another technique you can try. Write out the sentence in a way that makes its structure easier to follow. This "X-ray Method" puts the skeleton of the sentence on the outside, where you can see it.

Here, that would look—and sound—something like this:

For **Bardolph**,
> he is
>> *white-livered*
> and
>> *red-faced*—
> by the means whereof
>> a' *faces it out*,

but
> *fights not.*

For **Pistol**,
> he hath
>> *a killing tongue*
>
> and
>> *a quiet sword—*
>
> by the means whereof
>> a' *breaks words,*
>
> and
>> *keeps whole weapons.*

The X-ray Method makes the parallel structure unmistakable. The next sentence ("For Nim . . . ") begins in parallel to sentences 3 and 4 but then swerves away into its own form. Shakespeare loves pulling switches like that, as we have seen. If he sets up a pattern, he will soon break it, in this case by composing two similar sentences then making the third move in a new direction.

More parallelism occurs as the speech progresses. Sentences 7 through 11 follow an identical structure. In all five, the boy makes a general statement describing something the three antics have done or would do and then he develops it with a joke full of specific comic detail.

General statement:
> They will steal anything, and call it a "purchase."

Comic detail:
> Bardolph stole a lute-case, bore it twelve leagues, and sold it for three halfpence.

General statement:

Nim and Bardolph are sworn brothers in filching,

Comic detail:

and in Calais they stole a fire shovel. I knew by that piece of service the men would carry coals.

General statement:

They would have me as familiar with men's pockets as their gloves or their handkerchiefs—

Comic detail:

which makes much against my manhood, if I should take from another's pocket to put into mine, for it is plain pocketing up of wrongs.

Set-up, punch line. Set-up, punch line. Set-up, punch line. It's the parallel structure of the three sentences that makes the Boy sound as if he were onstage at a comedy club. Parallel structure also carries the actor through the bulk of this long speech, leaving only two short declamatory statements at the end.

S.O.S. THREE: THREE-PART BUILDS   The repetition of the same basic sentence structure three times is itself a structure, and one that is particularly well-suited to comedy: the three-part build.

We have run into Shakespeare's three-part builds before. There are a couple here. Bardolph 1) stole a lute-case, 2) bore it twelve leagues, and 3) sold it for three halfpence. Men's 1) pockets, 2) gloves, and 3) handkerchiefs.

The basic impetus for the Boy's speech—his need to talk about three antics—is another three-part build. It's one more piece of structure holding the speech together and giving the actor a simple but powerful organizing principle for the paragraph.

S.O.S. FOUR: ANTITHESIS Earlier we listed nine instances of antithesis in the Boy's speech. Of the speech's roughly 250 words, around 70 consist of these nine pairs of oppositions. That's a quarter of the speech. Simply by allowing them to do their work, the actor playing the Boy will find himself carried through the better part of the paragraph.

Try the speech again. Think the argument—*I know these guys. They're jerks. I've got to leave them*—and lift out this bounty of antithesis. The speech will immediately come to life. As in verse, antithesis is a reliable way to parse thought and attack a long speech.

MANY STRIKING STRUCTURES The four S.O.S.'s described above are just a few in a long list of the devices that govern Shakespeare's prose. Here are some more:

> **Numerical groupings**, such as the tripartite structure of the Boy's speech—Bardolph, Nim, Pistol. (See Falstaff discussing the twofold manner in which alcohol makes people drunk in *Henry IV, Part II* [4.2.82–111]).

> **A sequential, point-by-point retelling** of something that just happened. (See Launce in *The Two Gentlemen of Verona*, discussing how his dog, Crab, urinated on the floor in the duke's dining room [4.4.1–34]).

> **An orderly inventory** of something right in front of your eyes. (See Trinculo in *The Tempest* discovering what he thinks is a dead fish but turns out to be the monstrous Caliban [2.2.18–38]).

An extended riff on a single idea. (See Shylock in *The Merchant of Venice* teasing out instance after instance of his thesis that Christians and Jews are alike [3.1.45–61]).

A repeated phrase or phrases that thump like bass lines through a long disquisition. This S.O.S. occurs frequently in the early comedies. (See Benedick in *Much Ado about Nothing* repeating "yet I am well," and "or I'll never . . . " as he pontificates about the kind of woman he will one day love [2.3.8–31]).

A pileup of antitheses. This S.O.S. governs the prose spoken by many of the clowns in Shakespeare's middle and late plays. (See Touchstone in *As You Like It*, comparing life in the country to life in the court [3.2.13–20]).

The S.O.S.'s come in infinite varieties. An actor's job is to find them and use them to turn the long road of a big prose speech into a series of small, manageable, thinkable steps. Use the structures described on the previous pages as a starting checklist. Then read your speech a few times and listen carefully. Before long, you will see the S.O.S.'s that form the underlying architecture of thought and language and support you as you work through the text.

The Return of Punctuation

If you're having trouble identifying the S.O.S.'s, know that Shakespeare's punctuation provides a powerful way to speed your structural sleuthing.

Remember the first S.O.S.: the *sentence* is the basic building block of prose. Each sentence ends with a period, just as each verse line ends with a line ending. The sentence-ending period, along with all the other punctuation within the sentence, not only opens a window on structure but also sculpts each idea one thought at a time.

Look again at the X-ray of sentences 3 and 4 of the Boy's speech, paying particular attention to what's at the right-hand margin:

For Bardolph,
    he is
        white-livered
    and
        red-faced—
by the means whereof
        a' faces it out,
    but
        fights not.
For Pistol,
    he hath
        a killing tongue
    and
        a quiet sword—
by the means whereof
        a' breaks words,
    and
        keeps whole weapons.

Notice that when we X-ray the speeches in this way, we see more than their parallel structure. Their *parallel punctuation* also emerges. The commas, dashes, and periods are placed in *exactly the same spots* in both sentences. They inform the phrasing every bit as much as the antitheses and parallelisms do.

....

***THINKING SHAKESPEARE* RULE: Phrasing with the punctuation is helpful in prose.**

....

Back in chapter 7, we noted that when we phrase Shakespeare's verse according to the punctuation, rather than the line endings, we convert it into a kind of prose, flattening it, reducing it, and transforming its very nature. With Shakespeare's prose, however, the punctuation guides the way. Following it does not compromise its essential music. On the contrary, following the punctuation *reveals the basic structure of the prose.*

Mamet Moments in Prose

Ironically, by using the X-ray method on the two sentences "For Bardolph . . ." and "For Pistol . . . ," we have done the converse of what we didn't want to do in chapter 7. *We have transformed prose into a kind of verse.*

This "found verse" has its own loose and tumbling inner logic that cues thought and breath. It has *implied* line endings, MMMs that create questions that summon the next thought and move the language forward. You can use the Paper Trick on this improvised, found free-verse, moving through it one fragment at a time:

For **Bardolph**,　　　　　*(what about him?)*
　　he is
　　　　white-livered　　　*(what else?)*
　　and
　　　　red-faced—

```
by the means whereof          (he does what?)
        a' faces it out,      (yes?)
    but
        fights not.
For Pistol,                   (what about him?)
    he hath
        a killing tongue      (what else?)
    and
        a quiet sword—
by the means whereof          (he does what?)
        a' breaks words,      (yes?)
    and
        keeps whole weapons.
```

You might feel that you have broken up these sentences beyond recognition. For the record, it should be stated that no actor would actually say these lines in such a fragmented manner. But because you have taken them apart, their deeper structures will remain in your mind after you have put them back together. Try again:

For Bardolph, he is white-livered and red-faced—by the means whereof a' faces it out, but fights not. For Pistol, he hath a killing tongue and a quiet sword—by the means whereof a' breaks words, and keeps whole weapons.

All the detail you've worked so hard to identify is still there, helping you think your way forward in one long sweep rather than bit by bit. You are thinking Shakespeare's prose.

MORE REHEARSAL TIME

Here is one more speech in which the Prose Postulate and S.O.S's can be seen at work.

Launcelot Gobbo is Shylock's servant (we met him in the previous chapter's Things Further Thought On when his blind dad *tutoyer*-ed him). Ill treated and angry, he debates whether he should remain in the employ of Shylock ("the Jew") or get as far away as he can.

<table>
<tr><td>encourage; allow</td><td>Certainly my conscience will serve° me to run from this Jew my master. The fiend is at mine elbow and tempts me, saying to me, "Gobbo, Launcelot Gobbo, good Launcelot," or "good Gobbo," or "good Launcelot Gobbo—use your legs, take the start,121 run away." My conscience says, "No, take heed, honest Launcelot, take heed, honest Gobbo," or, as aforesaid, "honest Launcelot Gobbo—do not run, scorn running with thy heels."122 Well, the most courageous fiend</td></tr>
<tr><td>Italian for "away"</td><td>bids me pack. "Via!"° says the fiend; "Away!" says the fiend. "For the heavens, rouse up a brave mind," says the fiend, "and run." Well, my conscience, hanging about the neck of my heart, says very wisely to me "My honest friend Launcelot"—being an honest man's son, or rather an honest woman's son, for, indeed, my</td></tr>
</table>

---

121 take the start: i.e., get going already

122 scorn . . . heels: 1) don't allow your feet to do any running; 2) vehemently scorn the idea of running

father did something smack, something grow-to; he had a kind of taste[123] —well, my conscience says, "Launcelot, budge not"; "Budge!" says the fiend; "Budge not," says my conscience. "Conscience," say I, "you counsel well." "Fiend," say I, "you counsel well." To be ruled by my conscience, I should stay with the Jew my master who, God bless the mark,[124] is a kind of devil; and to run away from the Jew I should be ruled by the fiend who, saving your reverence, is the devil himself. Certainly the Jew is the very devil incarnation[125] ; and, in my conscience, my conscience is but a kind of hard conscience to offer to counsel me to stay with the Jew. The fiend gives the more friendly counsel. I will run, fiend. My heels are at your commandment. I will run.

(2.2.1–25)

This speech has it all—an antithesis that underpins the entire argument, changes in the height of the language, long and short sentences, poly- and monosyllables, repeated phrases, lists, numbered groupings—the works. X-rayed as free verse, those structures come clear.

....

123 **my father . . . taste:** all three phrases suggest euphemistically that his father was lustful and sexually adventurous

124 **God bless the mark:** a conventional phrase (like "saving your reverence" two lines later) that was used as an apology before saying something potentially offensive. Today's "excuse my language" or "pardon my French" are rough equivalents.

125 **incarnation:** Launcelot mispronounces *incarnate*, meaning *in the flesh*, but there is also a pun on *carnation* in its sense of "the color red," because in Shakespeare's period, a time of virulent anti-Semitism, Jewish characters were depicted onstage, bizarrely, wearing red wigs.

Certainly
> my conscience will serve me to run from this Jew my master.
>
> The *fiend* is at mine elbow and tempts me, saying to me
>> "Gobbo, Launcelot Gobbo, good Launcelot,"
>>> or "good Gobbo,"
>>>> or "good Launcelot Gobbo—
>> use your legs, take the start, run away."
>
> My *conscience* says
>> "No, take heed, honest Launcelot,
>>> take heed, honest Gobbo,"
>>>> or, as aforesaid, "honest Launcelot Gobbo—
>> do not run, scorn running with thy heels."
>
> Well,
>> the most courageous fiend bids me pack.
>>> "*Via!*" says the fiend;
>>>> "Away!" says the fiend.
>>>>> "For the heavens, rouse up a brave mind,"
>>>>> says the fiend,
>>>>> "and run."
>
> Well,
>> my conscience, hanging about the neck of my heart, says
>> very wisely to me
>>> "My honest friend Launcelot"—
>>>> being an honest man's son, or rather an honest
>>>> woman's son,
>>>>> for, indeed, my father did something
>>>>> smack, something grow-to;
>>>>> he had a kind of taste—
>
> well,
>> my conscience says,

"Launcelot, budge not";
"Budge!"

says the fiend;

"Budge not,"

says my conscience.

"*Conscience*,"

say I,

"you counsel well."

"*Fiend*,"

say I,

"you counsel well."

To be ruled by my *conscience*,

I should stay with the Jew my master who,

God bless the mark,

is a kind of devil;

and to run away from the Jew

I should be ruled by the *fiend* who,

saving your reverence,

is the devil himself.

Certainly

the Jew is the very devil incarnation;

and,

in my conscience,

my conscience is but a kind of hard conscience

to offer to counsel me to stay with the Jew.

The fiend gives the more friendly counsel.

I will run, fiend.

My heels are at your commandment.

I will run.

This found, free-verse rearrangement reveals a rich structure. With it, Launcelot Gobbo proves this chapter's central point: Shakespeare's prose is Shakespeare's verse without the meter. It has every brilliant facet the verse does.

All it's missing are the iambs.

··

THINGS FURTHER THOUGHT ON

··

Shakespeare's Old English

Both characters we met in this chapter are working men, not aristocrats. They are recognizable Renaissance London types: wisecracking serving men (despite the fact that Launcelot is Venetian and the Boy is from a time nearly two centuries before the Renaissance). Their grammar and vocabulary would have sounded as close as anything in Shakespeare to the language spoken by many in his audience. Of course, that day-to-day speech wasn't structured and made amusing by the greatest writer in the history of the world, but Launcelot's and the Boy's voices would have rung familiar to everyone who walked the streets just outside the Globe Theater, where the plays were first performed.

Despite its patina of ordinariness, however, the language of Launcelot and the Boy still sounds extremely complicated to our modern ears. If we could walk those London streets on the afternoons these speeches were being performed (if only!), we would surely fail to understand much of what people said to us. We would struggle with Elizabethan English just as we struggle with a foreign language we might encounter on our world travels today. It's a simple truth that every student of Shakespeare must grapple with: the English language as we speak it today is very, very different from the English spoken by the Bard.

For one thing, the Elizabethan and Jacobean English[126] language Shakespeare knew 400 years ago bore hallmarks of its recent ancestor, Middle English. That language, in turn, descended from Old English, essentially a Germanic tongue. For this reason, Elizabethan English in some ways resembles today's German more closely than it does today's English. The German-ness of Shakespeare's English is easy to see. For example, verbs often come at or near the ends of sentences. There are verb cases, declensions, and conjugations that still exist in German but that have disappeared from modern English (*doth* is actually the third-person singular form of *do*; today we use *does*. "The lady doth protest too much," says Gertrude in *Hamlet*, to which we would ask, "Does she?") As in German, Elizabethan English has two forms of the letter *s*. "ſ" was the English symbol for sharp *s*, the equivalent of *ß* found in such German words as *Straße*. The playwright's own name was in fact spelled "Shake-ſpeare" during his lifetime. Many nouns are capitalized ("And Time that gave doth now his gift confound"—Sonnet 60), as they still are in German. The list could go on and on. The similarities between Elizabethan English and German are so numerous that for hundreds of years, the most accomplished and nuanced translations of Shakespeare have been into German, and most linguists agree that after English, Shakespeare sounds best in that language.

But another factor, as the line from Sonnet 60 so aptly puts it, is that time effects vast changes. Shakespeare sounds formal and remote to us in part because of his temporal distance from

---

126 The adjectives are named for the monarchs who ruled at the time: Queen Elizabeth I and King James I, whose name in Latin was *Jacobus*.

us. Thousands of vocabulary words have fallen into and out of English since Shakespeare wrote. Rules of English grammar and syntax—even those not related to the German—have evolved dramatically in four centuries. In many ways, the miracle of Shakespeare in the modern world is not that he is so brilliant, but that we understand him at all. No less an authority than Sir Peter Hall, the iambic fundamentalist we discussed earlier and one of the great Shakespeareans in the world, predicts that English is now changing so much and so fast that in less than 200 years, Shakespeare will be completely incomprehensible to speakers of his own tongue!

It remains to be seen whether Hall's prediction will prove accurate. Shakespeare's is an old form of English, alien-sounding and sometimes hard to grasp. But it is English after all, and if you speak the language, you probably understand much more of Shakespeare, and much more readily, than you give yourself credit for.

ACT V

Ron Leibman as Shylock in *The Merchant of Venice*, directed by Barry Edelstein at the Public Theater, 1995. Photo © Michal Daniel, 1995.

CHAPTER
—№—
15

WHAT'S PAST IS PROLOGUE

SOME CONCLUSIONS

As amazing as it seems, even after working through all the techniques and exercises in the fourteen chapters of this book, an actress will still find herself at the beginning of her work on this material.

That's no reason to be discouraged. After nearly twenty years of working on Shakespeare's plays more or less without pause, I still find myself near the beginning of my understanding of them.

Shakespeare is a lifetime's occupation. Working on him is a process. It's cumulative, and it takes time.

But the process delivers. Step by step, technique by technique, and exercise by exercise, Shakespeare's words come closer and closer to being your own thoughts. When they finally do become yours, when thinking them is effortless and spontaneous, the thrill is unlike anything else in a theater artist's life.

"What's past is prologue," says Antonio in *The Tempest* (with wonderful use of antithesis), "what to come, in yours and my discharge."

The studies that have led you to what you now know about how Shakespeare works are merely spurs to the further knowledge your labors will bring as you continue forward. The more you analyze him, the more he lends you a hand. He reveals a lot on one reading, he unfolds even more upon careful scrutiny, and over time, through repeated visits, he yields great secrets.

Thinking Shakespeare is the foundation. *Knowing* Shakespeare, *mastering* Shakespeare, *living* Shakespeare—these are the edifices built upon it, one beam, one plank, one brick, at a time.

Loving Shakespeare is the life lived within those buildings.

The Mystery's Heart

Hamlet, that most opaque of Shakespeare's creations, scoffs at Rosencrantz and Guildenstern for their presumptuous attempt to understand him. In a memorable phrase, he warns them that it is impossible to "pluck out the heart of my mystery."

I think of this line whenever I marvel at how dense Shakespeare is and how difficult it sometimes can be to discover exactly what all that density is there to express. All of us who study Shakespeare are like Rosencrantz and Guildenstern in that regard, and Shakespeare is like our Hamlet: somewhat aloof, his mind always a few steps ahead of ours, his precise meaning infuriatingly difficult to ascertain. We study and delve, speculate and dream, as we labor to connect with his words. We make progress and then we stall; we inch forward only to hit some barrier. "The task [we] undertake," it seems, "is numb'ring sands and drinking oceans dry."

That's when we should remember another line, not from Shakespeare but from one of his greatest acolytes, the American-turned-British poet T. S. Eliot. "No! I am not Prince Hamlet, nor was meant to be." It might as well have been written by the Bard himself.

Shakespeare isn't Hamlet. Unlike the heart of Hamlet's mystery, the playwright's mystery is, finally, pluckable. We *can know* what his words express. We *can discover* the rules that govern their composition. We *can learn* which ones we need to stress for their sense to emerge and where to breathe so that their rhythms and structures have maximum impact.

All it requires is dedication. All it takes is practice.

My twenty years' devotion to Shakespeare may not have put me much beyond the foothills of my climb to his summit, but it has given me a pretty sure footing. To me, reading Shakespeare is little different from reading the newspaper. The language is clear, immediate, and accessible.

How did that happen?

Practice. Repetition. Hard work.

"Experience is by industry achieved, / And perfected by the swift course of time," says another Antonio, this one the father of a bright young man eager for knowledge, in *The Two Gentlemen of Verona*.

After all, the "mystery" Hamlet guards so fiercely isn't quite what we think of when we hear that word today. Hamlet uses the word not to mean an *enigma (that which eludes understanding)*. Rather, he intends an older definition: *a set of skills or knowledge unique to a particular group and reserved only for its initiates*. Hamlet's mystery is knowable only by insiders, not interlopers like Rosencrantz and Guildenstern. So it is with Shakespeare's mystery. He offers himself to those who have the keys. Happily, his keys are widely available. They can be had by those who are willing to devote time and energy to opening the lock.

Inside the door lie plentiful riches. They might be described, in a phrase the Duke of Clarence uses in *Henry VI, Part Three*, as "such rewards / As victors wear at the Olympian games."

Thoughts Speculative

Once you're a Shakespearean insider, what comes next?

The techniques in this book lead to what might be called *Further Thinking Shakespeare*, or perhaps, *Thinking More Deeply About Shakespeare*.

The clarity and specificity of utterance you have worked so hard to achieve, and the direct connection between thought and emotion you have forged, pose a whole series of questions about how Shakespeare should be performed in the contemporary theater and what place he should occupy in the culture of everyday American life.

These questions are fodder for insomniac rumination and over-a-beer jawboning. Now and then I bat them around with my students and my colleagues, or as I sit down to read the Shakespeare play I am about to direct.

> If Shakespeare's language feels as familiar as the morning paper, is it right if I speak it that way?

> If I'm from Oklahoma and I'm playing Cordelia, is it okay if she speaks with the same accent I have?

> If Shakespeare shouldn't sound like William Shatner, is it better if it sounds like Patrick Stewart?

If I really want Romeo to be someone I can relate to, would it be cool if I have him wear jeans rather than pumpkin pants?

If the Chorus in *Henry V* reminds me of war correspondents on CNN, how about setting the entire production during the invasion of Iraq?

"Much virtue in 'if,'" Touchstone proclaims in *As You Like It*, in one of my very favorite Shakespearean phrases. *If* provokes thought. *If* says that the way things are now isn't as good as the way they might be. *If* is the first step toward change. *If* brings growth.

These Shakespearean *ifs*, and the debates they inspire, are what keep these texts alive and fresh from generation to generation and production to production. Even the briefest survey of Shakespeare in today's theater will show the enormous range of ways in which these *ifs* are answered by our leading artists.

Many Ways Meet in One

There is a conservative view of Shakespeare. According to it, the plays are to be set in their own period and no other, interpretation is to be kept to a minimum, and the accents are to sound British, or certainly no further west than the middle of the Atlantic. There is also a progressive view. According to it, the connections between the play and our world are to be made maximally apparent, through design, conception, interpretation, casting, and diction, and the distance between Shakespeare's time and our own is to be so minimized that the play seems to have been written today.

There is an actor's Shakespeare, according to which the characters and their words are central, and a director's Shakespeare, according to which subjective insights about the texts are of paramount importance.

There is even a remnant of the eighteenth-century's scholiast's Shakespeare, according to which the theater is nothing more than a distraction from—and a vulgar insult to—the pure literary qualities of the texts. (We theater professionals don't discuss that school of thought in polite company.)

I've adhered to various doctrines over time. But after twenty years, I've come to recognize that there never really is, nor can there ever truly be, only one way to do Shakespeare.

In my own career, I've directed the plays in modern dress and in period dress. I've done heavily re-interpreted productions and straight, uninflected ones. The critics have rapped me on one hand for "ripping the stuffing out" of the plays and chided me on the other for "not lifting the play off the page." They have cheered me for my "stunning re-imagination" of one play and lauded my "commendable respect for the playwright's intent" in another. Eventually I realized that no common denominator unifies my attempts beyond my own gut response to the words themselves.

Each play has told me the right way to do it. Each moment has shown me how it must be staged. Each word has insisted on the one approach that makes it sound newly coined and fully real.

No preordained theory can solve all of Shakespeare. No manifesto can encompass him.

All we can do is study his words with all the rigor we can muster, bring our own interests, imaginations, and humanity to bear on them, and then resolve to be as sensitive and truthful as we possibly can be at every moment.

Shakespeare tells us what we must do in order to make him work.

They Knew in 1623

How do we listen for Shakespeare's voice so that we will hear it when we need to?

Here, I must defer to three of his greatest adherents and their two excellent pieces of advice.

One:

T. S. Eliot, mentioned above, said this: "We must know all of Shakespeare's work in order to know any of it."

There is not an idea anywhere in Shakespeare that isn't echoed somewhere else in Shakespeare. Lines, characters, even whole scenes he attempted in his early plays get recycled and revised in his later ones. Know one, and you know the other. *The Merry Wives of Windsor* illuminates *The Winter's Tale*. *Pericles* helps make sense of *The Comedy of Errors*. Know all, and you'll know any.

Which leads to . . .

Two:

John Hemings and Henry Condell, the actors in Shakespeare's company who gathered together and published their late friend's plays in the landmark First Folio of 1623, wrote an introduction to that volume. Addressed "To the great Variety of Readers," it was one part sales pitch ("what ever you do, Buy"), one part eulogy ("he was a happy imitator of Nature, was a most gentle expresser of it,"), and one part summary of this book's core premise that thought and speech are linked ("His mind and hand went together: And what he thought, he uttered").

Its most significant part, though, is a valedictory counsel for anyone who would ever set out to master the monumental and astonishing output of this preternaturally gifted writer who rose from a small town in the middle of England to shape the imagination of the world:

Reade him, therefore; and againe, and againe.

That's about as good a tag line to *Thinking Shakespeare* as any I can imagine.

You now have a new and versatile set of tools with which to read these marvelous works. Use them. Read the plays. Listen to them. Luxuriate in them. Love them. They will take you places you never dreamed existed, and they will tell you things you never even knew you didn't know.

All you have to do is read him, therefore.

And again.

And again.

EPILOGUE

WORKS WORTH KEEPING CLOSE AT HAND

A comprehensive bibliography of helpful Shakespeare resources would run many times longer than this entire book. However, smart and curious *Thinking Shakespeare* actors and directors can use the following list of essential works as a starting point for their explorations.

The books listed below are the ones I turn to most frequently in my own work. Some are new and cutting edge, and some are old standards. Some are straightforward, and others are quirky. Most are still in print. All are available in good libraries or at vast online bookstores such as *www.bn.com.*

I've derived much pleasure and enlightenment from them all. I recommend that you make room for them on a short shelf that could, in time, grow into a comprehensive Shakespeare library.

The Text

The words come first. The ability to answer the question *Why am I using this word now?* depends on the accuracy of that word, and accuracy requires an authoritative edition of the plays.

COMPLETE WORKS   One of my rules is that in order to live a good life, you should own a *Complete Works* of Shakespeare. (It's a rule I encourage in others whenever I can: the *Complete Works* is my standard gift for all weddings, bar mitzvahs, confirmations, and graduations.) There are many editions currently in print. Two of them are, to my mind, superior:

The Norton Shakespeare, **edited by Stephen Greenblatt, W. W. Norton and Company, 1997.**

> The general introduction by Greenblatt, the doyen of contemporary Shakespeareans, in itself explains almost everything you could want to know about Shakespeare. Featuring a scrupulously well-edited text, concise introductions to each play, clear notes and glosses, and helpful supplementary materials, this is my top choice in one-volume Shakespeares.

The Riverside Shakespeare, **Second Edition, Houghton Mifflin Company, 1997.**

> I list this second to the Norton only because it lacks the imprimatur of the great Greenblatt. Otherwise, it's a fantastic volume. Some argue its text is superior to Norton's, which is based on the very idiosyncratic Oxford edition of the mid-1980s, but in my view that's splitting hairs.

SINGLE-VOLUME EDITIONS In Things Further Thought On at the end of chapter 6, we discussed the texts printed in Shakespeare's period and the modern editions that derive from them. Of those modern editions, the cream of the crop are world-class single-volume scholarly editions of the plays available from three great publishers. I never go into rehearsal without them.

Oxford University Press publishes the plays in its Oxford World's Classics series.

Cambridge University Press has its New Cambridge Shakespeare series.

The Arden Shakespeare was for many years the standard in scholarly texts, but don't be confused—the titles in its First and Second Series date from decades ago in some cases; only the Arden Third Series is as up to date as either Oxford or Cambridge.

Each volume from these three series features a carefully edited text made by one of the world's leading experts and based on the very latest scholarship. These editors provide thorough introductions, copious notes, some illustrations, usually a stage history of the play under consideration, and, in some cases, excerpts from Shakespeare's sources or other relevant material.

Here's the rub: neither the Arden Third nor the Oxford or Cambridge has yet tackled every single play. Between the three publishers, though, you can cover almost the entire canon. Wonderfully, in the case of a handful of the plays, you can get all three publishers' editions and look at them side by side. That's an embarrassment of riches.

For students and general readers who don't necessarily need these sometimes overwhelmingly high-octane and heavily technical scholarly editions, the Barnes & Noble Shakespeare series is a godsend. Edited by David Scott Kastan, one of America's major Shakespeareans, the texts in this series feature concise and very readable introductory and historical material, newly and scrupulously edited texts, and, best of all, superb glosses and marginal notes that make even Shakespeare's strangest turns of phrase transparent and immediately comprehensible. Kastan strikes just the right balance between too much information and not enough, and the series hews to what's important while omitting the minutiae that's the province of Oxford, Cambridge, and Arden. Barnes & Noble even manages to include some material that the big three don't, such as wonderful short essays on works in other media inspired by the Shakespeare play in each volume and a selective list of recommendations for further reading. The series is destined to become the standard single-volume Shakespeare for non-specialist readers. It's a fantastic addition to the literature. (One further terrific feature: the volumes are small enough to fit in the back pocket of a pair of jeans. This is an important consideration when rehearsal time rolls around, and it's sure to make Barnes & Noble Shakespeare a favorite of actors.)

I also try to consult the *New Variorum Shakespeare* edition of the play I'm working on. Published in the late nineteenth century and edited by H. H. Furness, the Greenblatt of his day, the *Variorum* is full of quirky delights. It takes a trip to a library to find, though.

SparkNotes' *No Fear Shakespeare* series is another useful single-volume resource. It presents on facing pages both the original Shakespeare text and also a translation into modern English. These can help enormously as you prepare your paraphrase. They're also just great fun to read. (I've done a few of them myself, so you can trust my recommendation!)

PERIOD TEXTS   Every good library will have reproductions of the First Folio and, usually, the early Quarto editions of Shakespeare. Both are valuable to keep around during rehearsals. If you want to own one, a few publishers print copies.

Applause Theater Books is my favorite. They publish a First Folio in facsimile (a photographic reproduction that looks exactly like the original text), another in modern type that preserves the original spelling, and single-volume editions of the Folio texts. Atria Books and Taylor and Francis also publish Folio texts. Cambridge University Press publishes modernized versions of the Quarto texts, in the cases of some of the major plays that were first published in that format. A facsimile of the Complete Quartos is harder to come by, but your library will have one, and you may be able to find a used copy somewhere online.

INTERNET TEXTS   In my productions and in my classes, I always prepare my own texts by downloading the play from the Internet and then word-processing it and making whatever cuts I deem necessary. Shakespeare's plays are ubiquitous online. My first stop, though, is often *www-tech.mit.edu/Shakespeare/*. And Google recently rolled out a Shakespeare site at *www.google.com/ Shakespeare*. It's limited in scope for now, but like everything else that innovative company provides, it's sure to grow into a major Internet resource in the time ahead.

Reference Works
DICTIONARIES   *The Oxford English Dictionary* (OED) remains the most important reference work for the rehearsal room. It tells you what a word means, where it came from, and what it has meant over the years of its existence. The twenty-volume set costs

around $1,500 new. A web-based version is available by monthly or annual subscription. But don't worry; every library has one you can use for free, and most even have a CD-ROM version or access to the online version.[127]

Less all-encompassing dictionaries of the type most people already have on their bookshelves, such as the *Concise Oxford*, can be useful, but often specialized or rare words—the very sort Shakespeare loves—aren't there. In those cases, glossaries or lexicons, which provide definitions of a limited list of words, can be helpful.

LEXICONS

***Shakespeare Lexicon and Quotation Dictionary*, edited by Alexander Schmidt, in two volumes, Dover Publications, 1971.**

The standard, in paperback. It supplies brief definitions of most of the unusual words in Shakespeare and gives the context in which they're used.

A *Shakespeare Glossary*, edited by C. T. Onions and Robert Eagleson, Oxford University Press, 1986.

A very similar work but in one volume, the *Glossary* was first compiled by one of the original editors of the *OED*. Onions simply looked up the *OED* definitions of each odd Shakespeare word he could think of, and listed them. Eagleson added a few that Onions omitted.

---

127 I once got a copy of the Compact Edition of the *OED* as a free gift for signing up with a book of the month club. It consists of two huge books containing all twenty volumes photographically reduced so that four original pages fit on every one. The set comes with a cute magnifying glass in a little drawer. I feel like Sherlock Holmes every time I use it. You can get the same sensation by buying one of these on eBay for about $50. I quit the club, by the way, but I kept the dictionary!

OTHER REFERENCE WORKS

Complete Concordance to Shakespeare, **edited by John Bartlett, St. Martin's Press, 1969.**

This is an alphabetical listing of every word in Shakespeare, with citations to the place in each play that word occurs. If, say, you're working on Portia and are baffled by her sudden decision to talk about the song of the nightingale, you can look up the word in your *Concordance* and see if one of Shakespeare's other references to that bird sheds any light on your speech. This standard Shakespeare *Concordance* was complied by John Bartlett (famous for his book of *Familiar Quotations*) in the 1870s and then updated periodically. Still in print, it would run you close to $200 today. Check a library or use a limited online version at *www.bartleby.com*.

Shakespeare's Names: A New Pronouncing Dictionary, **edited by Louis Colaianni, Quite Specific Media Group, 1998.**

Gives the pronunciation of most of the proper names (of both people and places) in Shakespeare. Helpful in particular in the English histories and Roman plays.

Narrative and Dramatic Sources of Shakespeare, **edited by Geoffrey Bullough, Columbia University Press, 1957.**

An epic eight-volume set that compiles all the source material Shakespeare used in writing his plays. It can be very useful to look at how Shakespeare's imagination transformed the material that inspired him. This is definitely a library-only resource, but worth consulting.

Shakespeare's English Kings, **Peter Saccio, Oxford University Press, 2000.**

> A kind of mini-version of Bullough's eight-volume bomber, concentrating only on the sources Shakespeare used in writing his English history plays and the changes he made to those sources to suit his dramatic purposes.

Shakespeare A to Z, **by Charles Boyce, Delta Press, 1991.**

> A one-volume encyclopedia of the plays. Very useful to consult for a quick refresher on some character, action, or event in one of the texts. And a lot of fun to read. I always keep it handy.

On Acting and Directing

Of the thousands out there, these are the handful of books I recommend to students who ask. In order of interest:

Respect for Acting, **by Uta Hagen, Macmillan, 1973.**

> A toolkit that will help you get the job done, this is the perfect first book to read on the subject of acting, written by one of the great actresses of the twentieth century.

Audition, **by Michael Shurtleff, Bantam Books, 1978.**

> There's no more concise and concrete how-to acting guide available.

On the Technique of Acting, **by Michael Chekhov, Harper Perennial, 1991.**

> Somewhat more sophisticated than the previous two, with more emphasis on physical acting and less on the text. But a joy to read and very practical.

How to Stop Acting, **by Harold Guskin, Faber and Faber, 2003.**

> The best and most influential acting coach at work today offers advice and practical exercises in this clear, energetic guidebook.

Thinking Like a Director, **by Michael Bloom, Faber and Faber, 2001.**

> Fourteen concise chapters covering all aspects of the director's art, from research, to casting, to working with designers, to rehearsal. An ideal introduction to the subject.

Four books by great twentieth-century directors also merit attention. I often dip into them and always find rewards:

The Empty Space, **by Peter Brook, Atheneum, 1983.**

The Presence of the Actor, **by Joseph Chaikin, Atheneum, 1980.**

My Life in Art, **by Constantin Stanislavski, Methuen, 1985.**

Theatre, the Rediscovery of Style, **by Michel Saint-Denis, Theatre Arts Books, 1960.**

On Shakespeare's Life, Times, and Theater

Good works on Shakespeare himself and the world he lived in can offer invaluable aid in understanding arcane references in the text. They are also helpful and interesting on a general level. Here's a selective list:

BIOGRAPHIES

William Shakespeare: A Compact Documentary Life, **by Samuel Schoenbaum, Oxford University Press, 1987.**

> For years, this has been the standard narrative telling of Shakespeare's life based on the historical record (much of which is reproduced in this book). It gives the basic outline of the known facts.

Shakespeare, **by Michael Wood, Perseus Publishers, 2004.**

> Summarizes the basics and adds to them the discoveries about Shakespeare that have been made in the years since Schoenbaum's groundbreaking work. This volume is a companion to the fine PBS television series *In Search of Shakespeare*, and its pace and tone are therefore quicker and livelier than the average academic work. A good introduction to the subject for non-specialists.

Will in the World, **by Stephen Greenblatt, W. W. Norton and Company, 2005.**

> The master thinker on Shakespeare turns his attention to the playwright's life in this "speculative biography." One of the best Shakespeare books of the past twenty years, this dazzling work not only tells Shakespeare's life story but also draws connections between that life and the creations it left behind.

A Year in the Life of William Shakespeare: 1599, **by James Shapiro, HarperCollins, 2005.**

> Shapiro does Greenblatt one better by concentrating not on Shakespeare's entire life but on one eventful year in it. From there he branches out to every corner of the playwright's life, psyche, world, and canon. A wonderful and informative read.

SHAKESPEARE'S WORLD

This Stage Play World, **by Julia Briggs, Oxford University Press, 1997.**

> Originally published in 1983 and since revised, this is my favorite short introduction to the English Renaissance world in which Shakespeare lived. It is concise, readable, and thorough.

Companion to Shakespeare, **edited by David Scott Kastan, Blackwell, 1999.**

> This work is similar to Julia Briggs's book, but it includes nearly thirty essays by different critics, each addressing some aspect of Shakespeare's society and how it worked.

The *Cambridge Companion to Shakespeare* and the *Oxford Companion to Shakespeare* are also excellent places to start for a broad overview of the context in which the plays were written.

SHAKESPEARE'S THEATER   There are many works on specific aspects of Shakespeare's stagecraft, ranging from who his actors were and how they were trained, to the architecture of the playhouses he wrote for, to the financial arrangements that got his plays produced.

English scholar Andrew Gurr is one of the renowned experts in this area; his books *The Shakespearean Stage, Playgoing in Shakespeare's London, The Shakespeare Company,* and *Staging in Shakespeare's Theaters* will give you as much information as you need.

SPECIALTY SUBJECTS   There are books for just about every Shakespeare subject you can think of. Working on Falstaff? Try *Shakespeare and Alcohol,* by Buckner B. Trawick. Doing the "white rose / red rose" scene *from Henry VI, Part One?* Look at *Shakespeare's Flowers,* by Jessica Kerr. Playing the doctor in the sleepwalking scene in *Macbeth?* Have a glance at *The Medical Mind of Shakespeare,* by Aubrey C. Kail. Dismayed by the anti-Semitism in *The Merchant of Venice?* Crack open the stunning *Shakespeare and the Jews,* by James Shapiro, which revolutionized scholarly thinking on the subject. It's hard to think of an area that someone hasn't deemed worthy of a book-length study. Shakespeare's birds, Shakespeare's animals, food in Shakespeare, clothing in Shakespeare, Shakespeare's religious thought, Shakespeare's views on family, race, history, women, men, sex, dogs, horses, children, humor, politics, bicycles, barbecues . . . there is a book—possibly several books—on each.

Follow your nose. You're bound to find something useful. But let the buyer beware—there are as many stinkers as masterworks out there. Don't expect books like these to unlock the deepest mysteries of the canon. Delve into them instead with specific queries in mind. You'll not be disappointed. And you'll be amazed at the tidbits you pick up along the way.

On Shakespeare in the Culture

Two idiosyncratic but very worthwhile books address William Shakespeare as worldwide icon and cultural phenomenon.

Maverick scholar Gary Taylor's *Reinventing Shakespeare* (Oxford University Press, 1991) traces the history of Shakespeare's reputation from the beginning of his professional life until today, telling a story in the process about how cultures determine the values they celebrate and those they reprove. Polymath journalist, historian, and essayist Ron Rosenbaum tours the many places Shakespeare is found in our society—the theater, the study, the street—in his virtuoso *The Shakespeare Wars* (Random House, 2006) and delivers a personal and revelatory look at the struggle over what the Bard means, and what he represents, to today's world.

Criticism

Like the specialty books listed above, Shakespearean criticism is also a bottomless endeavor. It is so complex, and there is so much of it, from so many points of view, that it's now an academic subject in and of itself. You can actually read books about the history of criticism of Shakespeare and even study it for an advanced degree. Despite the overwhelming amount of criticism out there, I always try to keep up with what the most influential minds are thinking. If you discover just one provocative idea that makes a moment on stage more alive and electric than it would have been, you have justified hours and hours of reading.

Two prominent journals allow you to keep abreast of the latest trends in Shakespearean criticism. One is the English *Shakespeare Survey*, published annually by Cambridge University Press. In addition to wonderful essays on diverse subjects by leading critics, each volume includes a summary of the past year's important books on Shakespeare and productions of his works on stage, television, and film. Most libraries shelve it.

The second is American. *Shakespeare Quarterly* is published by Washington D.C.'s Folger Library, one of the world's great Shakespeare institutions. It's similar to the *Survey* in every respect, with slightly more focus on work happening on this side of the Atlantic. Again, most major libraries have it.

In addition to browsing through these two periodicals, I like to dip into the work of some contemporary critics I've come to respect over the years. This subjective and incomplete list includes Emrys Jones, who was my supervisor in graduate school; the unavoidable, if too celebrated, Harold Bloom; Stephen Greenblatt, of course; Columbia University's brilliant James Shapiro; Stephen Orgel; and Frank Kermode. Terry Eagleton, Graham Holdnerness, and Jonathan Dollimore should also be added to this list, although not in a position as high as the law firm of Greenblatt, Shapiro, and Orgel.

Critics from the past whom I admire include Eliot, who is indispensable on all the Elizabethans, and Coleridge, whose prose shimmers. W. H. Auden is breathtaking on Shakespeare, though at times a bit nutty. A. C. Bradley ("These little things in Shakespeare are no accidents," a favorite aphorism), G. Wilson Knight, John Dover Wilson, and E. M. W. Tillyard (the initials, spectacularly, stand for Eustace Mandeville Wetenhall) are rewarding. The critic I consult most frequently, because he was a major director of the plays in addition to a commentator on them, is Harley Granville-Barker. His "Prefaces to Shakespeare" are must-reads. These superb short essays about the plays detail their themes and—best of all for the thinking Shakespearean—the nuts and bolts of how they work on stage.

Production Histories / Shakespeare on Stage and Film

The past fifteen years or so have seen great progress on academic work that takes theatrical production seriously. Whereas in the bad old days theater wasn't considered worthy of real scholarly attention (you still can't get a degree in it at Harvard, only a certificate), now there are wonderful books that discuss the insights great actors and directors can bring to the texts.

Alan C. Dessen of the University of North Carolina is one of the trailblazers. His books, *Elizabethan Stage Conventions and Modern Interpreters*; *Rescripting Shakespeare: The Text, the Director, and Modern Productions*; and *Recovering Shakespeare's Theatrical Vocabulary* all regard the theatrical side of Shakespeare as interconnected with the way his work functions intellectually and emotionally. Manchester University Press's fine *Shakespeare in Production* series is also a standard-bearer, discussing how artists have interpreted the plays on stage scene by scene, choice by choice, and sometimes even line by line. (James Loehlin's volume on *Henry V* is staggeringly good.) The Arden Shakespeare has launched a similar series, *Shakespeare at Stratford*, focusing on the productions of the Royal Shakespeare Company in great detail. So far, *The Winter's Tale* is the only play that has been covered.

Shakespeare on film has also attracted its share of scholarly attention. Kenneth S. Rothwell's *History of Shakespeare on Screen: A Century of Film and Television* is a great place to start, as is Diana E. Henderson's *Concise Companion to Shakespeare on Screen*, a book that takes a more theoretical approach.

It's fun to read what the best Shakespearean actors have to say about their art. Cambridge University Press's *Players of Shakespeare* series, featuring interviews with leading actors, is as fascinating as it is fun. Don't overlook biographies about and memoirs of great Shakespeare actors, like Olivier, Peggy Ashcroft, Gielgud, and Burton. They are chock full of great thoughts on the player's art.

Your local video store is also worth a visit. Laurence Olivier's films of *Henry V*, *Hamlet*, *Richard III*, and *Othello* are masterpieces. Kenneth Branagh's *Henry V* and *Much Ado about Nothing* are beguiling. Orson Welles's *Chimes at Midnight*, a condensation of *Henry IV, Part One* and *Part Two* and *Henry V*, is considered by many to be the greatest Shakespeare film ever made. Kevin Kline's television *Hamlet* is wonderful. Michael Almereyda and Ethan Hawke's *Hamlet* is a personal favorite, as is Baz Luhrmann's *Romeo and Juliet*. I also love Peter Brook's *King Lear*, with Paul Scofield in the title role. The Shakespeare films of the Soviet-era Russian auteur Grigori Kozintsev are hard to find, but well worth the effort. His *Hamlet*, starring a genius named Innokenti Smoktunovsky, and his *King Lear* are unforgettable. In these films, the plays can seem even more compelling in Russian translation (by Boris Pasternak) than they are in English.

And Finally . . .

One of the best ways to learn more about *Thinking Shakespeare* and the intersection of the actor's craft, the critic's theories, and the Bard's words is to go to the theater and watch the plays. Every city in America has Shakespeare playing at some time or another during the year, whether at the local professional or community theater, the high school or college, or the church group or cinema.

Go see them.

Start with this list of the members of the Shakespeare Theatre Association of America: *www.staaonline.org/index/member_index.php*.

Go see them.

In the summer, outdoor Shakespeare festivals dot the country. There's one no more than a day's drive from anywhere in the United States. Check this list for the company nearest your town: *www.unc.edu/depts/outdoor/dir/shakes.html*.

Go see them, go see them, go see them.

CURTAIN CALL

LIST OF ILLUSTRATIONS

ACKNOWLEDGMENTS

No one who works on Shakespeare in the English-speaking theater does so anew. It's important to remember that generations of artists have trod this ground before and that your contribution, whatever its dimensions, would have been impossible without theirs. I've been fortunate to have had brief contact with a handful of modern Shakespeare's giants, and I wish to acknowledge how much I've learned from them and how much this book is indebted to their important work: John Barton, Cicely Berry, and Peter Hall. Rob Clare and Jeffrey Horowitz belong on that list too, as do James Shapiro, John Dias, JoAnne Akalaitis, Michael Greif, and the late A. J. Antoon. I knew Joseph Papp briefly; the vivid thoughts he shared with me about Shakespeare continue to resonate.

Mr. Papp introduced me to my friend and mentor Kevin Kline, the finest Shakespearean working today. He has shown me the infinite splendors a smart, talented, thinking actor can create from five iambs, and his ideas on how to do it, more than those of any other single individual, have informed and shaped mine. I thank him.

The structure of this book derives from courses I've taught at this country's leading actor-training institutions. Arthur Bartow, Zelda Fichandler, Michael Kahn, Madeline Puzo, Michael Miller, Rosemarie Tichler, and others who lead those institutions gave me opportunities to discover my own ideas even as I taught them to others. I thank them. I also thank in particular the distinguished faculties of the Juilliard School and the Graduate Acting Program at NYU's Tisch School of the Arts, whose insights into the technique of acting, shared so generously, helped me sharpen mine. The hundreds of students I've had the pleasure to instruct over the years have also taught me much, and I'm grateful.

Classic Stage Company, the Public Theater, the Williamstown Theater Festival, the Tennessee Repertory Theater, and the Idaho and New Jersey Shakespeare Festivals are wonderful American theaters. I've directed Shakespeare on their stages, and I'm honored. The hundreds of actors I've worked with have dazzled me with their talents and educated me with their skills. I thank them.

John Crowther at Spark Publishing took me through my first experience as a book author with a gentle hand, much wisdom, ample humor, and a superabundance of patience. I'm very grateful to him and also to the gifted and smart Emma Chastain.

Richard Abate and, of course, Sam Cohn at ICM were helpful as always.

My friends Jeffrey Rosen, David Segal, Ben Sherwood, and David Wright encouraged me to write. My prose may never measure up to theirs, but their excellence inspires me to continue trying.

This book is dedicated to my brilliant, talented, sparkling, and loving wife Hilit. She knows the energy she had to expend to get these pages into the world. I know it too, and I'm more thankful than I can say.

Finally, this. William Shakespeare has shown me the world. My work on his plays as an artist and teacher has taken me around the United States, much of Europe, and parts of Asia. The places he's led me in my imagination are even more thrilling and varied. Though I know he won't hear it, I nonetheless thank him for expanding and enriching my life in so many astonishing ways. This book's strengths are nothing more than pale reflections of his genius. Its shortcomings, however, are entirely mine. If I ever get to meet him, as I hope to do one day not too soon, I shall ask him to forgive them.

Barry Edelstein
Wonder Valley,
Twentynine Palms, California
2006

ABOUT THE AUTHOR

Barry Edelstein is a theater director noted for his work on the plays of William Shakespeare. He has staged over half of the Bard's plays at theaters around New York City and the United States. Some highlights: *The Winter's Tale*, starring David Strathairn, which the *New York Times* called a "stirring production"; *As You Like It*, starring Gwyneth Paltrow; *Julius Caesar* starring Jeffrey Wright for New York's Shakespeare in the Park; *Richard III* with John Turturro and Julianna Margulies; *The Merchant of Venice*, starring Ron Leibman in an OBIE Award–winning performance as Shylock; and Kevin Kline in three separate one-night-only Shakespeare "concerts"—one with Sigourney Weaver, one with Roger Rees, and one solo performance.

Edelstein teaches Shakespearean acting at USC's School of Theater and has taught the subject at the Juilliard School, the Graduate Acting Program at NYU, the Public Theater's Shakespeare Lab, and in lectures and master classes around the United States and abroad.

From 1998 to 2003, Edelstein was artistic director of New York's award-winning Classic Stage Company, where he directed a half-dozen plays and produced a dozen more. He has directed classical and contemporary work on stages around New York and across the United States, and he directed the film *My Lunch with Larry*. He has written about theater-related subjects in the *Washington Post*, the *New York Times*, the *New Republic,* and *American Theater* magazine. A graduate of Tufts University, he holds an M.Phil. in English Renaissance Drama from Oxford University, where he studied as a Rhodes Scholar.

He lives in Los Angeles and Twentynine Palms, California, with his wife, Hilit.

Please send him your questions and thoughts: *thinkshakes@ yahoo.com.*

Mr. Edelstein's book is the next best thing to being in one of his eye- and ear-opening classes on Shakespeare. Read it aloud, and, as with Shakespeare, you will be appreciably wiser.

—*Kevin Kline*

Barry Edelstein has a wonderful grasp of how Shakespeare's plays work. Rich in insight and beautifully written, *Thinking Shakespeare* is the best guide I know of to the challenges that confront every student and actor who reads or performs the plays.

—*James Shapiro, Author of* 1599: A Year in the Life of William Shakespeare, *Professor of English, Columbia University*

Barry Edelstein really knows his Shakespeare. When he directed me in *As You Like It*, the depth of his knowledge about the text unlocked the character of Rosalind. His knowledge really served to deepen my work. His book *Thinking Shakespeare* puts this knowledge in a fun, accessible form. I highly recommend it.

—*Gwyneth Paltrow*

At last an accessible answer to "what the heck does all this mean?!" Barry Edelstein addresses the myriad demands of acting an Elizabethan text clearly and with passion. Here's someone who knows what he's talking about—and it's a pleasure to read.

—*Roger Rees, Artistic Director, Williamstown Theater Festival; Member, Royal Shakespeare Company*

Barry Edelstein's class in performing Shakespeare has very quickly become one of the most popular courses in the school. Anyone reading *Thinking Shakespeare* will understand why. Edelstein's knowledge and love of Shakespeare's writing, as well as his humor and generosity, are apparent on every page. His approach to the text is perfect for all of us who have ever been intimidated by Shakespeare's greatness or who have thought that somehow we weren't smart enough to "get it." Edelstein gently eases the reader into a deeper understanding not only of Shakespeare's words but also the process by which actors bring those words to life. It doesn't matter what your previous experience with Shakespeare has been, whether it has been a little or a lot; this is a wonderful book for anyone—actor or audience, professional or student—who would like to know our greatest writer better.

—*Madeline Puzo, Dean, USC School of Theatre*

Taking a workshop on speaking Shakespeare with Barry Edelstein was revelatory to me. I think I learned as much or more than I had from any single book, and it struck me that he is one of those rare individuals with insight into both the literary and the dramatic power of the language.

—*Ron Rosenbaum, Author of* The Shakespeare Wars

Barry Edelstein is one of the great teachers of Shakespeare's text, and this book will be invaluable for actors and audiences alike.

—*Michael Kahn, Former Director, Juilliard Drama Division; Artistic Director, Shakespeare Theater, Washington, D.C.*

A witty, knowledgeable, and eminently stage-worthy book.

—*Zelda Fichandler, Chair, Graduate Acting Program, NYU / Tisch School of the Arts*